KISS 'EM GOODBYE

CHICAGO B. B. C., 1871.

Fred Treacy, *L.F.*, J. Simmons, *C.F.*, E. Pinkham, *R.F.*
E. Duffy, *S.S.*,   M. McAtee, *1st B.*
C. Hodes, *3d B.*,   JAS. WOOD, *2d B.*,   Mart. King, *C.*
E. P. Atwater, *Sub.*, G. Zettlein, *P.*,   T. J. Foley, *Sub.*

KISS 'EM GOODBYE

AN ESPN TREASURY
OF FAILED, FORGOTTEN,
AND DEPARTED TEAMS

DENNIS PURDY

BALLANTINE BOOKS | NEW YORK

Copyright © 2010 by Dennis Purdy

Published in the United States by ESPN Books,
an imprint of ESPN, Inc., New York, and Ballantine Books,
an imprint of The Random House Publishing Group,
a division of Random House, Inc., New York.

BALLANTINE and colophon are registered
trademarks of Random House, Inc.
The ESPN Books name and logo are registered
trademarks of ESPN, Inc.

Photographs on pages iv, 20, 80, 171, and 216 courtesy of Robert Edward
Auctions. Photographs on pages 26, 39, 46, 64, 71, 115, 146, 183, 236,
267, and 337 courtesy of Hunt Auctions. All other photographs
are from the author's private collection.

LIBRARY OF CONGRESS CATALOGING-IN-PUBLICATION DATA
Purdy, Dennis.
Kiss 'em goodbye : an ESPN treasury of failed, forgotten,
and departed teams / Dennis Purdy.
p. cm.
ISBN 978-0-345-52012-8 (pbk.)
eBook ISBN 978-0-345-52047-0
1. Sports—United States—Miscellanea. 2. Sports teams—United
States—Miscellanea. 3. ESPN (Television network) I. Title.
GV583.P87 2010
796.0973—dc22   2009051076

Printed in the United States of America on acid-free paper

www.ballantinebooks.com
www.espnbooks.com

2 4 6 8 9 7 5 3 1

First Edition

Designed by R. Bull

This book is dedicated to Lyle Oswood, my ninth-grade typing teacher at BGM High School in Brooklyn, Iowa, who in 1967 not only taught me one of my most important life skills, but cared enough to teach, mentor, advise, and watch out for a young man whose own father had abandoned him.

Acknowledgments

Most books are the product of more than just the author, and this book is no exception. As with most authors, I assume, we get so wrapped up in our book projects that, as the old saying goes, we can't see the forest for the trees. In that regard, I have been fortunate for a third time to have Richard Rosen as my lumberjack editor. He not only cleared away the brush and toppled the deadwood, but he helped plant new seedlings to get me going in the right direction. For his efforts I am once again truly appreciative.

While many of the images in this book are of items in my own extensive collection of cards, photographs, and memorabilia, for others I would especially like to thank Rob Lifson of Robert Edward Auctions in New Jersey (www.RobertEdwardAuctions.com), and David Hunt of Hunt Auctions in Pennsylvania (www.huntauctions.com), two of the finest and most reputable sports and Americana auction houses in the country.

I would also like to single out for special thanks two sports memorabilia dealers who assisted on this book. The first is long-time dealer and Pacific Coast League historian Mark Macrae of Castro Valley, California, who not only gave me a great deal on many items I purchased from him over the last twenty years, but has been a fountain of knowledge for many of my writing projects, and who was only a phone call away at any hour of the day or night. The second is Don Knutsen of Northwest Sports Cards in University Place, Washington (www.nw-sportscards.com), who has graciously allowed me to borrow many cards when I needed images.

And finally, I'd like to thank my wife, Kathy, who for months brought lunch and dinner to me so I wouldn't have to stop working on this book.

—Dennis Purdy

Table of Contents

Introduction

So, why a book on eighty-six failed, forgotten, and departed teams? Because their stories are so damn fascinating! For forty years I have researched and written about sports, and whenever I've come across teams that played for only a few seasons, a few months, or a few games before folding, I've wondered why their time was so short. The answers contain both surprising information and valuable historical lessons. Just as we learn more from our own mistakes than our successes, so we can appreciate the history of professional sports more completely through the tales of the failures.

When I think about it now, it seems inevitable I would write *Kiss 'Em Goodbye*. When it comes to sports history, especially baseball, I have always been obsessed with the obscure and the rare. As a teenager in 1968, I began compiling handwritten journals of baseball statistics, records, and achievements for my own pleasure. Later, I began collecting newspaper and magazine clippings of baseball-related stories. I expanded to books, assembling a baseball library that now contains more than 1,000 volumes, including many rare books, some dating back to the 1860s. From 1995 to 2000, I published *The Vintage & Classic Baseball Collector* magazine, a scholarly journal devoted to baseball's history and its rare collectibles.

My interest in embracing all of baseball's history resulted in two ambitious exhibits I created in the 1990s to complement the baseball card show–promotion business I owned from 1990 to 2006. The first was an exhibit called The History of Baseball Exhibit, for which I used 137 30" by 40" panels—one panel per year—to illustrate with pictures and stories the history of base-ball from its inception to the present. It took thirty-five tables to hold it all, but card-show enthusiasts loved it and many would study it for hours, mesmerized.

My other creation was The Traveling Baseball Card Museum, an ever-growing exhibit of baseball cards dating back to the 1860s. It grew from six 2' by 4' wood and Plexiglas panels to more than one hundred and twenty, and while it contained the obliga-tory and common Topps, Fleer, and Upper Deck cards from re-cent years, the real treasures, and my particular favorites, were the obscure and the rare, like my Elizabeth Resolutes carte-de-visite from 1873.

In *Kiss 'Em Goodbye,* I share not just this only known image of an Elizabeth Resolutes player in uniform, but also the story of the Resolutes' strange twenty-three-game journey as a major league baseball team. And that goes for the intriguing stories of eighty-five other franchises—from those that lasted decades be-fore disappearing to those that suited up for only a single game.

I can honestly say that of all of the books I've written, *Kiss 'Em Goodbye* is my favorite because, while exhuming the graves of so many defunct franchises, I was amazed by the stories and facts that had been buried with them. I examined more than six hun-dred dead teams to come up with the eighty-six histories that make up this book, and I'm grateful to have the chance to bring these faded franchises to life again.

KISS 'EM GOODBYE

TOO GOOD-LOOKING

THE ALTOONA MOUNTAIN CITYS
Union Association
1884

Be careful what you ask for, because you might get it.

Even in Altoona, Pennsylvania.

The Altoona Mountain Citys had established themselves as a prominent amateur baseball team in the early 1880s, but they wanted more. Two local men, attorney Arthur Dively and clothier William Ritz, gave them their chance in 1883 when they agreed to become the team's financial backers. In return for their support, Dively and Ritz were allowed to sell stock in the team and they found sixteen investors willing to help the popular team reach a higher level.

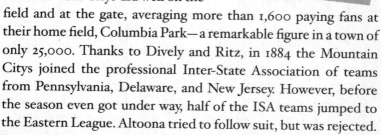

Shortstop Germany Smith began his 15-year major league career with Altoona in 1884.

As a semi-pro team in 1883, the Mountain Citys did well on the field and at the gate, averaging more than 1,600 paying fans at their home field, Columbia Park—a remarkable figure in a town of only 25,000. Thanks to Dively and Ritz, in 1884 the Mountain Citys joined the professional Inter-State Association of teams from Pennsylvania, Delaware, and New Jersey. However, before the season even got under way, half of the ISA teams jumped to the Eastern League. Altoona tried to follow suit, but was rejected.

Then Henry Lucas came calling. Lucas was the force and cash behind the formation of a new major league, the Union Association. Lucas had tried in vain to land a Pittsburgh franchise for his new league, since the city was conveniently located halfway between the eastern teams and Chicago and St. Louis in the west. When Lucas heard about the orphaned Altoona team on his scouting mission to Pittsburgh, he met with Dively and Ritz and quickly offered them a spot in his new UA. Never one to let either facts or reality get in the way of a sales pitch, the enthusiastic Lucas told the two Altoona directors that joining his new league would no doubt encourage the railroads to invest in both Altoona, nestled one hundred miles east of Pittsburgh, and its major league team. Lucas told them the operating cost of the team would be five thousand dollars, of which he was willing to contribute half. Dively and Ritz dove in.

When the local citizenry heard about Altoona's jump to major league status, they could hardly contain their pride, especially two stockholders, tailor James Goetz and hatter Malcolm Westfall. Goetz contracted with the team to make home and road uniforms (at $18 each) as well as brown traveling suits ($35) for every member of the team. Westfall provided uniform hats ($10) and brown derbies to match the suits ($8). Together, the two stockholders siphoned off over $1,000, more than 20 percent of the team's operating capital. But boy, the team looked good when it left in April for a seven-game road trip to Cincinnati and St. Louis. Hundreds of well-wishers joined a local band at the Altoona train station to send off the team, which was led by Germany Smith, the team's rookie shortstop, who was embarking on a fifteen-year major league career.

After losing their first three games in Cincinnati to the Outlaw Reds, the Mountain Citys were embarrassed in four straight by the St. Louis Maroons, outscored by a combined 35–7. When the team stepped off the train in Altoona from their winless road trip, there was no band to welcome them and considerably fewer fans. But they sure looked good.

First up for the Mountain Citys at Columbia Park were the visiting Maroons, who were stopping off in Altoona for a four-game series before heading east on a long road trip. The Maroons resumed their dominance by routing Altoona, 15–2, in the first-ever home game for the Mountain Citys before thrashing them in the next three games as well. When the infield dust had settled, Altoona was 0–11.

Lucas informed them not only that neither the railroad's money nor his own would be forthcoming, but also that he had already arranged for a new team in Kansas City to take Altoona's place.

The Boston Reds, en route to Chicago, were next. The Mountain Citys managed to win the first game, 9–4, and won five of the next twelve home games against Philadelphia, Washington, and Baltimore, but many of their losses were embarrassingly one-sided, thanks to porous defense and pathetic pitching. Attendance dwindled to less than 1,000 a game, and sometimes as low as 200—not even enough to pay the players' salaries. By the end of May of the team's inaugural professional season, a number of the players had jumped to other teams.

In an emergency meeting with Lucas on May 29, Dively and Ritz asked about the promised railroad money as well as any further possible subsidy from Lucas himself. Lucas informed them not only that neither the railroad's money nor his own would be forthcoming, but also that he had already arranged for a new team in Kansas City to take Altoona's place! The stunned Dively and Ritz had no choice but also to cease operations after just six weeks as a major league team. With a 6–19 record, the Mountain Citys were the Union Association's first casualty.

But they sure looked good.

TOO SMALL FOR BALL

THE ANDERSON PACKERS
National Basketball Association
1949-50

When the National Basketball Association was created in 1949 by merging seventeen teams from two separate professional basketball leagues—the Basketball Association of America and the National Basketball League—there were a handful of "Davids," like the Packers from Anderson, Indiana, and a bunch of "Goliaths," like the Celtics, Knicks, and Lakers. But this story didn't play out like the Old Testament one.

The Packers, named after millionaire Ike Duffey's meat-packing business in Anderson, Indiana, first took to the court in 1945 as a semi-pro team called the Chiefs in rural Indiana, a hotbed of basketball activity. A year later, they changed their name to the Duffey Packers and joined the NBL, where they played quite well for three years, even winning the NBL Playoffs in 1949 after a 49–15 regular season. Later that summer they joined the new NBA, shortening their name to just the Packers.

1947 Anderson Packers warm-up jacket.

While the Knicks played their games in 17,000-seat Madison Square Garden, and the Celtics often hosted 15,000 at Boston Garden, the Packers performed before crowds averaging

2,500 at the Wigwam, the town's high school gymnasium. And while the Knicks, Celtics, Lakers, and other Goliaths of the league signed marquee college players for large salaries, the Packers had to content themselves with players in the fifty to seventy-five dollars per game range, and who were willing to be paid on a game-by-game basis. Most of the Packers were young, single men who lived at the local YMCA and were employed as car salesmen, janitors, and the like when they weren't playing basketball. But while there weren't any college All-Americans playing for the Packers, they did have players like Charlie Black, a local hero known for his fifty-one flying missions over Europe during World War II, and Howie Schultz, a 6'6" multisport athlete who achieved an unusual sort of fame as the white guy the Brooklyn Dodgers let go in 1947 to make room on their roster for Jackie Robinson.

> Most of the Packers were young, single men who lived at the local YMCA and were employed as car salesmen, janitors, and the like.

On the court, Black, Schultz, and the other Packers held their own against the NBA's best. The Packers, to the delight of their rabid fans, called "Packer Backers," started off the season with six wins in seven games, including an 83–80 upset shocker over George Mikan's Minneapolis Lakers, a team already in the midst of its dynasty years. Halfway through the season, the Packers' record stood at 19–13, with five of their losses by four points or less. When the regular season ended, the Packers were 37–27, just two games behind the Indianapolis Olympians in the Western Division, easily qualifying for the playoffs.

Except for the finals, a best-of-seven format, all the other rounds of the playoffs were best of three. In the first round, Anderson knocked off the Tri-Cities Blackhawks, 2–1. They did the same to Indianapolis in the second round. In the semifinals, the Packers were faced with the unenviable task of playing the Lakers, who swept them in two straight on their way to the NBA title.

Though the Packers held their own on the court, they couldn't compete with the Goliaths' large arenas. Nor could they profit by the NBA's incredibly uneven schedule in 1949–50. Some teams played sixty-eight games while others played as few as sixty-two. Also, the Packers played the Lakers (the NBA's biggest drawing card) only twice, while facing other Davids such as Tri-Cities, the Denver Nuggets, and the Waterloo Hawks seven to nine times each. What's more, the Lakers typically traveled with the Harlem Globetrotters, usually booking a double-header on the road with a Globetrotter game, a guaranteed sellout. What was the point of selling out the Wigwam when you could sell out Madison Square Garden?

Midway through the season, Duffey could see the writing on the backboard: The NBA's formula of including big-city teams with small-town ones, mixing large arenas with high school gyms and armories, spelled doom for the Davids. Deep in red ink, Duffey announced to his Packer Backers during halftime of a league game that he wasn't sure he could keep the team afloat for the rest of the year, but he would try if every one of the 1,500 fans in attendance that night brought at least one friend with them to the next home game. He also told them he had an offer of $25,000 from a group of Toledo investors who wanted to move the team to Ohio, but he would hold off as long as he could.

Alarmed at the prospect of losing their team, fifty of Anderson's leading citizens convened at the YMCA and formed the Packers Civic Committee. They were successful in their effort to sell $10,000 in tickets to the season's remaining games. The civic-minded Duffey then sold the team to the community for the $10,000 they had raised, but it was no use. After the season, the Packers and five other teams were forced out of the NBA when the league required all teams to post a $50,000 "performance bond" as security.

Several months later, under the leadership of Doxie Moore, the old NBL commissioner, the Packers and seven other former NBA, NBL, and BAA teams formed a new eight-team league, the National Professional Basketball League. The Packers had another fine season on the court, but when the league folded at the end of the season, so did the Packers.

As for Duffey, whose other passion was railroading, he sold his meatpacking business for three million dollars and took a job as president of the Indiana Central Railroad for a salary of one dollar a year.

CLAWLESS AND CLUELESS

THE BALTIMORE CLAWS
American Basketball Association
1975

I n one of the strangest cases in all of sports history, the Baltimore Claws of the American Basketball Association can actually lay claim to being defunct before they were defunct.

The Claws came to Baltimore in 1975 after playing the previous five seasons in Memphis under various names, most recently the Sounds. While in Memphis, the team had struggled financially because of low attendance, forcing the league to take over operation of the team in midseason and subsidize it the rest of the way. After the 1974–75 season had ended, ABA commissioner Tedd Munchak gave the Sounds a three-pronged ultimatum: 1) line up some new investors; 2) sell at least 4,000 season tickets; 3) get a better deal on their lease with Mid-South Coliseum. The Sounds were unable to meet any of the conditions by the deadline, so the league put the team up for sale.

A group of Maryland businessmen agreed to purchase the team for $1 million and moved it to Baltimore. But when the group didn't meet all their financial obligations, new ABA commissioner Dave DeBusschere awarded the franchise to another Memphis group. The next day, however, the

1975 ABA basketball.

new Memphis group withdrew their offer and DeBusschere was forced to give the Baltimore group a second chance.

The Baltimore owners came up with enough of an initial payment that the league cut them a little slack in meeting their entire obligation. In the meantime, the team was named the Hustlers, but due to league and public criticism (Larry Flynt's *Hustler* magazine had been founded in 1974), they changed the team's name to the Claws.

A month before the season was set to begin, the Claws stirred up the basketball world when they announced the acquisition of superstar Dan Issel of the defending ABA champion Kentucky Colonels. Issel had come to Baltimore in exchange for center Tom Owens and $500,000 in cash, but when Baltimore couldn't raise the money, Issel was instead sold to the Denver Nuggets. The Claws then traded high-scoring guard Rick Mount to the Utah Stars in another move that perplexed their new fan base, a fan base that hadn't seen them play a game yet.

When the preseason finally rolled around, the Claws still had several name players on the roster, including Mel Daniels, Stew Johnson, and Skip Wise. Wise had jumped to the ABA from Clemson, where the year before he had become the first freshman ever to make the ACC's all-conference first team.

The Claws were a mess off the court too.

On October 9, 1975, the Claws played their first exhibition game, losing 131–121 to the Virginia Squires in front of a widely spaced 1,150 fans in Salisbury, Maryland. They took the court wearing red Memphis Sounds uniforms with a green "Claws" patch sewn over "Sounds." Their warm-up suits hadn't yet been altered. Two nights later in Cherry Hill, New Jersey, the Claws were 21-point losers to the NBA's Philadelphia 76ers. Then they lost to the Squires again, 100–88, with only five hundred in attendance at St. Mary's College in Emmitsburg, Maryland.

But the Claws were a mess off the court too. With only a week to go before the regular season began, Commissioner DeBusschere heard from several Claws players that not only were they not being paid their salaries, they weren't even receiving their per diem meal money. DeBusschere next received word that the Claws' bank had revoked its line of credit. He gave the team four days to post a $500,000 "performance bond" to cover team expenses or face expulsion. The Claws raised $250,000 and had another $320,000 in escrow with the city of Baltimore, but they couldn't get their hands on it. It seems the city was having difficulty with the Claws' president, David Cohan, who wasn't paying the team's bills at the Baltimore Civic Center. The city not only refused to release the escrow funds as long as Cohan was affiliated with the team—it ordered the Claws' offices locked up.

A few days later, the ABA disbanded the Claws, just days before the regular season was to open. The Claws threatened legal action, hoping to delay the start of the ABA season since they hadn't been given ten days' notice, a period called for in league bylaws. The league and the city responded with threatened lawsuits of their own.

Realizing they were fighting a losing battle, the Claws finally accepted their dissolution, allowing the players to take whatever equipment and office furniture they could carry in exchange for unpaid salaries.

While even the shortest-lived professional franchises lasted at least one regular-season game, Baltimore's ABA entry clawed its way to extinction without being able to claim even that.

COLT COMFORT

THE BALTIMORE COLTS
National Football League
1953–83

No franchise shift in all of sports history led to as much controversy, ill will, and legal and legislative action as the Baltimore Colts' surreptitious move to Indianapolis in 1984. The popular belief is that it was just another case of a greedy owner with an eye for greener grass and greener bucks, and the way he snuck out of town proved how slimy he was. But the real story is somewhat different.

Baltimore became home to its first professional football team in 1947 when the bankrupt Miami Seahawks of the All-American Football Conference, an NFL rival, moved to the city and took the name Colts in honor of the region's long history of horse racing and breeding. Following the 1949 season, the 1–11 Colts and three other AAFC teams merged with the NFL. After another 1–11 season in 1950, the Colts folded due to financial problems. Baltimore got a second chance at an NFL team in 1953 when the league agreed to expand to the city after folding the Dallas Texans, a team the league had been forced to take over in midseason 1952.

1969 Baltimore Colts pennant.

The Colts had losing seasons from 1953 to 1956, but their fortunes turned around in 1957 when a young quarterback who had been drafted and released by the Pittsburgh Steelers—Johnny Unitas—led the Colts to a 7–5 record, one win short of the playoffs. In 1958, the Colts burst out of the gate, winning their first six games, finishing 9–3 and winning a spot in the NFL Championship game against the New York Giants in Yankee Stadium. This historic contest was the first nationally televised game in NFL history at a time when the league was still struggling to compete with the more popular college football. In regard to exposing the professional product to a mass audience, the NFL couldn't have scripted a better game. The Colts held a 14–3 lead at the half, but the Giants stormed back to take a 17–14 lead while Colts kicker Steve Myhra missed two field goals. Then, with time winding down in the fourth quarter, Unitas led the Colts all the way down the field to set up a game-tying field goal by Myhra with just seven seconds left, leading to the first-ever overtime game in NFL history. The Giants won the toss, but their offense stalled and Unitas then led the Colts on another long drive that culminated in an Alan Ameche one-yard touchdown run and a 23–17 Colts victory in what many football historians consider the greatest game in NFL history. Not only did it give the Colts their first NFL title, it marked the beginning of a boom in the NFL's popularity. In 1959, the Colts repeated as NFL champs, knocking off the Giants again, 31–16.

However, from 1960 to 1963 the Colts were barely a .500 team, missing the playoffs each year. Then, in 1964 Unitas won the league's MVP Award by leading the Colts to the title game against Cleveland, although the Jim Brown–led Browns trampled the Colts, 27–0. In 1967, the Colts and Rams tied for the Coastal Division championship with identical 11–1–2 records, but because Los Angeles had a win and a tie in the teams' two meetings, they went to the playoffs while the Colts went home, despite Unitas's second MVP Award.

While Unitas missed most of 1968 with injuries, backup quarterback Earl Morrall stepped in and led the Colts to a record-breaking 13–1 season, copping the MVP Award in the process. The dominant Colts were eighteen-point favorites over Joe Namath's New York Jets in Super Bowl III. Nonetheless, Namath almost blithely guaranteed a Super Bowl victory for the AFL, and he was as good as his word, leading the Jets to the biggest upset in NFL history, 16–7.

Irsay stunned the football world by trading teams.

The Jets' surprising victory helped forge an AFL-NFL merger. The Colts, Steelers, and Browns moved to the AFC, one of two conferences in the newly reconfigured NFL. In the first year under the new format, the Colts won the AFC Championship and the right to play the Cowboys in Super Bowl V. In a turnover-rife Super Bowl that would be nicknamed "the Blunder Bowl," the Colts defeated the Cowboys, 16–13, on a field goal by Jim O'Brien with five seconds left.

On July 26, 1972, Colts owner Carroll Rosenbloom and Rams owner Robert Irsay stunned the football world by trading teams. Players, coaches, and staff stayed put as only the owners switched offices. With the first losing record in sixteen years (5–9), Irsay further angered Colts fans when he traded the aging Unitas to the San Diego Chargers. In another move that would become an Irsay trademark, he fired popular coach Don McCafferty after five games (1–4) and replaced him with John Sandusky (4–5). Before the next season, Irsay replaced him with Howard Schnellenberger (4–13), who lasted just three games into his second season when he, too, was fired. His replacement, Joe Thomas, lasted just eleven games (2–9) before he was replaced by Ted Marchibroda in

1975. Marchibroda, popular with the players, led the Colts to a rebound season (10–4), though the Steelers quickly knocked them out of the playoffs.

Early in the 1976 season, when Marchibroda resigned after a falling-out with the irascible Irsay, the players threatened a strike unless their beloved coach returned. Irsay relented, reinstated Marchibroda, and the team responded behind Bert Jones, their latest MVP-winning quarterback, by advancing to the playoffs, where the Colts were again bounced by the Steelers.

The Colts had their last winning season (10–4) and playoff appearance (a 37–31 double OT loss to Oakland) in 1977. Over the next six seasons, Colts fans became increasingly weary of Irsay's ownership tactics, miserly ways, and public rants, and it showed in dwindling attendance figures. Irsay's reputation was so tainted in football circles that when the Colts drafted Stanford's John Elway with the number one pick in the 1983 NFL draft, he refused to play for them. Only after Elway threatened to play baseball instead of football—he was also drafted by the New York Yankees—did Irsay gave in, trading him to the Denver Broncos for Mark Herrmann, Chris Hinton, and a draft pick. Colts fans, already upset over the team's 19–53–1 record over the previous five years, were furious over losing Elway, and so the chasm between owner and fans widened.

Because Irsay—and Rosenbloom before him—felt strongly that Baltimore's Memorial Stadium was an inadequate venue for football, he tried to get city officials to increase seating capacity, add luxury boxes, build separate locker rooms for the Orioles and Colts, and build additional office space and restrooms. The protracted battle between Irsay and city officials escalated into a public feud with both the Orioles and the local press. City officials kept promising improvements, and even developed plans for some of them, as well as for a domed stadium. But in 1974, Maryland governor Marvin Mandel put the brakes on talk of a new stadium. Baltimore comptroller Hyman Pressman went a step further, placing an amendment to the city's charter on the fall ballot. The measure, titled Question P, prohibited the use of public funds for the construction of a new sports stadium and was passed by a 56 to 44 margin, effectively ending all hope of a new stadium for the Colts or the Orioles.

As early as 1976, Irsay was in discussions with other cities about relocating the Colts. The public disclosure of these talks with officials in Phoenix, Memphis, Los Angeles, and Jacksonville only incited fans further. In 1979, Irsay gave Maryland governor Harry Hughes a list of $25 million in requested improvements to Memorial Stadium. The state legislature cut it to $23 million, but earmarked much of it as improvements for the Orioles. When the legislature asked both teams to sign long-term commitments before the improvements would be made, both the Colts and Orioles refused, so the planned improvements were shelved.

Irsay appeared at a press conference, screaming,
"This is my goddamn team!"

Irsay intensified his efforts to find a new home, and in early 1984 he was approached with strong offers from Phoenix and Indianapolis, the latter having already constructed a new domed stadium in the *hope* of attracting an NFL team. When word leaked out about the secret meetings Irsay had been conducting with both cities, the state of Maryland took action. On March 27, 1984, one chamber of the state legislature passed a law allowing the city of Baltimore to seize the Colts under eminent domain laws, something the city and county were already threatening to do. The other chamber was poised to take up the same matter a few days later. An angry Irsay appeared at a press conference, screaming, "This is my goddamn team!"

Irsay didn't wait to see what the other chamber would do. On the morning of March 28, when Phoenix officials told Irsay they were dropping out of the bidding, Irsay immediately called Indianapolis mayor William Hudnut and told him he was moving his team to Indiana. Hudnut turned to his good friend, John B. Smith, owner of Mayflower Transit, who then arranged at his own expense for a fleet of large moving trucks scattered from New Jersey to Virginia to converge on the Colts' offices. At ten o'clock that evening, sixty men quietly began to load fifteen trucks with all the Colts' equipment, books, and furniture. By dawn, the trucks were on their way to Indiana via fifteen separate routes in case the Maryland State Police tried to stop them. At the Indiana state line, the trucks were met by Indiana state troopers who, with lights flashing, escorted them to the Colts' new home in downtown Indianapolis.

The Indianapolis Star featured a photo of a jubilant Irsay and Hudnut, hands clasped, arms raised, as 20,000 *new* Colts fans cheered them. Baltimore's mayor, William Schaefer, appeared on the front page of *The Baltimore Sun* in tears. Colts attorney Michael Chernoff expressed Irsay's exasperated position best when he told the media, "[The Maryland legislature] not only threw down the gauntlet, but they put a gun to his head, cocked it, and asked, 'Want to see if it's loaded?' They forced him to make a decision *that* day."

Within two weeks of announcing ticket sales for the upcoming 1984 season, Irsay received 143,000 requests for season tickets. Although the Colts struggled on the field for most of their first fifteen years in Indianapolis, they were very successful at the box office, and for the last decade have been one of the NFL's best teams.

The city of Baltimore and the state of Maryland, both of which had threatened to take Irsay's personal property away from him through eminent domain, realized the error of their ways and declared the building of a new public stadium a priority. In that fall's election, Maryland voters repealed Question P by a 62–38 margin. The people of Maryland also learned how to attract an NFL football team: build a new stadium that meets the needs of a modern team. Once they promised to construct a new stadium for Art Modell, owner of the Cleveland Browns and, ironically, once the loudest voice against Irsay's relocation to Indianapolis, Modell moved his team to Baltimore in 1996 and renamed them the Ravens.

In the aftermath of the Colts' move to Indianapolis, a flurry of legal activity attempted to force the Colts back to Baltimore, but all efforts failed. Johnny Unitas summed it up best for Colts fans when he declared that he was a *Baltimore* Colt only, and would not associate in any manner with the Indianapolis Colts, a position he maintained until the day he died, nearly twenty years later.

DIAMOND THIEVES

THE BALTIMORE ORIOLES
National League
1892–99

I
f the 1890s were baseball's Wild West Era, the Baltimore Orioles of that decade were definitely the guys in the black hats.

In the years from 1892 to 1899, the twelve-team National League was the only major league in operation. Despite the frequent on-field fisticuffs and rampant gambling, baseball was at peace at last. The NL had recently vanquished the competing Players' League (1890) and American Association (1891), and for

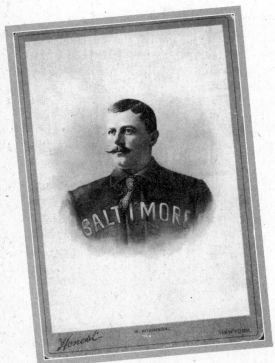

Hall of Fame catcher Wilbert Robinson, one of baseball's most popular players and managers for more than forty years.

the next eight years not a single franchise went out of business or relocated. It was a stable period dominated by two teams, the Boston Beaneaters, who won five pennants, and the Orioles, who won three.

The Orioles were managed by Ned Hanlon, a master of baseball strategy who achieved almost mythical status because of his talent for making seemingly strange trades that always seemed to work out in the Orioles' favor. In one 1892 trade, Hanlon sent George Van Haltren, a proven .320 hitter, to Pittsburgh for a rookie outfielder named Joe Kelley, who went on to hit over .350 for the Orioles and wound up in the Hall of Fame. More mysteriously, in 1893 Hanlon traded shortstop Tim O'Rourke, hitting .363 at the time, to Louisville for a youngster by the name of Hughie Jennings, who was hitting only .136. All Jennings did was hit .359 for the Orioles over the next seven years, including .401 in 1896, on *his* way to the Hall of Fame.

Orioles owner Harry Von der Horst got so tired of trying to explain his manager's moves to reporters that he wore a lapel button that simply read, "Ask Hanlon." Hanlon worked so many wonders that Von der Horst rewarded Hanlon by allowing him to purchase 25 percent of the team's stock and giving him complete and unquestioned control over the entire organization.

On the field, Hanlon expected his players to be aggressive and play sound fundamental baseball. More than any team of the era, the Orioles practiced long hours to perfect such basic baseball skills as bunting, hitting the correct cutoff man, taking the extra base, backing up one another in the field, executing the hit-and-run, and testing the arms of the opponents' outfielders. Hanlon's brilliance extended to strategic groundskeeping as well. He had the baselines sloped toward fair territory to help keep bunts from rolling foul. The dirt in front of home plate was packed hard to aid his team's "Baltimore chops"—Hanlon's tactic of having batters hit down on the ball to get a high bounce that could be beat out for a hit. Hanlon also had the dirt in the base paths packed hard to assist his team's base stealers, which included almost everyone. In 1894, six Orioles stole more than thirty bases. Finally, Hanlon kept the outfield grass long as a hiding place for extra balls that could conveniently be brought into play in case an opponent hit one in the gap.

But it was more than just shady groundskeeping that gave the Orioles their "black hat" reputations. Hanlon schooled his players in many illegitimate tactics. One Oriole would try to distract or shield the game's only umpire while a teammate cut ten feet off second base as he went from first to third; infielders would trip opposing runners as they ran the bases; John McGraw in particular would try and hook his finger in an opposing base runner's belt; Wilbert Robinson would throw his catcher's mask in a runner's path in an attempt to trip him; and, with a runner on third, the Orioles' third-base coach would sometimes bolt toward home in an effort to confuse the opposing pitcher and/or catcher, hoping that one of them would throw the ball away. Most brazen of all their schemes was to file their spikes to razor-sharp edges in full view of their opponents, then slide at both opposing players and umpires with their weapons high.

So notorious was Baltimore's reputation that almost everyone rooted against them. When Boston's Beaneaters won the pennant on the last weekend of the 1897 season, it was hailed around the league as a triumph of clean baseball over dirty. John Heydler, an umpire in the 1890s before becoming NL president in 1918, said of the Orioles, ". . . they were mean, vicious, and ready to maim a rival player or umpire." But in spite of the Orioles' reputation, the fans around the league loved to see them come to town. All theater needs a villain, and the Orioles filled the bill magnificently. And because Hanlon masterminded the Orioles' dirty methods, he was always happy to pay any fines imposed on his players.

In 1894, William Temple, owner of the Pittsburgh Pirates, decided the NL needed some sort of postseason series, and for the purpose donated a large silver trophy called the Temple Cup that the league's top two teams would compete for after the season. In what was billed as the World's Championship Series, Baltimore won the pennant, but lost the Cup in four straight to the runner-up New York Giants. The Orioles, who claimed they hadn't tried that hard because it was the pennant that really mattered, won the pennant again in 1895, but lost the Temple Cup again, this time to the Cleveland Spiders. The Orioles won the next two Temple Cup series before the event was discontinued for lack of interest among players and fans alike.

> Hanlon kept the outfield grass long as a hiding place for extra balls.

In 1899, the Orioles and Brooklyn's Superbas (later called the Dodgers) were brought together under one ownership group in a system, legal at the time, called syndicate ownership. Charlie Ebbets and Ferdinand Abel owned 50 percent of both teams while Von der Horst owned 40 percent and Hanlon ten. Hanlon managed Brooklyn while McGraw took over in Baltimore. The teams were allowed to transfer players back and forth, and Hanlon took advantage of this by taking Baltimore's best players with him to Brooklyn and sending lesser players to the Orioles, which irritated the highly competitive McGraw. This tactic was met with much cynicism by baseball fans and reporters of the day, calling into question the integrity of the game itself.

Although Hanlon guided Brooklyn to the pennant in 1899, Baltimore outdrew them on the road, an embarrassment for Hanlon. McGraw also made a number of player moves that further irritated Hanlon, including hiding the ability of ace pitcher Joe McGinnity from Hanlon by not allowing McGinnity to throw his excellent curveball whenever Hanlon was present.

When the NL decided to contract to eight teams after the 1899 season, Baltimore, in spite of its huge success on the field and at the gate, was unanimously voted out of the league, a move intended to quiet baseball's critics of the syndicate system. Baltimore's owners (Brooklyn's, essentially) were given a $30,000 buyout and allowed to dispose of its players as they saw fit. As it happened, the best of the Orioles' black hats all went to Brooklyn.

IT'S WAR

THE BALTIMORE ORIOLES
American League
1901–02

When the National League contracted from twelve teams to eight following the 1899 season, Ban Johnson and his minor league Western League partners saw their opening; along with Charles Comiskey and several other major financial backers, the determined and irascible Johnson decided to transform his league into a newly renamed American League for the 1900 season.

The National League had dropped Baltimore, Washington, Louisville, and Cleveland from their ranks in an effort to provide more financial stability for the remaining eight teams, and Johnson's American League group immediately targeted the forsaken cities. Because the Western League was still a member of the National Agreement, organized baseball's ruling body, they had to have permission to transfer franchises and open new ones. Unfortunately for Johnson, the National League was the real power behind the National Agreement, and when he asked to relocate one of his franchises (Comiskey's St. Paul team) to Chicago, the NL reluctantly agreed, but only with severe stipulations that hamstrung the new Chicago franchise, such as giving the NL's Chicago club the right to draft two players each year off the new AL club. The NL also forbade the new Chicago franchise from using the word "Chicago" in its name, so Comiskey called his team the White Stockings, borrowing a former, popular name of the NL club, which was now being called the Orphans.

These and other stipulations were a sore point for the new American Leaguers, who dropped out as members of the National Agreement after the 1900 season and declared themselves a major league in 1901. No longer bound by the rules and restrictions of the National Agreement, the new league felt free to raid the NL teams of their players and place new teams wherever they wanted. The war was on.

Ban Johnson was a no-nonsense man who saw that one of the National League's major problems was the drinking, gambling, and rowdiness that flourished among players and managers alike, so he imposed strict rules regarding on- and off-field behavior. He dealt out harsh punishments for violators, the most prominent of whom was player-manager John McGraw of Baltimore, whose temperamental history had preceded him to the new league.

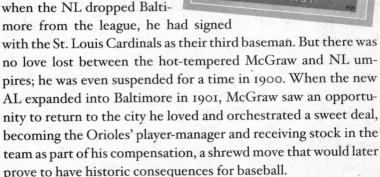

Oriole Mike Donlin later became a silent movie star.

After McGraw had lost his job following the 1899 season, when the NL dropped Baltimore from the league, he had signed with the St. Louis Cardinals as their third baseman. But there was no love lost between the hot-tempered McGraw and NL umpires; he was even suspended for a time in 1900. When the new AL expanded into Baltimore in 1901, McGraw saw an opportunity to return to the city he loved and orchestrated a sweet deal, becoming the Orioles' player-manager and receiving stock in the team as part of his compensation, a shrewd move that would later prove to have historic consequences for baseball.

Before the 1901 season, McGraw secured a lease for Baltimore's Union Park, but the owners of the property (including Ned Hanlon, who had business ties to NL owners) insisted that the lease applied only to the land, not the park. When McGraw tried to use the ballpark anyway, Hanlon sent over armed guards to occupy the clubhouse and first base. McGraw recruited a bunch of thugs and stormed the ballpark, beating up the groundskeepers and physically occupying third base. When the police arrived, they set up a neutral peacekeeping station in left field and unsuccessfully tried to sort things out. The courts finally settled the matter by evicting McGraw and his cohorts, forcing the Orioles to build a new ballpark before the season got under way. The feisty McGraw began raiding NL teams for their players, including eventual Hall of Famers Joe McGinnity and Roger Bresnahan.

> McGraw simply sat down in the batter's box
> and refused to leave.

McGraw's feuds with umpires continued in the American League in 1901. In one particularly nasty incident, mounted policemen had to escort the umpire out of the ballpark, earning McGraw another suspension from Johnson. In 1902, McGraw's on-field battles with umps escalated. He was thrown out on Opening Day, punched a Brooklyn team official several days later, and engaged in a prolonged dispute with umpire Jack Sheridan when the ump refused to let him take first base after being hit by a pitch because he felt McGraw hadn't tried to get out of the way. The next day, McGraw was hit by pitches five times, and each time Sheridan refused to let McGraw take first base. After the fifth time, McGraw simply sat down in the batter's box and refused to leave until Sheridan had him physically removed. This earned him a five-day suspension in May.

By now, Johnson and McGraw were bitter enemies. Johnson might have been ruthless, but McGraw was vicious—and vindictive. On June 18, shortly after serving his latest suspension, McGraw met secretly with Andrew Freedman, owner of the NL's New York Giants, and together they concocted a plan to take revenge on both Johnson and the upstart American League.

The first part of the scheme required McGraw to again get suspended, not a difficult task. On June 28, McGraw chose his opportune moment and orchestrated a wild team-wide performance that resulted in the umpire ordering an Orioles forfeit. This, of course, earned McGraw another indefinite suspension from AL president Ban Johnson. Next, McGraw had to get out of his Baltimore contract. The Orioles had had their fill of McGraw, so they quickly agreed to let him go when McGraw offered to forgive the club their $7,000 debt to him for club expenses in exchange for his outright release. Once this was done, McGraw sold his stock in the Orioles for $6,500 and signed a four-year contract with the Giants.

The next part of the scheme involved a silent financial partner who was a front for Freedman, Joseph C. France, who used money from Freedman and Cincinnati Reds owner John T. Brush to purchase 201 of the 400 shares of Baltimore Base Ball Club stock. For one very painful day—July 16, 1902—the owner of the American League's Baltimore Orioles was the owner of the National League's New York Giants. In those twenty-hours, Freedman released all the best Orioles players from their contracts, signing McGinnity, Bresnahan, and several others with the Giants, while letting others sign with the Reds as a thank-you to Brush for his help in financing the deal.

The next day, when only five Orioles players showed up for their game with St. Louis, the umpire awarded a forfeit to the Browns. When Ban Johnson uncovered the scheme, he quickly invoked an American League rule that allowed the league to take over any franchise that for any reason couldn't field a team. Johnson took over the Orioles, negating Freedman's purchase. After appointing Wilbert Robinson as team manager, Johnson ordered the other teams in the league to each send a player to Baltimore so the Orioles could field a team and continue the season.

As a further measure of revenge against the National League, Andrew Freedman, and John McGraw, Ban Johnson moved the Orioles franchise to New York after the 1902 season to compete directly with Freedman's New York Giants. The new team was known as the New York Highlanders, but eventually took the name Yankees, and became the most storied team in baseball history.

Ban Johnson's crown now had its jewel.

SLOWLY BUT SURLY

THE BALTIMORE TERRAPINS
Federal League
1914–15

The Baltimore Terrapins, of baseball's short-lived Federal League, survived only two seasons, but they nonetheless started baseball on its long, slow road to finally emancipating its players.

The team was one of the few true community teams in major league history, owned by a group of six hundred shareholders rather than one or two large investors. The leading shareholder was Ned Hanlon, a Baltimore legend who had managed three Orioles teams to National League pennants in the 1890s after a stellar career as an outfielder, primarily with the Detroit Wolverines, the combination of which eventually earned him a spot in the Hall of Fame. Together, the stockholders raised $164,000 to purchase and operate the franchise, half of which was spent constructing 15,000-seat Terrapin Park.

Hanlon's squad got off to a great start in 1914 and by May 27 Baltimore was in first place, seven and a half games ahead of the Brooklyn Tip-Tops and the only team in the FL with a winning percentage over .500. Then the Terrapins went into a shell, losing seventeen of twenty, and settled for an 84–70 finish, good for third place. The Terrapins added ace pitcher and future

1914 Baltimore Terrapins program.

Hall of Famer Chief Bender of the Philadelphia A's for the 1915 season, but Bender and the rest of the pitching staff flopped and Baltimore was last in batting average and ERA, finishing in the cellar, a whopping twenty-four games behind the seventh-place Brooklyn Tip-Tops.

By the end of the 1915 season, the Federal League itself was beginning to crumble, so when the NL and AL, both hurt badly in the two-year bidding war, approached FL president James Gilmore about a possible peace settlement, Gilmore readily listened to their proposition. The FL, through its Baltimore franchise, had undertaken an antitrust lawsuit against Organized Baseball before the season began (*Federal Baseball Club of Baltimore v. National League*), but now all three leagues wanted the lawsuit to go away—especially in light of the proposed settlement agreement that satisfied everyone except Terrapins stockholders.

Besides disbanding the Federal League, the peace settlement among the three major leagues called for some FL owners to get buyouts of varying amounts while others were allowed to buy into existing NL and AL teams. Terrapins stockholders, however, were very unhappy with their proposed buyout of $50,000; their attorney, Stuart Jawrey, countered that the team's stockholders should be allowed to purchase an existing AL or NL team for $250,000 rather than take the buyout. Jawrey's offer was not only rejected, but he, the Terrapins, and the city of Baltimore were soundly ridiculed, primarily by Charles Ebbets of the NL's Brooklyn Robins. Among other things, Ebbets said, "Baltimore is one of the worst minor league towns in this country. You have too many colored population, to start with. They are a cheap population when it gets down to paying their money at the gate."

Rejected by the major leagues, the Terrapins stockholders, led by team president Carroll W. Rasin, next attempted to combine their team with the International League's Baltimore Orioles, owned by Jack Dunn. Dunn refused that offer and a subsequent offer to buy the Terrapins outright for $100,000. He did, however, purchase Terrapin Park for $25,000 and moved his Orioles in for the 1916 season.

Federal League president James Gilmore made one last attempt to resolve the issue with the Terrapins, raising the buyout offer to $75,000. Rasin turned down the offer and the FL washed its hands of the Terrapins, leaving the team out of the final settlement agreement among the three leagues. The Terrapins appealed to the U.S. Justice Department, claiming that Organized Baseball was in violation of federal antitrust laws, but the agency refused to get involved.

With their investment in the Terrapins now worthless, the stockholders next voted to spend $50,000 to take the matter to court. The first suit, filed by Jawrey on May 19, 1916, in U.S. District Court in Philadelphia, sought $900,000 in damages from Organized Baseball for destroying the Federal League and establishing a monopoly. On the day the trial began, June 11, 1917, Jawrey inexplicably withdrew the suit. On September 20, he refiled the suit, this time in Washington, D.C., including as additional defendants Charles A. Weegham (owner of the Chicago Whales), Harry F. Sinclair (owner of the Newark Peppers), and FL president Gilmore.

Nearly two years later, the trial was held. After nineteen days of testimony and jury deliberation, the Terrapins stockholders were awarded $254,000. Organized Baseball immediately appealed, and on December 6, 1920, the award was overturned on the grounds that baseball was not commerce and therefore was not subject to restraint-of-trade laws.

Now it was the Terrapins stockholders' turn to appeal and the case made its way to the U.S. Supreme Court. On May 29, 1922, seven years after it began, Baltimore's case against Organized Baseball ended. Justice Oliver Wendell Holmes wrote the unanimous opinion that upheld the appellate court's decision denying any damages to the Terrapins stockholders because "... while baseball is played for money, it is not trade or commerce in the commonly accepted use of those words. [It is] personal effort, not related to production [of goods]." Even more fatefully, Holmes upheld baseball's reserve clause.

But the efforts of the Terrapins to cast Organized Baseball as a business, not simply a pastime, were hardly in vain. They opened the door a crack for what followed fifty-three years later, when arbitrator Peter Seitz ruled baseball's reserve clause was illegal in the cases of Dave McNally and Andy Messersmith, pushing the door wide open for the free agency system in place today.

HELL ON WHEELS

THE BAY CITY BOMBERS
Professional Roller Derby
1954-73

In the 1950s and '60s, the Bay City Bombers drew crowds that made the Green Bay Packers, New York Yankees, and Boston Celtics green with envy. And they did it on roller skates.

During the Great Depression, Americans sought various forms of entertainment to distract themselves from their crushing economic worries. One of the most popular diversions was marathon dancing, which created a spin-off, marathon skating, in which participants roller-skated around a circular track, sometimes for weeks or months with only short rest periods. Enterprising promoter Leo Seltzer took things a bit further. When he noticed how spectators enthusiastically cheered when two skaters collided on the track, he devised a game that incorporated the contact, and then some. Roller derby was born.

Roller derby was a simple game in which two teams of five helmeted skaters and one jammer would skate around a banked, circular track with guardrails in an attempt to pass one another. If one team's jammer passed the other's, they scored a point. It was the duty of the other five skaters to block the opposing team's jammer. Sometimes this meant an elbow to the face or getting knocked over the guardrails. Teams consisted half of men, half women, with men skating against men and women against women most of the time, though occasionally the teams would mix.

It wasn't long before professional teams and organized leagues of roller derby enthusiasts hit the American scene. The most popular of these teams by far was the Bay City Bombers, based out of San Francisco, the hotbed of roller derby activity.

The Bombers routinely skated before crowds of 15,000–20,000 in America's armories and arenas, and even more—up to 50,000—when they performed in outdoor stadiums. Television jumped on the roller derby bandwagon early, making it one of the first sports to be telecast nationally in the late 1940s, and the Bay City Bombers were the star attraction. All Bombers matches were televised in the San Francisco Bay Area, while a select number were telecast nationwide to an audience of 19 million viewers, huge numbers in the early days of television. In addition, the Bombers filmed their matches, syndicating these to more than 120 stations nationwide.

The Refrigerator was known for one move that was short on finesse: jumping on an opposing skater and trying to squish him.

The Bombers increased their fan base by touring the country, playing hundreds of one-night stands every year, often skating seven nights a week with doubleheaders on Saturdays and Sundays. The Bombers also spawned a number of traveling squads that traveled the country to match wits—and elbows—against the best local teams. Typically, these local matches were televised after viewers had been warmed up by a taped Bombers match.

Never mind that roller derby was as spontaneous as professional wrestling. Americans loved the largely harmlessly brutal theater of it, and the Bombers became America's team, with fans tuning in nightly to watch "America's sweethearts"—captains Charlie O'Connel and the beautiful Joanie Weston (the Blonde Amazon) battle against the bad guys, usually the Los Angeles Thunderbirds or the New York Demons.

A typical Bombers match would include baddies like Terrible Teresa, the Fiery Calvello, and Banana Nose—all played by Ann

1960 Bay City Bombers program.

Calvello. Calvello, known as the "Demon of the Derby," and other villains were famous for their wild clothes, hair, and makeup, and their dirty tactics on the track. The Refrigerator, a behemoth on skates, was known for one move that was short on finesse: jumping on an opposing skater and trying to squish him. Regardless of the opposition's flagrant violations, the Bombers usually eked out a victory just as time was about to expire. And when they suffered a rare loss, it made for even better TV ratings the next night.

The roller derby and Bombers phenomenon that swept America from the 1940s to the early 1970s spawned many copy-cat Bombers teams and numerous feature movies, including *Fireball,* starring Mickey Rooney, and *Kansas City Bomber,* starring Raquel Welch. By 1973, however, the Bay City Bombers had become victims of their own success and overexposure; the Bombers had appeared on television almost nightly for years, and the fans eventually tired of them, seeking new avenues of entertainment. When the television ratings tanked virtually overnight, the Bombers skaters and promoters suddenly found themselves out of work for the first time in a generation. Over the years, both roller derby and the Bombers tried to revive themselves with a variety of gimmicks, such as incorporating a figure-eight track for more collisions, a "wall of death," a ski-jump, and even an alligator pit. But not even teams comprised of lesbians, go-go girls, or midgets could attract the huge crowds that had once flocked to America's favorite sport.

FIRST THINGS FIRST

THE BOSTON BRAVES
National League
1876–1952

The long-running Boston Braves were a team of firsts. Unfortunately, they also led the league in owners who could squeeze blood out of a rosin bag.

When baseball's first professional league, the National Association, folded after the 1875 season, Boston's entry, winners of four consecutive NA pennants, became a charter member of the National League, changing its name from the Red Stockings to the Red Caps. Boston finished fourth in the NL's inaugural season of 1876, but was already beginning to pile up the firsts: It won the very first NL game, 6–5, over Philadelphia, a twenty-error contest witnessed by 3,000 fans, and it was the only team to complete its entire seventy-game schedule in 1876.

The team's owner, Nathaniel Apollonio, was also the first name in frugality. When pitcher Joe Borden, nicknamed "Josephus the Phenomenal," was unable to live up to his three-year contract due to an injury after one year, Apollonio insisted that Borden work off his $2,000 per year salary as the team's overpriced groundskeeper, reasoning that Borden would be too embarrassed to accept and agree to a smaller buyout. But Borden called his bluff and immediately set to work cutting the grass and mending the fences at the South End Grounds. Apollonio got Borden to agree to take three-quarters of his remaining salary.

That lone season was all Apollonio could stand in the baseball business, and in 1877 he sold out to a group headed by Arthur H. Soden, the man who would control the team for the next thirty years. Soden, who made his fortune in pharmaceutical supplies, banking, roofing, and railroads, was a leading voice on the side of baseball management and the first to propose the idea of baseball's reserve clause, which bound players to one team indefinitely. When NL president William Hulbert died in 1882, Soden became the NL's first interim president.

Soden made Apollonio look like a philanthropist. He often did his own ticket selling and collecting to save on staffing. He abolished complimentary passes, limiting himself to just two per game. Soden encouraged his players to retrieve foul balls and, if necessary, wrestle with the fans to get the balls back. He made players pay for their uniforms and their cleaning. Broken bats were discarded, but cracked and splintered ones were repaired and put back in use. Soden always found an excuse for refusing to pay dividends to the team's stockholders. And when outfielder Charlie Jones once complained, while on a road trip in Cleveland, that Soden owed him $378, Soden promised to look into it, then left Jones in Cleveland when the team departed for Boston. Soden then claimed Jones had jumped his contract and succeeded in having him banned for two years.

1914 celluloid pin of the "Miracle" Boston Braves.

Oddly, though, the miserly Soden became the first owner ever to purchase a player outright for cash when he bought King Kelly from Chicago for $10,000. His team won two pennants in the 1870s, another in 1883 (when the team changed its name to the Beaneaters), then became the league's powerhouse in the 1890s, winning five more pennants behind second baseman Bobby Lowe (the first player ever to hit four homers in one game), shortstop Herman Long, and pitcher Kid Nichols. The Beaneaters were the first (and only) team to win the NL pennant during a split season (1892), when the first-half winner (Boston) played the second-half champ (Cleveland Spiders) in a postseason playoff. Boston swept Cleveland five straight, but fan interest was low and the NL abandoned the split-season format after one season.

> Soden proceeded to make one of the worst
> decisions in baseball history.

While dominant in the nineteenth century (it was the first team ever to win one hundred games in a season, in 1892), Boston turned into a doormat in the next, becoming the first twentieth-century team to lose one hundred games in consecutive seasons (1905–06). With the team's fortunes and its fan base deteriorating, Soden proceeded to make one of the worst decisions in baseball history, as far as the National League and his Boston Beaneaters were concerned. When Ban Johnson first aspired to turn his fledgling American League into a major league in 1900, he asked the NL for their endorsement, promising that if they agreed to the AL's equal status as a major league, he would not locate any AL team in an NL city. Soden, acting as NL spokesman, not only rejected Johnson's offer, but announced that he and the other NL owners would revive the American Association (AA), and together they would ruin the AL. When Soden provocatively took preliminary steps to set up an AA franchise in Boston, an angry Johnson established a franchise called the Somersets, which quickly became the more popular team in Boston, changing their name in 1907 to the Red Sox.

By 1905, the Beaneaters, wallowing in the cellar, had achieved another first: They became the first team with four twenty-game losers in the same season. In 1906, they did it again, and no other team has turned the trick since. This was the last straw for Soden, who was so far in debt that his only option was to sell the team to two brothers, George and John Dovey, who fronted for a Pittsburgh theater owner named John Harris. So involved were the Dovey brothers that by 1907 reporters were calling the team the Doves. But a name change, new electric scoreboard, and refurbished stadium all failed to help. The Doves had two more one-hundred-loss seasons before being purchased by New York lawyer William Russell, who in his one year of ownership renamed the team the Rustlers in his honor, then finished in last with a record of 44–107. The huge financial bath he took likely contributed to the heart attack that killed him shortly after the season.

In a forced sale, millionaire contractor James Gaffney purchased the team. Although he owned the team only four years, Gaffney made numerous contributions to the team's history. First, he gave the franchise the name it would keep—with a five-year exception—until today. Second, he brought in a number of quality players, which turned the team's fortunes around. Third, he built a new ballpark in 1915, Braves Field, with a playing area so big it was ten years before anyone hit a home run into the left-field bleachers. Gaffney's main source of pride, however, was leading the team to the 1914 NL pennant with a streak so incredible the team was aptly dubbed the Miracle Braves. By early July, the team was in last place. Worse, when they played an exhibition game against the employees of a soap company, they lost. Then the "miracle": The Braves reeled off fifty-two wins in their final sixty-six games, staging the greatest comeback in baseball history. So energized was the city of Boston that even Red Sox owner Joseph Lannin became a fan, offering the use of his bigger and nicer stadium, Fenway Park. The Braves set regular season single-game and series attendance records while playing in Fenway, then topped it off with a World Series sweep of the heavily favored Philadelphia A's.

But Gaffney left as quickly as he had come, selling the team after the 1915 season. For the next thirty-two years, the Braves languished mostly in the second division, finishing last or next to last fifteen times. During one five-day stretch in 1929, the Braves established another first when they lost ten games, all double-headers. To boost attendance, the Braves signed former stars in the twilight of their careers, such as Babe Ruth, to attract fans. In an effort to break out of the doldrums, in 1936 Boston held a contest to rename the team; Bees beat out suggestions like the Boston Basements or Boston Bankrupts, but the rechristened team created little buzz before reverting to the name Braves for the 1941 season.

They had one last hurrah, though, in 1948 when, now owned by Lou Perini and led by the dynamic pitching duo of Johnny Sain and Warren Spahn, the Braves won the pennant, drawing 1.5 million fans. But after they lost the World Series to the Indians, things fell apart. Key injuries, combined with the sale of several star players to raise cash, led right back to mediocrity. In 1952, the Braves finished in seventh place, drawing a measly 282,000 fans.

But the franchise wasn't through achieving "firsts": On March 18, 1953, in the middle of spring training, the Braves became the first twentieth-century NL team to relocate to another city when they moved to Milwaukee.

BROKEN

THE BOSTON/NEW ORLEANS/ PORTLAND BREAKERS
United States Football League
1983–85

No team in sports history has been the subject of as much teasing as the United States Football League's Breakers. After playing in Boston in 1983, New Orleans in 1984, and Portland in 1985, fans of the team—if they had any left—were wondering where the Breakers would be playing in 1986. Anchorage? Honolulu? *Tokyo?* One reporter suggested the Breakers place a classified ad: "Pro football team looking for a home. With water view, if possible."

The Boston Breakers were charter members in the newly created United States Football League, which began play in 1983. Owners George Matthews and former New England Patriots wide receiver Randy Vataha had sold their chain of local racquetball centers to finance the team's purchase.

Vataha and Matthews knew it was a risky proposition, especially considering the USFL's decision to avoid head-to-head competition with the NFL by playing a spring schedule. But what put the Breakers at risk right from the start was the lack of a proper stadium in which to play their games. They couldn't afford Sullivan (now Foxboro) Stadium, home of the Patriots, nor were they able to negotiate a lease with their second choice, Harvard Stadium. This relegated them to Boston University's 21,000-seat Nickerson Field, the smallest venue in the USFL, which sat on the former site of the Boston Braves baseball field. The Breakers tried to put the best spin on it. The inaugural season's media guide trumpeted, "We're already associated with a New England Football Tradition," an apparent attempt to play on owner

Vataha's career with the Patriots. They also hired a big name offensive coordinator—Roman Gabriel, the former NFL MVP quarterback of the Los Angeles Rams.

On the field, the Breakers were successful, going 11–7 in 1983, but failed to make the playoffs. Their initial concern over Nickerson Field's small size proved to be unwarranted as the Breakers averaged only 12,817 per game, worst in the USFL. As it turned out, the Breakers lost money even when they did sell out because the visiting teams got a cut of the gate receipts.

Disillusioned over their one-season fiasco, Vataha and Matthews sold the Breakers to Joseph Canizaro, a Louisiana real estate developer who moved the team to New Orleans. Canizaro, who was much better financed than the previous owners, leased the 73,000-seat Superdome for the Breakers' new home. Former NFL tight end Dan Ross and rookie halfbacks Marcus Dupree and Buford Jordan helped the Breakers get off to a 5–0 start, but the Breakers lost 10 of their remaining 13 games, including their last six in a row, disappointing their new fans, which averaged 30,557 in the team's second season.

Following the disappointing 1984 season, the USFL's owners decided to go to a fall schedule in 1986. Canizaro, realizing that his team could never win a head-to-head battle for fan loyalty with the NFL's Saints, decided to get a jump on things by moving the Breakers to Portland, Oregon, for the 1985 season, figuring that a city without a pro football team would be thrilled. Coach Dick Coury reasoned that "Portland is only an hour from the ocean, so the name Breakers still makes sense."

The name may have made sense, but the move didn't. The citizens of Portland had already rejected pro football back, when the World Football League's Portland Storm/Thunder franchise (incidentally, also coached by Dick Coury) folded without a whimper. But Canizaro optimistically leased Portland's 32,500-seat Civic Stadium, and he didn't help his own cause by establishing the team's training facility at California State Polytechnic

University in Pomona, 1,000 miles away from the Breakers' new home.

The Breakers recorded their worst season yet, finishing 6–12. Attendance was modest at 19,919 per game, but the financial loss was staggering. Canizaro, like all USFL owners, hoped that the league's antitrust suit against the NFL would lead to some kind of merger or financial settlement between the two groups, but it was winding slowly through the courts. After falling behind $500,000 in his payroll, Canizaro was unable to wait any longer for a favorable court decision. Citing the team's combined $17 million loss over three seasons, Canizaro suspended operations.

1985 Portland Breakers pennant.

At a press conference to announce the team's decision, Breakers president John Ralston was a bit more sanguine. "Our image may be tarnished a little bit, but we will make a go of it here in Portland. We're in the habit of changing lemons into lemonade, and we're confident we'll field a much stronger team in the fall of 1986."

But when the court decided to award the USFL just three dollars in damages, the Breakers were finally broken, and folded along with the league.

TOO GOOD TO LAST

THE BOSTON RED STOCKINGS
National Association
1871–75

E very league has its dynasty team. The NBA has the Celtics, the NHL the Canadiens, the NFL the Packers, and major league baseball the New York Yankees. But for five years a long, long time ago, baseball's unquestioned kings were the Boston Red Stockings. They were so dominant, in fact, that it destroyed them.

When baseball's first professional team, the formidable Cincinnati Red Stockings, was disbanded in 1870 and its great players scattered, the leading amateur teams in the country de-

1873 Boston Red Stockings.

cided to form a professional league that would make it easier to determine each season's champion. Cincinnati's former manager and center fielder Harry Wright, by all accounts the best all-around baseball player in America, and his brother George, the team's shortstop, ended up in Boston, where George found investors who were very interested in bringing a top team to their city. Harry then persuaded former Cincinnati teammates Charlie Gould and Cal McVey to join their new team, the *Boston* Red Stockings.

The backers of the new Boston Red Stockings team had raised an incredible $15,000 for salaries and expenses, but Harry balked at the thought of paying large salaries to players; paying players $1,000 to $1,500 for the eight-month season was a dizzying proposition to Harry, in an era when the average Boston factory worker was making just $2.30 a week plus board for a sixty-nine-hour workweek. Harry wanted to keep the Red Stockings an amateur team. But the seeds of baseball professionalism had been sown in America and the team's backers forced Harry to go the professional route.

Harry Wright was able to secure the playing services of a veritable all-star team that included Jim O'Rourke, Al Spalding, Ross Barnes, and Deacon White.

For their entire five-year National Association existence, the Red Stockings played their home games at South End Grounds, which would later be the home for the NL's Boston team through the 1915 season. It had ample seating and a nice grandstand, but the field was unusual for its time: It was almost entirely dirt, which was rolled before games to compact it. The dimensions were also quite odd: 250 feet to left, 255 to right, and 445 to dead center field.

It was the perfect ballpark for the right kind of hitters, and Harry packed his lineup with them. In 1875, the last year of the NA, Boston had the top four batters in the league and eight of the top twenty. Second baseman Ross Barnes led the way at .372 (winning his second NA batting title), followed by Deacon White

(.355), Cal McVey (.352), and George Wright (.337). Andy Leonard chipped in with a .323 average, and even pitcher Al Spalding hit .318. The other three regulars were Harry Schafer (.295), Jim O'Rourke (.289), and Jack Manning (.285). Of course, hitters of the era were also abetted by the underhand pitching, which allowed teams to carry only one primary pitcher. For the Red Stockings, that man was Al Spalding, the man who would later create the Spalding Sporting Goods empire. Spalding's 57–5 record in 1875 gave him a five-year record in the NA of 207–56. Spalding easily outdistanced the pitcher with the second-best five-year record, Dick McBride of the Philadelphia Athletics, who was 152–76.

The NA schedule expanded every year of its five-year existence. In 1871 it was about thirty games. The next four years it was approximately fifty, sixty, seventy, and eighty games. Approximately, it should be emphasized, because it was left up to each team to set its own schedule as the season went along. Some teams preferred playing more league games and fewer non-league games while other teams preferred fewer league games with more tournaments and barnstorming tours.

The 1871 Red Stockings finished in third place with a record of 20–10, two games behind the Philadelphia Athletics and percentage points behind Chicago, the only year Boston didn't win the NA pennant. Boston took the 1872 pennant by a comfortable seven-and-a-half-game margin over both the Baltimore Canaries and Philadelphia Athletics with a 39–8 record, but the 1873 race was much more interesting. The Philadelphia White Stockings had gotten off to a strong start, leading the league at one point with a 32–10 record, four games ahead of Boston. But when star Philadelphia first baseman Denny Mack was run over by a horse, the distraught Philadelphia team lost five games in a row, allowing Boston to get back in the race, go on a tear, and win its second straight pennant, this time by four games.

In 1874, Boston walked away with yet another pennant, this time by a solid seven and a half games over the New York Mutuals. They and the Philadelphia Athletics interrupted the season for a nearly two-month midseason tour of England and Ireland to play each other in exhibition baseball games and challenge their hosts in cricket matches. Attendance was poor, however, and the adventure was financially crippling for both teams. In 1875, the pennant race was a rout. The Red Stockings finished an incredible 71–8 (a winning percentage of .899), averaged more than ten runs per game, and were a perfect 37–0 at home.

By now, though, resentment over Boston's predictable success hurt attendance on the road, and complacency hurt it at home. Nobody wanted to watch a rout every day. A *Chicago Tribune* article of the time reported, "... a thunderbolt from a serene sky would cause less astonishment in this city than the news of [Boston's] defeat...." Many of the better amateur teams of 1875 were outdrawing Boston. To make matters worse, in July four of Boston's star players—Spalding, White, McVey, and Barnes—announced that they had signed with William Hulbert's Chicago White Stockings for the 1876 season. For the rest of the season fans were openly abusive to the departing players, although it seemed only to spur the team on to its remarkable record.

The dimensions were also quite odd: 250 feet to left, 255 to right, and 445 to dead center field.

It wasn't just the Red Stockings who had trouble. The NA had expanded from eight teams to thirteen in 1875, and the increased demand for quality players drove salaries higher. For a league already suffering from rampant gambling, rowdiness, game throwing, and teams' refusal to complete their schedules, the expansion proved fatal. Nearly half the teams in the league failed to finish the 1875 season. Boston's runaway pennant simply drove the last nail into the NA's coffin, and the league disbanded before beginning play in 1876.

When Hulbert launched his plan for a new owner-controlled league with stricter rules of behavior and accountability, six of the strongest NA teams—including Boston, which renamed itself the Red Caps—joined new franchises in Louisville and Cincinnati to become the eight charter members of the new National League. The need for reform was so obvious to virtually everyone that there was no serious opposition to Hulbert's reformist zeal. Only the great baseball writer Henry Chadwick was upset over the move to a new league, and mostly because he had been left out of the loop.

DEM HEROES

THE BROOKLYN DODGERS
National League
1890-1957

The Brooklyn Dodgers were famous for their innovations, historical precedents, cheap owners, and rabid fans, but ultimately the team's greatest—and ambiguous—legacy was pointing the way to the megabusiness that baseball was about to become.

The team's roots were in another era of great baseball change. When a group of rebellious players announced in 1889 their intention to form a third major league the next season, the Players' League, executives of both the American Association and National League met in simultaneous sessions in Manhattan's Fifth Avenue Hotel to discuss mutual strategy and possible retaliatory measures. Two AA owners, Charles Byrne of the Brooklyn Bridegrooms and Aaron Stern of the

c. 1950s Brooklyn Dodgers pennant.

Cincinnati Reds, were so upset over St. Louis owner Chris Von Der Ahe's attempt to install a puppet American Association president that they left their own league meeting and walked down the hall to the NL meeting. By the end of the day, both teams had joined the National League.

Byrne was an owner ahead of his time. Since he was already

paying some of the highest salaries in the major leagues, the 1890 player revolt had almost no effect on his Bridegrooms, so named because of the many players who got married in 1888. The only player he lost to the Players' League was backup catcher Joe Visner, so it was a relatively easy matter for the Bridegrooms—defending AA champs—to win the 1890 NL pennant by six and a half games.

Attracting fans was more difficult. The Bridegrooms suffered from the presence of two other major league teams in Brooklyn, the Gladiators of the AA (quickly brought in to replace the Bridegrooms) and the Wonders of the PL. In the settlement that followed the 1890 season, the Bridegrooms agreed to absorb the Wonders, led by manager John Montgomery Ward.

Over the next four decades, the team changed its name many times, and was often referred to by unofficial nicknames as often as official ones. The Grooms, the Wonders, Foutz's Fillies, Hanlon's Superbas, the Trolley Dodgers, and the Robins all took their turns. For one year, 1913, the team was even known as the Dodgers, but it dropped the name after the season and went by the Robins from 1914 to 1931. It wasn't until 1932 that it officially adopted the name Dodgers.

In 1892, Brooklyn set one of baseball's earliest precedents when pitcher Tom Lovett, who was 30–11 in 1890 and 23–19 in 1891, declined a $3,000 contract for 1892 because it was less than he had made the year before. The Dodgers refused to budge, citing the huge financial losses during the 1890 season because of the PL revolt. Lovett didn't budge either, and became the first player ever to hold out for an entire season over a salary dispute. In 1899, in the midst of a tense pennant race, Brooklyn canceled another of their innovations—Ladies Day—because many men complained that the women chattered constantly during the game and allowed their children to run wild in the aisles.

Yet another Brooklyn innovation—playing on Sunday in defiance of blue laws—also backfired. In 1904, the team was in the midst of a fifteen-year run of weak finishes and pitiful attendance. Owner Charles Ebbets came up with the idea of "free entertainment" to circumvent the NL's ban on Sunday games. On April 17, he promoted a "free" game against the Boston Braves. All fans had to do was buy color-coded scorecards priced suspiciously like regular box, grandstand, and bleacher seats. He got away with it, but when he tried it a week later against the Phillies, the police marched onto the field and arrested Brooklyn's starting battery of Ed Poole and Fred Jackson as well as Philadelphia's leadoff hitter, Frank Roth. The three players were initially acquitted at a court hearing of violating city Sabbath laws, but that verdict was later overturned and fines were levied against all three players and their clubs. The other NL owners warned Ebbets not to include them in any future schemes.

Brooklyn canceled Ladies Day because men complained that the women chattered constantly and allowed their children to run wild.

Thirteen years later, Ebbets, figuring everything had been forgotten and forgiven, tried a new Sunday promotion. On July 1, 1917, he arranged with the U.S. Navy for a band concert to take place at Ebbets Field. Donations would go to the Red Cross and other war-related charities. And oh, by the way, anyone who paid admission to the concert would get to see a "free" baseball game between the Dodgers and Phillies. When the 1,500 marching sailors left the field and the game began, Ebbets and his manager, Wilbert Robinson, were arrested and later found guilty of violating the city's blue laws. The Dodger executives' desire to help the military in time of war did make an impression because, two years later, state senator and future mayor Jimmy Walker sponsored a successful bill that allowed each city to decide whether or not to allow Sunday ball games, thus ending New York's blue laws.

Ebbets also received his share of negative publicity, particularly from local sportswriters who blamed the team's many years of second-division finishes on his miserly ways. When the 1922 season opener featured a lavish parade with Ebbets at the front, a sarcastic *New York Herald* columnist reported, "President Ebbets was in the parade but dropped a dime just before the band signaled the start of the procession, and the parade moved on while he was searching for it." When Ebbets objected to the characterization, the columnist reported, "I was in error when I wrote that squire Ebbets held up the Opening Day parade by searching for a dime he had dropped. The president of the Brooklyn club has informed me that the amount involved was fifteen cents."

The press didn't have Ebbets to kick around much longer, however, because he died the night before Opening Day in 1925. His successor, Edward McKeever, died eleven days later from a bout of influenza he caught while standing in a chilling rain at Ebbets's grave while gravediggers struggled to enlarge the hole because of the unexpectedly large coffin.

The void led to an internal struggle that resulted in twenty years of chaotic rule by often uncaring executors. By 1937, the deterioration of the Brooklyn organization was so severe that other league owners were calling for something to be done. Attendance was averaging little more than 6,000 per game; the ballpark was literally rotting away, with crumbling outfield walls and thousands of broken seats; ushers who were little more than thugs were hired to remove complaining fans from the ballpark; and the telephones were frequently shut off at the team's main office for nonpayment, circumstances that inspired *World Telegram* cartoonist Willard Mullin to first call the team "Dem Bums."

Finally, Brooklyn Trust Company, which held the mortgage on Ebbets Field as well as a $500,000 note, asked Commissioner Ford Frick to intervene and appoint a baseball man to run the team instead of the revolving door of executors, something that would be in everyone's best interests. Frick agreed, and brought in Larry MacPhail, who had recently helped turn around Cincinnati's fortunes.

MacPhail was given a free hand and convinced Brooklyn Trust to give the team another $400,000 for stadium improvements and the purchase of better players. MacPhail gave Ebbets Field a complete overhaul with new seats, concession stands, and a paint job. He also added lights for night games, the first of which drew 38,738 fans who witnessed Johnny Vander Meer's second consecutive no-hitter. In 1938 he hired Babe Ruth to be the team's first-base coach, although, of course, he really wanted the extra fans brought into the park by Ruth's batting practice moon shots. By the time the season ended, the Dodgers had drawn 750,000 fans, more than double the year before.

In 1939, MacPhail made some enemies in New York when he unilaterally broke the team's agreement with the Giants and Yankees not to broadcast the team's games on the radio—an agreement made in the belief that it would help attendance. It was a decision that put the Dodgers into every living room and bar in the greater New York area, helping increase the team's popularity and fan base, paving the way for the Dodgers' exploitation of television.

MacPhail broke more new ground in the 1940s when he began to use air travel instead of rail to transport the Dodgers to St. Louis and Chicago. After two of his top players—Joe Medwick and Pee Wee Reese—were beaned, he hired researchers at Johns Hopkins University to design protective bands that could be sewn into players' caps, the forerunner of batting helmets. He hired organist Gladys Gooding to play the National Anthem before each game and other songs during the game, though she and MacPhail both got into a bit of hot water when she played "Three Blind Mice" as the umpires came on the field. And he instituted a grandstand band called "Dodger Sym-Phony," whose specialty was following an opposing player back to the dugout after he made an out and taunting him with the tune, "Go wash your feet, go wash your feet," then clanging cymbals and booming a bass drum when he sat down. MacPhail also built the Dodgers' farm and scouting systems into the best in baseball.

MacPhail left the team in 1942 for the military and was replaced by Branch Rickey, who built on his predecessor's work by sending out 20,000 letters to high school coaches around the country asking for player recommendations. But Rickey's greatest achievement was using the Dodger organization to integrate major league baseball. Under the guise of participating in the newly created Black United States Baseball League in 1945, Rickey created the Brooklyn Brown Dodgers and signed Jackie Robinson. In 1946, Rickey sent Robinson and black pitchers John Wright and Roy Partlow to the Montreal Royals, the Dodgers' International League farm team. That same year, Roy Campanella filled in for Walter Alston for one game as manager in a Nashua Dodgers minor league game, thereby becoming the first black to manage in the modern minor leagues. And in 1947, Rickey brought Robinson up to the Dodgers, having given white players two years to get used to the idea of playing with blacks.

The Dodgers' pioneering integration helped usher in a decade of unprecedented team success. From 1947 to 1956, the Dodgers won six NL pennants (and finished second three times), though their AL opponent in all six Series, the Yankees, five times foiled their dreams of a World Championship. Despite it all, the team had trouble drawing the kind of crowds needed to pay all the new high-priced talent the Dodgers were bringing on board.

Most disconcerting—and eye-opening—to Dodger owner Walter O'Malley in 1953 was that the Braves, playing their first season in Milwaukee, had outdrawn the NL champ Dodgers by more than 650,000. He also understood the reasons why: a bigger stadium, more parking spaces, and a television blackout of home games. By 1956, O'Malley noted that the Dodgers' peak attendance year had been 1947, so he scheduled a handful of games at Jersey City's Roosevelt Stadium in an effort to convince city officials that if the Dodgers didn't get a new stadium, they could lose their team.

The Jersey City ploy didn't work, so O'Malley pushed harder, selling Ebbets Field to real estate developer Melvin Kratter for $3 million, taking out a three-year lease. When local officials remained unfazed, O'Malley swapped minor league teams with the Cubs' Phil Wrigley in early 1957, giving O'Malley the territorial rights to Los Angeles. In August, the New York Giants announced that they would be moving to San Francisco in 1958. O'Malley continued to insist the Dodgers were staying put in Brooklyn—until a week after the season ended, when he announced the Dodgers *were* moving to Los Angeles after all, a move that helped propel major league baseball into an era of unprecedented expansion and prosperity.

And while O'Malley moved the team for practical business reasons ("The borough had its chances for ten years"), Brooklyn Dodger fans couldn't help but be angry ("We was robbed!"). To paraphrase more than a few of the brokenhearted, now there really *wasn't* going to be a next year.

SQUEAKY WHEELS

THE BUFFALO BISONS
Players' League
1890

Maybe there's no crying in baseball, but there's definitely whining, and there was no bigger example of it than in 1890. And although the whining got two influential players what they wanted in the short run—a Players' League team in Buffalo—they came to regret it by season's end.

The Players' League probably never would have come about had not the National League in 1889 implemented its radical new salary classification system, whereby all players (except player-managers, who could make a little more) were required to be paid between $1,500 and $2,500 depending on the player's position, performance on the field, and behavior off the field. For the players, who had long been at odds with the owners, this was the last straw. A core group of 120 players, approximately one hundred

from the NL and twenty from the American Association, decided to form their own new league in 1890, with the intent of placing a team in each of the NL's eight cities. Just before the start of the 1890 season, however, two AA teams—Cincinnati and Brooklyn—jumped to the NL (enabling the NL to dump its two weakest teams, Washington and Indianapolis). The PL quickly shifted gears

Third baseman Deacon White, who averaged .303 over 15 years, ended his career with Buffalo.

and placed a team in Brooklyn, though they decided against placing one in Cincinnati.

That Buffalo, a city with a strong baseball history, got the other team was largely due to the influence and whining of Deacon White and Jack Rowe, who had been third baseman and shortstop for the Detroit Wolverines in 1888 when, at the end of the season, Detroit owner Frederick Stearns held a fire sale to dispose of the team and its players. He sold White and Rowe to Pittsburgh, but both players refused to report. Instead they wanted to go to Buffalo's International League team, in which they both owned stock. White was even the team's president. Of White's refusal to report to Pittsburgh, Stearns warned, "White may have been elected president of the Buffalo club or president of the United States, but that won't enable him to play ball in Buffalo. He'll play ball in Pittsburgh or get off the Earth."

By June of 1889, both White and Rowe still had not reported. It took the intervention of John Montgomery Ward, president of the Players' Brotherhood, to resolve the mess by convincing both players to report to Pittsburgh without signing a contract. The two did so, but made sure that Ward knew he owed them one. When the PL was formed in 1890, with Ward taking the lead, White and Rowe called in their markers and got the new league to agree to make the Buffalo Bisons the last franchise to join the new league.

Because the PL truly was a league of the players, some of them became investor-players in the new league. Eventual Hall of Fame catcher Connie Mack and deaf outfielder Dummy Hoy both became part owners of the Bisons franchise. The Cincinnati *Enquirer*, still miffed over the PL's choice of Buffalo over Cincinnati for the final franchise, called the Bisons team ". . . a home for respectable old men," an obvious swipe at the forty-two-year-old White's age.

On the field, the Bisons, led by manager Rowe, got off to a fast start with a four-game sweep of the Cleveland Spiders, scoring 28, 15, 19, and 18 runs. Inexplicably, the Bisons then lost twenty of their next twenty-five games, falling into a hole too deep to climb out of. Of the sixty-eight blowouts they played (games won or lost by five or more runs), they lost a pathetic fifty-three. Their pitching staff had the highest ERA in the league at 6.11 (the next worst team's ERA was 4.23). They had the lowest team batting average—.260. They scored the fewest runs (793) while allowing the most (1,199). It's no wonder they averaged only 924 paid attendance at home. And the Bisons couldn't blame their poor attendance on a competing major league team in the same city, as was the case with the PL's other seven teams. Even Buffalo's International League team had relocated to Montreal on June 3.

Given the nature of nineteenth-century baseball, it almost seems a miracle that the PL remained intact for the whole season. Not one team disbanded, not even the overmatched Bisons, who finished with a record of 36–96, forty-six and a half games out of first and a whopping twenty games behind the seventh-place Spiders, the team they had ravaged to begin the season. In the end, though, it didn't matter because, even with the cream of the crop when it came to players, the PL folded after one season. When the NL approached the PL and AA with a peace settlement, the PL was in the hole more than $125,000. The PL Brotherhood didn't know it at the time, but the NL was more than $500,000 in the red. Had they known, they might have held out for another year and actually put the NL out of business.

When the dust settled, the PL franchises in Boston, Pittsburgh, Brooklyn, and New York merged with their NL counterparts. The Chicago Pirates were sold to Al Spalding, owner of the NL's Chicago franchise. The NL's Philadelphia franchise purchased the AA's Philadelphia franchise, and the PL's Cleveland franchise was paid a buyout by the NL's Cleveland franchise. The four best AA teams (Louisville, Washington, Baltimore, and St. Louis) transferred to the NL while the others were given cash payments and disbanded. When the PL music stopped in this game of musical chairs, only the Buffalo Bisons were left without a chair. Since the Bisons had been the only team in their market and hadn't damaged another league's team, no one felt any obligation to compensate the Buffalo owners for the contraction of the Bisons.

Besides, with only one major league left standing (the NL), and barely so, baseball's rulers wanted a return to business as usual, in which the owners had total control, the reserve clause was fully in force, and there were no squeaky wheels, such as Deacon White and Jack Rowe, neither of whom ever played major league baseball again.

GOPHER BALLS

THE BUSTIN' BABES AND THE LARRUPIN' LOUS
Professional Barnstorming
1927–early 1930s

No television, little radio, and no major league baseball team west of the Mississippi River: It was 1927 and for folks in small-town America the biggest attraction of all was the chance to experience firsthand the batting exploits of the game's two greatest hitters, the legendary Babe Ruth and Lou Gehrig. At a time when many Americans ventured no more than a few miles from their own towns during their lifetimes, the barnstorming games between the Bustin' Babes and Larrupin' Lous were truly an event of a lifetime, a memory to pass down through the generations.

For Babe Ruth, of course, it was hardly community service. He had a well-known appetite for everything—food, drink, women, money... *life*—that his 1926 Yankee salary of $52,000 (ten times what the average major leaguer earned) barely covered. There was another $200,000 that year from endorsements, a movie, and various business deals—and still it was not enough. So even though the Yankees raised his salary to $70,000 in 1927, immediately after he and his Yankee teammates had swept the Pittsburgh Pirates in the World Series, he undertook a barnstorming tour to further supplement his income. Ruth had already experienced the income potential for exhibition games because the Yankees routinely scheduled them for the team's off days during the season, in large part to raise money in order to pay Ruth's huge salary.

Although Ruth's Bustin' Babes relied primarily on local talent to fill out his team, Ruth sometimes took along a few of his major league buddies. In 1927, Ruth enlisted the services of Lou Gehrig, largely as a thank-you for having done such a great job of protecting him in the batting order, giving him more opportunities to hit his record 60 home runs. The prospect of next facing Gehrig, who in 1927 hit 47 homers, 52 doubles, and 18 triples with 175 RBIs, left pitchers with no choice but to pitch to Ruth.

For the twenty-one-game tour that started on the East Coast and took them to California, Ruth originally agreed to give Gehrig 10 percent of the gate receipts, but changed his mind and instead paid him a flat $10,000, $3,000 more than the twenty-four-year-old Gehrig's Yankee salary. Ruth received a flat fee of $2,500 per game from the local promoter, from which he paid the tour's expenses. The local players who joined in the game (minor leaguers, college players, servicemen, or semi-pros) were content to contribute their services free of charge for the chance to share the field with gods.

At every stop, Ruth invariably made other money from local promotions and endorsements, as well as from selling autographed baseballs. Bob Feller remembers going to a Bustin' Babes–Larrupin' Lous game with his father in Des Moines, Iowa. "Baseballs with their autographs were sold for five dollars from a bushel basket," Feller said. Five bucks was a fortune for a young Feller, however, and the future Hall of Famer had needed a scheme: "At the time, farmers in our area were being plagued by gophers. They offered a bounty of ten cents a pair for gopher claws. I caught enough gophers to pay for my own ball."

When Ruth's Bustin' Babes, decked out in black uniforms, took the field against Gehrig's Larrupin' Lous, in white, hundreds of fans would usually, at some point, pour onto the field, seeking autographs or at least a closer look at the immortal baseball stars. Although thirteen of the twenty-one games of the 1927 tour were never finished because of mass fan interference, no one went home disappointed. Ruth and Gehrig always got their homers, and fans (sometimes more than 20,000) always got their brushes with greatness.

1927 photo of Babe Ruth and Lou Gehrig in their barnstorming uniforms.

To make sure folks got their money's worth, Ruth and Gehrig led off every inning for their respective teams. When Ruth would hit one over the fence, it wasn't unusual for hundreds of young boys to race onto the field and accompany the Bambino around the bases. It was organized pandemonium. And Ruth loved it.

But it was a business. At one stop in Asbury Park, New Jersey, the local promoter had failed to come up with his $2,500 cashier's check as promised. So, while thousands of fans stomped their feet and clapped their hands in anticipation of the great Babe, Ruth sat in his easy chair in the hotel across the street from the ballpark, smoking a cigar while the panicky promoter scurried about to come up with the fee.

A few years later, Ruth, Gehrig, and their families took an off-season cruise together, during which at one point Gehrig found his wife alone in Ruth's compartment. Although it may have been innocent, Gehrig, a known mama's boy, reported the incident to his mother, who retaliated by chiding Ruth's wife over her lack of supervision of Ruth's daughter, Dorothy. An angry Ruth told Gehrig to tell his mother to mind her own business. Gehrig took offense at Ruth's remark and the two men stopped speaking for a long time. Needless to say, it put an end to their barnstorming days together. The Golden Goose that had been the Bustin' Babes and Larrupin' Lous teams died, not from incompetence, financial woes, or even greed, but rather from very large and very bruised egos.

THE PITS

CARD-PITT
National Football League
1944

W hen Art Rooney won $250,000 in a series of long-shot parlay bets at Saratoga Race Course in 1932, he used $2,500 of it to pay the franchise fee for his newly founded NFL team, the Pittsburgh Pirates. It was a gamble that didn't look like it would pay off. The Pirates—whose name Rooney changed to the Steelers in 1940—would not have a winning season until 1942. And then things really took a turn for the worse.

Because of a severe player shortage during World War II (more than 600 NFL players either enlisted or were drafted into the military), every team in the NFL was adversely affected, but none more than the Pittsburgh Steelers. In 1943, the six remaining Steelers players and sixteen Philadelphia Eagles had merged to form a new team called the Steagles, which finished a respectable 5–4–1. In 1944, the situation was even more acute because the player shortage had worsened while the league actually grew to eleven teams. The Cleveland Rams were returning after sitting out a year because of the war, and the Boston Yanks joined the league as an expansion team.

Since the odd number of teams was going to make scheduling difficult, NFL commissioner Elmer Layden asked the Steelers and Eagles to merge for a second year. The Eagles were willing, but only if all home games were played in Philadelphia. Rooney refused. Rooney also rejected a merger with both Boston and the Brooklyn Tigers. He finally agreed to merge his Steelers with the Chicago Cardinals, owned by his longtime friend Charlie Bidwill, with half the home games to be played at Pittsburgh's Forbes

Field and the other half at Chicago's Comiskey Park. The merged team was inelegantly called Card-Pitt.

When training camp opened on August 15 in Waukesha, Wisconsin, Card-Pitt's collection of misfits (those rated 4-F by the military, former high school players, college dropouts, and one player with only a single eye) showed up in ninety-degree heat. Six of them fainted from heat exhaustion. It was evident from the start that there would be another problem—the coaching. The two merged teams agreed to a "coaches by committee" system. Since 1944 was the first year coaches were allowed on the sidelines, it meant four coaches (two heads and two assistants) would be walking among the players, barking orders. Rooney's son Dan later said, "You know that old saying that too many chefs will spoil the soup? Well, we had too many chefs." The coaching awkwardness was apparent in Card-Pitt's two exhibition games, both shutout losses, 22–0 to the Eagles and 3–0 to the Redskins.

Could things get any worse? You bet they could.

Card-Pitt opened the regular season on September 24 against the Cleveland Rams in Forbes Field. A crowd of 21,000 watched as Card-Pitt snatched defeat from the jaws of victory. Late in the game, Card-Pitt was leading, 28–23, with Cleveland driving deep in Card-Pitt territory. When an interception gave Card-Pitt the ball at its own one-yard line with seconds to go, everyone thought the game was over. But instead of running out the clock or taking a safety to ensure victory, the committee of coaches decided to punt—on first down! The punter shanked the ball and it went only 10 yards. Three plays later the game was over, with Cleveland a 30–28 winner.

Could things get any worse? You bet they could. Before the next game, the team's quarterback, Coley McDonough, was drafted and left for the Army. Card-Pitt lost at Green Bay in week two, 34–7, before heading to Wrigley Field, where they were mauled by the Bears, 42–7. The coaches were so furious over the debacle that they handed out $200 fines for "indifferent play" to halfback Johnny Butler, fullback John Grigas, and guard Eberle Schultz. Already upset with the dictatorial style of coaching employed by the committee, the players staged a strike, refusing to practice until the three fined players were given a fair hearing. After Rooney met with the players, Butler was suspended and waived to Brooklyn. Schultz and Grigas agreed to pay their fines, but Rooney eventually rescinded them.

After a road loss to the New York Giants, 23–0, Card-Pitt went to Washington, the team's fourth straight road game, where the team jumped from the frying pan into the fire. In an attempt to change their luck, Card-Pitt had a new blue jersey designed to replace the Cards' red-and-white ones they wore in Chicago and the Steelers' black-and-gold ones they wore in Pittsburgh. Washington was color-blind. Card-Pitt lost their new quarterback, Johnny McCarthy, when he was carried off the field with two broken ribs. Then, just before the end of the first half, three separate fights broke out, the last of which included the coaches and escalated into a near riot. It took dozens of police officers to restore order. Even Art Rooney, an ex-boxer, was running to join the fray when he thought better of an owner being involved in a fight with the opposing team's players. When the final gun sounded, Card-Pitt was a 42–20 loser.

The team returned home and lost to the Detroit Lions, 27–6. In a letter to the *Pittsburgh Post-Gazette,* a disgruntled fan wrote, "We should start calling them the Car-Pits (carpets) as every team in the league walks all over them." The name stuck and the team continued to stink, losing its remaining four games to finish the season with an 0–10 record, the first of only five teams in NFL history to play a full schedule without a win.

Before the final game, Johnny Grigas had a shot at winning the NFL rushing title, but rather than play on frozen Forbes Field in a rematch against the brutal Bears, he went home to Massachusetts. Grigas left a note for Rooney, explaining that his soul wasn't in the game after taking a pounding week after week. Sixty years later, Dan Rooney said that Grigas might have been the smartest guy on the team since the Bears handed Card-Pitt their worst loss of the year, 49–7, outrushing them 308 yards to minus 2.

Their 0–10 record was not an adequate measure of how bad they were; said Rooney at the time, "We were the worst team in the history of the NFL." In their ten games, Card-Pitt was outscored 328–108; missed both of its field goal attempts; missed 4 of its 15 extra point tries; set the still-standing record for lowest punting average, 32.7 yards per kick; completed only 31 percent of its passes for just eight touchdowns and 41 interceptions, still the third highest total in NFL history; and committed 64 turnovers (41 interceptions and 23 fumbles) to their opponents' 27. Quarterback Johnny McCarthy didn't throw a TD pass while having 13 intercepted for a QB rating of 3.0.

By the time the 1945 season began, the war had ended and the Cardinals and Steelers returned to fielding their own teams, with somewhat better results. The Steelers actually won two games in 1945, the Cardinals one. But their owners never gave up on them. When the two teams met in the 2009 Super Bowl sixty-five years later, the Steelers were still owned by the Rooney family and the Cardinals by the Bidwills.

1944-style football helmet.

RINKY-DINK

THE CHICAGO COUGARS
World Hockey Association
1972-75

The 1974 Chicago Cougars were the Cinderella team of the World Hockey Association. Then Peter Pan turned them into pumpkins.

When the World Hockey Association was first organized in 1971, the league was counting on the Cougars to be one of its cornerstones. Unfortunately, six months of chaos left the franchise with no owner, no players, and no arena, just a few months before the league was set to begin play in 1972. After two ownership groups fell apart, brothers Jordon and William Kaiser, Chicago area real estate developers and restaurant magnates, stepped in and purchased the franchise for $25,000 from league cofounder Gary Davidson.

But by midsummer, the Cougars had only a single veteran player under contract, Bob Kelly, and he jumped back to the NHL before the season started. Pressed for time, the Kaisers settled on a team of minor leaguers, fringe NHL players, and one former Chicago Blackhawk, Reg Fleming. The Kaisers did make a strong bid for Chicago Blackhawks star Stan Mikita, offering him a multiyear contract at $300,000 per season, but the Blackhawks, having already lost Bobby Hull to the WHA's Winnipeg Jets, beat the Cougar offer, kept Mikita, and averted a total fan revolt.

Surprise, surprise—the Cougars got off to a disastrous start, 2–12–1, and finished with an even more inept 1–12–0 run, ending up 26–50–2, the worst record in the league.

Before the 1973 season, however, the Cougars bolstered their team when they signed a number of NHL stars, including two former Blackhawks, center Ralph Backstrom and defenseman

Pat Stapleton. Stapleton, a fan favorite, had spent the previous eight seasons with the Blackhawks, while Backstrom had spent most of his seventeen-year career with the Montreal Canadiens before joining the Blackhawks for just part of the 1972–73 season. With the Cougars he would set career highs in both goals and assists in 1973–74.

The invigorated Cougars became the league's Cinderella story in 1974 when they finished with a 38–35–5 record, for 81 points. A remarkable 10–3–2 run to close the season (including two wins over Quebec) allowed the Cougars to edge the Quebec Nordiques out of the playoffs by a single point. In the playoffs, the upstart Cougars had the unenviable task of playing the formidable New England Whalers, the defending league champs. In the 1973 playoffs, the Whalers had taken all three series by a four-games-to-one margin.

The Cougars quickly dropped the first two games in Boston. But 1974 was Cinderella's year, and the Cougars responded by winning the next three straight. After losing Game 6 at home, the Cougars returned to Boston for Game 7, where the Cougars edged the Whalers, 3–2, for an unexpected first-round victory. Then they faced the Toronto Toros, a team against which they had gone 5–2–1 during the regular season, but their real adversary, suddenly, was Peter Pan. The dilapidated International Amphitheatre, the

1972 Chicago Cougars uniform.

Cougars' home arena, had booked a presentation of *Peter Pan* starring gymnast Cathy Rigby over the same dates as the Cougars' home playoff games against Toronto. The Cougars tried to rent Chicago Stadium, but the Blackhawks were using it for their own Stanley Cup playoffs. After briefly considering moving their home games to the Cleveland Arena in Ohio, the Cougars finally settled on Randhurst Twin Ice Arena, a hockey rink at a suburban shopping mall. The good news: It was in the Chicagoland area. The bad: It had 2,000 seats, 7,000 fewer than the Amphitheatre's 9,000.

Despite it all, the Cougars prevailed again in seven, winning the final game on the road. This sent the Cinderella Cougars to the big ball, the Avco Cup Finals, against the Houston Aeros, for the WHA championship. The Aeros, led by aging hockey legend Gordie Howe and his two sons, Mark and Marty, had romped to the league's best record in 1973–74, but the Cougars were ready for them.

The Amphitheatre, however, wasn't. Once the *Peter Pan* show hit the road, for some inexplicable reason the Amphitheatre's crew melted the ice surface and dismantled the copper pipe system used to create the ice. Forced to return to rinky-dink Randhurst Twin Ice Arena for their home games, the disheartened Cougars were swept in four straight by the powerful Aeros.

Already frustrated over their failure for more than two years to get a badly needed new arena constructed, the Kaiser brothers viewed the *Peter Pan* public relations disaster as the last straw and put the financially struggling team up for sale. However, midway through the team's next season, its third, the Kaisers still hadn't found a buyer. Finally, they sold the team to three of their Cougars players—Backstrom, Stapleton, and Dave Dryden, the team's new goalie—for $2 million, a tidy profit.

The three purchased the team with the hope of finding a better-heeled buyer before the next season, but when no prince with a cash-filled glass slipper arrived, the new player-owners folded the Cougars and the players were scattered around the league in a dispersal draft.

BIG FISH

THE CHI-FED WHALES
Federal League
1914–15

I f you can't join 'em, beat 'em. And if you find you can't beat 'em, then rough 'em up enough that they finally *ask* you to join 'em.

That pretty much describes the Federal League's approach to becoming a third major league in 1914. Established as a minor league in 1913, the Federal League sought major league status in 1914 from Organized Baseball, the ruling body that had been established in 1902—a year after the formation of the American League—to oversee both major leagues and most minor ones as well. Soundly rebuffed, the FL withdrew from Organized Baseball, declared war on the other two major leagues, and began raiding them for players.

The FL president, John T. Powers, was a cautious man who opposed his league's owners' desire for major league status, so they voted him out of office and replaced him with James A. Gilmore, a coal magnate with an aggressive nature who was a minority owner of the FL's Chicago franchise (called the ChiFeds in 1914 and the Whales in 1915). Gilmore first convinced the FL owners to act as a group, not as individual proprietors within the league, whereupon the owners approved his plan of requiring each team to contribute $25,000 to a war chest with which to battle the other two major leagues. Gilmore also lined up other wealthy investors in each city to support their local team.

Chicago's deep pockets belonged to Charles Weegham (who became the majority owner), the millionaire owner of a chain of cafeterias; William Walker, owner of the largest fish wholesale business in the Midwest; and chewing gum magnate William

Wrigley. Together, these three men provided an initial infusion of $412,000. Of this, $250,000 went for the construction of Weegham Park, a state-of-the-art, completely fireproof stadium on Chicago's North Side.

Excluded by Organized Baseball, and therefore not bound by its reserve rule, the flush FL owners aggressively pursued players already under contract with other teams. When AL and NL owners cried foul, Gilmore's response was simple: Grant us major league status and we'll play ball according to your rules. Again they were refused.

The first major player signed by Weegham was Joe Tinker of the Cincinnati Reds, a former Chicago Cub and local fan favorite who would be the team's manager and shortstop. Next up was former twenty-four-game winner for the Pittsburgh Pirates, Claude Hendrix, who in 1914 would lead the FL in wins (29–11) while posting the second best ERA (1.69, just behind teammate Adam Johnson's 1.58).

Weegham's signing of Philadelphia Phillies outfielder Bill Killefer, however, opened a legal can of worms. After verbally committing to the Phillies, Killefer signed a three-year deal with the Chi-Feds for $17,500, a hefty raise. Less than two weeks later, Killefer signed a three-year deal with the suddenly generous Phillies for $19,500. Weegham sued the Phillies, but when the case came to court, the judge told both parties that as far as he was concerned, Killefer should be like any employee, free to sell his services to the highest bidder. In an omen of things to come sixty years later, the judge also opined that, as far as he was concerned, baseball's reserve clause didn't hold much legal weight.

On the field, Chicago finished second in 1914, one and a half games behind Indianapolis, outdrawing the Cubs, but not the White Sox. Encouraged, Weegham initiated a promotion in his lunchrooms for the 1915 season that gave each person who purchased a meal a free ticket to a Whales game (the team was renamed after a fan contest). He gave away other free tickets through his lunchroom raffles. Weegham also did away with the noisy food vendors who walked through the stands during Whales games, hawking their wares and obstructing views. He replaced them with concession stands located behind the last row of seats that were manned by professional food service workers and offered a major upgrade in the food traditionally offered at ballparks.

In 1915, Weegham signed pitcher George McConnell from the crosstown Cubs and Les Mann, an outfielder who had helped Boston's "Miracle Braves" win the World Series the year before. (Weegham almost lured the great Walter Johnson away from the Washington Senators, but Washington owner Calvin Griffith,

1914 Chicago
Chi-Feds pennant.

playing on Johnson's sense of loyalty, got him to stay with the stingier Senators, a decision he later admitted regretting.) McConnell led the FL with a 25–10 record, and when the dust settled the Whales had won the closest pennant race in major league history, a single percentage point ahead of the St. Louis Terriers.

Following the 1915 season, Weegham challenged the Phillies and Red Sox, winners of their respective leagues, to a three-way World Series. They ignored him. Weegham then challenged the Cubs and White Sox to a round-robin city championship series. They ignored him, too. Weegham then printed up a form letter addressed to the mayor of Chicago, demanding that such a city series be played, and gave them to his cafeteria customers to send in. The letter stressed that the Whales had outdrawn the Cubs two years in a row, and the fans demanded it. The mayor refused to get involved. Not to be outdone, the Federal League minted championship medallions that declared, "Chicago Whales— Champions of the World."

While poised to do battle again in 1916, the Federal League awaited an important legal decision in a suit filed against Organized Baseball early in 1915, seeking to have all OB contracts declared void because they contained the reserve clause. *(See the Baltimore Terrapins, page 30.)* The FL officials expected a quick verdict in their favor because Standard Oil had recently been fined $29 million for antitrust laws violations by the same judge hearing their case—Kenesaw Mountain Landis. However, Landis, a die-hard baseball fan, had sat on the case for nearly a year, refusing to rule.

While waiting for Landis's ruling, the NL, which had been hit particularly hard in the war with the FL, proposed a peace settlement among the three leagues—which were financially, if not emotionally, exhausted by the drama—following the 1915 season. The three leagues reached an agreement, but none of them wanted to implement it because of the unresolved court case. The AL and NL thought they'd be held in contempt of court for interfering in an open court case. Because the settlement preserved the reserve clause, the FL was afraid of being justly accused of now supporting the very reserve clause they had brought a suit against. When officials of all three leagues finally met with Landis to timidly report their settlement, Landis was the most relieved person in the room. After quickly dismissing the case, Landis told them he was just a big baseball fan who was afraid of screwing up the game by making the wrong ruling and was glad they had worked it all out.

The settlement revealed the Federal League's submissive side. It called for the FL to disband, with FL owners being paid buyouts of varying amounts. FL owner Philip Ball was allowed to buy the AL's St. Louis Browns and Weegham was permitted to purchase the financially strapped Chicago Cubs for $500,000, with the NL kicking in $100,000 of that amount. After combining the best players of the Cubs and Whales to make his new Cubs team, Weegham moved the Cubs out of West Side Park and into his stadium, which was renamed Cubs Park in 1920 and Wrigley Field in 1926.

CRIPPLING CHAOS

THE CHICAGO WHITE STOCKINGS
National Association
1871

I n 1869, the Cincinnati Red Stockings put together the first all-professional team in baseball history. They toured the country over the next two years, taking on all comers for a hefty portion of the gate receipts. They also put together (depending on the source) a fifty-seven, sixty-nine, seventy-nine, ninety-seven, or 130-game unbeaten streak that created intense interest among fans and extreme jealousy among opposing teams. Everyone wanted a shot at the Red Stockings, and this led to a mushrooming of professional teams around the country, all of which had visions of drawing, like Cincinnati, 10,000–20,000 fans per game.

In March 1871, this sudden craze to turn pro led nine of the best teams in the country to form the first professional league, the National Association of Professional Baseball Players (NA). The charter members were the Boston Red Stockings, Cleveland Forest Citys, Fort Wayne Kekiongas, New York Mutuals, Philadelphia Athletics, Rockford Forest Citys, Troy Haymakers, Washington Olympics, and Chicago White Stockings. The Brooklyn Eckfords had attended the organizational meeting, but declined to join the NA. Each of the nine teams paid a ten-dollar entry fee for the right to compete for the first professional pennant.

Conspicuously absent from this group were the great Cincinnati Red Stockings themselves, whose bubble had burst. After suffering their first loss in June 1870, they then lost five more games before the end of their second season. Interest in the team, absent its incredible winning streak, had declined. Following the 1870 season, the team disbanded. About half the team went with Harry and George Wright to Boston, where they became the Boston Red Stockings. The other players went to Washington, forming the Olympics, and a natural rivalry was born. Boston was clearly the class of the league, but both Philadelphia and Chicago put formidable teams on the field.

The Chicago White Stockings had much the same team in 1871 as they had had the year before. Most of their players had come from the New York City area, prompting the *New York Times* to refer to them as ". . . the Chicago branch of the old Eckford club, known as the White Stockings." Captain Jimmy Wood, the team's second baseman and the man most responsible for forming the team, had assembled an impressive array of New York talent while ignoring two local players—Al Spalding and Ross Barnes—who would become two of the sport's biggest stars in the league's early years. Moreover, team manager/outfielder Tom Foley had a chance to sign twenty-year-old Cap Anson right out of Marshalltown, Iowa, but passed, preferring to go with players who had more experience.

The White Stockings had a new home in 1871. Lake Front Park was a wooden facility with covered grandstands that could hold more than 7,000 fans. Season tickets were a pricey fifteen dollars. Men and women were seated in separate sections, with men getting preferred seating, while a separate section of the municipally funded ballpark was reserved strictly for city officials.

However, the knock against the White Stockings remained— that they were just a collection of hired guns from out of town who had no sense of local pride. They also had a reputation as a bunch of sluggers who had little interest in baseball strategy. In any event, Chicago got off to a great start, posting twenty-nine consecutive wins, including seven straight in National Association play. By September, Chicago, Boston, and Philadelphia were embroiled in a tight pennant race. On September 29 in Chicago, the White Stockings edged the Red Stockings, 10–8, in an exciting game to move into first place. With two outs and runners on second and third, Boston's Ross Barnes hit two long drives over

CHICAGO B. B. C., 1871.
Fred Treacy, *L.F.*, J. Simmons, *C.F.*, E. Pinkham, *R.F.*
E. Duffy, *S.S.*,   M. McAtee, *1st B.*
C. Hodes, *3d B.*,   JAS. WOOD, *2d B.* Mart. King, *C.*
E. P. Atwater, *Sub.* G. Zettlein, *P.* T. J. Foley, *Sub.*

*The 1871 Chicago White Stockings, who lost everything
including their ballpark in the Great Chicago Fire.*

the left field fence that hooked just foul at the last moment before he finally popped out.

Unfortunately, the league had given no thought to whether the champion would be the team that won the most games, the most series, or had the best winning percentage.

The tight pennant race, however, accentuated several glaring problems with the league's rules in 1871. One impetus for the creation of the National Association was the need for an orderly process of establishing who was the best team in the country. When the 1870 season had closed, numerous teams claimed to be the national champions, based either on wins over Cincinnati or some combination of wins against the other top teams. To avoid confusion, the NA stipulated that each team's regular season would consist of five-game series against all the other teams to determine the league champion, leaving the scheduling of the games up to the teams. Unfortunately, the league had given no thought to whether the champion would be the team that won the most games, the most series, or had the best winning percentage. As a result, some teams just quit their series after winning the third game, regardless, and some visiting teams discontinued play simply because the crowds weren't big enough to justify their presence in town. Also left unresolved was what to do if a team used illegal players, or whether games won against a team that failed to finish the season would still count.

Worse still, each team had the right to identify games as either a league match or an exhibition game, and to do it ex post facto—meaning that losses could immediately be reclassified as exhibition games! The lack of foresight and oversight was unfathomable. It was so chaotic that not even the great sportswriter

Henry Chadwick, "the father of baseball," could keep it straight. His journals and other papers of 1871 are littered with asterisks and disclaimers, reflecting his frustration.

In early October, with a month still to go in the season (it was routine to play as late as early November), the league's Championship Committee got together with representatives of most of the teams in an attempt to figure out how the league champion would be decided. Based on series won, Chicago was the league leader, having won five series during the season to four each for Boston and Philadelphia. But Boston was the leader based on won-lost record at 24–12. Philadelphia's representative, however, pointed out that not all of the games should count, because some games had involved now-defunct teams, illegal players, or were exhibition games. Using Philadelphia's logic, *they* were the leaders.

Before a decision was made, tragedy struck Chicago and its team. On Sunday night, October 8, the Great Chicago Fire killed hundreds and destroyed more than 2,000 acres of the city, including Lake Front Park. The White Stockings lost all their uniforms, equipment, money, and other personal effects. New York and Philadelphia, both mindful of the large payouts they had received from the huge crowds that had attended their games at Lake Front Park, put on exhibition games to raise money for the White Stockings. Peck and Snyder Sporting Goods was not so charitable, refusing to sell the team new uniforms and equipment on credit, forcing the White Stockings to finish the season in various assorted and borrowed garments.

Although forced to finish the season entirely on the road, the White Stockings still entered the final game of the year with a chance to win the league. It was decided that Philadelphia and Chicago, the two teams with the best overall records, would square off in the championship-deciding game on October 30 in Brooklyn's Union Grounds, the new emergency home park of the White Stockings. Only 500 fans bothered to show up, a far cry from the thousands that routinely attended the games in Lake

Front Park. The Athletics prevailed, 4–1, in a game that took only ninety-five minutes.

After the game, the White Stockings disbanded. Players returned to their pre-Chicago homes, then joined new teams in 1872. The devastated city of Chicago went without a team in both 1872 and 1873, the only years since 1871 that the city of Chicago hasn't been represented by at least one major league baseball team. A new White Stockings team joined the NA in 1874, eventually moving to the National League in 1876 and becoming another ill-fated franchise, known today as the Chicago Cubs.

LEFTOVER HAMS

THE CINCINNATI PORKERS
American Association
1891

From their very inception, the American Association's Cincinnati Porkers were an embarrassment. A *desperate* embarrassment. It was the kind of thing that happened in the early, Wild West days of professional baseball, when you could barely tell the teams without a scorecard.

The Porkers' sad story began in 1890, when the Players' League folded after a single season, leaving the American Association and the National League to fight it out for the talent orphaned by the PL's collapse. The signing frenzy turned into an all-out war between the two leagues. When the AA's Cincinnati Reds franchise jumped to the NL in 1890, along with Brooklyn, the AA, desperate to put a new franchise in Cincinnati in 1891 to compete against the departed Reds, fashioned one from leftover PL players who hadn't found a job by the time the 1891 season rolled around. The new team, called the Porkers, was 75 percent owned by St. Louis Browns owner Chris Von Der Ahe and 25 percent by the other AA owners. The conglomerate installed Edward Renau as team president, but Von Der Ahe called the shots.

What the Porkers lacked in baseball talent, they made up for in rowdiness. Von Der Ahe guaranteed that when he chose the legendary King Kelly, one of the greatest players of the nineteenth century, as the Porkers' manager. Though he hit a respectable .297, and played seven different positions for the Porkers that year, Kelly was well past his prime as a player, managing only one homer and 53 RBIs. He had long been one of baseball's hardest drinkers; years earlier, although he was one of the biggest stars in the game while playing with the White Stockings,

Chicago owner Al Spalding sold Kelly to Boston after tiring of his drunken exploits on and off the field. While in Boston, Kelly opened a bar, where he was rarely seen without his pet monkey on his shoulder, and would on occasion perform a bastardization of "Casey at the Bat" called "Kelly at the Bar." In an era when baseball was played with only one umpire, on the field Kelly would often skip second or third when the umpire turned his back, trip base runners, or intentionally drop easy pop flies to get a double play.

Hall of Famer King Kelly, baseball's biggest star at the time, played with Boston before coming to Cincinnati in 1891 near the end of his career.

As Porkers manager, Kelly let the players decide each game which position they wanted to play. He also made sure to have plenty of food and drink on hand for what would become postgame parties at Pendleton Park, the Porkers' ball field. An inebriated Kelly once stripped off his clothes and swam across the Kentucky River. Whereas the National League charged fifty cents admission to their games, prohibited the sale of beer, and did not play Sunday games, the AA charged just twenty-five cents, played on Sundays, and not only sold beer in their parks, but promoted its sale heavily since a number of the AA owners had brewery interests.

Although the Cincinnati police were often called to the park, they didn't often come, since it was accessible only by a one-hour steamboat ride. Nonetheless, Kelly was cited three times for playing baseball on a Sunday at Pendleton Park, and three times he marched the whole team down to the local police station immediately after Sunday's game. And three times he was found not guilty, after which he signed many autographs for police and other public officials.

The team was commonly called, and is often still referred to as, the Cincinnati Kellys or Kelly's Killers—partly because there were no other players of note on the team. It's hardly surprising that the Porkers' forte was fighting. An Opening Day brawl with Von Der Ahe's Browns set the tone for the season, and the Porkers' drunkenness at games led to scraps with their opponents on an almost daily basis. Even though Pendleton Park was a remote destination for Cincinnati baseball fans, a certain clientele relished being out of the watchful eye of the police as they enjoyed the National Game. Players and fans alike were having too good a time to mind—or maybe even notice—that they floundered near the bottom of the league standings.

Cincinnati Reds owner John T. Brush certainly noticed that the dissolute Porkers were cutting into the Reds' fan base. In August, he paid a visit to Von Der Ahe, the Porkers' majority owner, who was as tired of the Porkers' antics as Brush and the Cincinnati police. Brush offered Von Der Ahe $12,000—not to buy the team, just to move the team elsewhere. Von Der Ahe, privy to secret negotiations already under way to replace the troublesome Porkers with the Western Association's Milwaukee Brewers, agreed.

> The Porkers' drunkenness led to scraps
> on an almost daily basis.

Von Der Ahe didn't bother to inform Kelly and the gang that their team had been disbanded until after the Porkers had played the first two games of a series in St. Louis against his Browns

(King Kelly still had drawing power, after all), after which Milwaukee replaced them. Kelly left it up to the former Porkers to find, and fund, their own way home.

The sale proved to be especially propitious for Von Der Ahe. Following the 1891 season, the two leagues struck a deal by which the NL absorbed the four best AA teams, including Von Der Ahe's Browns, and discarded the other five. This new twelve-team league would have just one team per city and no small cities, such as Milwaukee—the very franchise that had paid Von Der Ahe a substantial fee for the right to replace his Cincinnati team in the AA.

THE BEST AND YET NOT-SO-BRIGHTEST

THE CINCINNATI RED STOCKINGS
Independent Baseball Team
1866–70

The Cincinnati Red Stockings hold the distinction of being the first professional baseball team in American history. In one incredible stretch, from 1868 to 1870, they were undefeated in 130 consecutive games (129 wins and one tie), a streak during which they routinely drew crowds of 10,000–20,000 and were the toast of America, feted at banquets and given awards and presents at almost every stop. All of which makes the story of their sudden and inexplicable demise one of the strangest stories in baseball history.

The Cincinnati Red Stockings Base Ball Club was formed on July 23, 1866, in the law offices of Tilden, Sherman & Moulton. Most of the players were attorneys who had graduated from Harvard and Yale. Including their various "nines" and numerous junior teams, the club had more than 500 members who supported the teams through dues and nominal admission charges at their games. After playing just four games their first year, winning two and losing two, the club moved to the field the Union Cricket Club had been using since 1856. Once exposed to the American sport, many cricketers became members of the baseball team, including their bowler, Harry Wright. Wright, a jeweler during the off-season, previously had been the bowler for the New York Cricket Club at a salary of twelve dollars a week. He moved to Cincinnati in 1865 to take the same position on the Union club but at a substantially higher salary, $1,200 for the season.

Cincinnati had an excellent team that year, finishing with a 17–1 record. The team's only loss was a 53–10 embarrassment to the Washington Nationals, one of America's top amateur teams. The game would have been closer had the Red Stockings not lost catcher John McLean, one of their top players, four days before. In a tune-up game, McLean was hit in the face by a foul ball and suffered so disfiguring an injury that his mother forbade him ever to play again. Strangely, it would be another decade before the catcher's mask was invented.

In a September game in which the Red Stockings dismantled the Holt Base Ball Club of Newport, Kentucky, 109–15, former cricketer Wright and first baseman John Howe each clubbed seven home runs (it's good to remember that pitchers pitched underhanded). Five days later they mauled the Washington Olympics, another top team, 77–17. On November 22, Wright signed on as the team's pitcher, manager, and captain for 1868, at the same $1,200 salary he'd been making with the cricket club.

Given the need to now pay four professional players, including Wright, the Red Stockings tripled their scheduled games in 1868, compiling a 41–7 record, and pursued the "gold baseball" offered by the New York *Clipper* newspaper to the 1868 national

1869 Cincinnati Red Stockings.

champions. The championship, decided by head-to-head play with *Clipper*-approved contenders, moved around during the season as clubs knocked off the current titleholder in what were called "championship matches." As it happened, the Red Stockings were deprived of the chance to win the championship when the Unions of Morrisania, New York, refused to play them in a rubber game in order to avoid even the possibility of losing the national championship to a "western" team. The Unions' cowardly refusal to play the Red Stockings was met with national outrage, even in the eastern newspapers.

In 1869, the Red Stockings fielded the first totally professional team in history, with salaries ranging from $600 to a high of $1,400—paid to Harry Wright's brother, George, the team's shortstop. The club's directors, still miffed about 1868, were determined to field a dominant team—and got what they wanted. The Red Stockings toured the country, winning 64 of 65 games. The only blemish on their record was a controversial 17–17 tie with the Haymakers of Lansingburgh (a suburb of Troy, New York, though the team is often referred to as the Troy Haymakers). With the game tied at 17 after five innings, the Haymakers walked off the field under the pretext of an argument, but it was later revealed that New York gamblers had bet heavily on the Haymakers to win and, afraid of losing, had pressured Troy's manager to quit while tied. The undefeated team of 1869 achieved, along with the national championship, an almost mythical status. Everywhere they went, the Red Stockings drew huge crowds. And all the top teams in the country wanted to reap the financial rewards of playing a team that packed the house, and at double the usual admission prices.

After dispatching its first twenty-seven opponents in 1870, scoring 100 or more runs in three of those games, Cincinnati's day of reckoning finally came. On June 14, the Red Stockings met the Atlantics at Brooklyn's Capitoline Grounds. The ballpark held 9,000, but 20,000 fans showed up, standing wherever they could find room, including on the outfield grass and right up to the foul lines on both sides of the field. (Newspaper reports of the game noted that many fans were "plunked in the head" by foul balls.) After nine innings, with the game tied 5–5, Atlantic manager Bob Ferguson proposed to Harry Wright that the game end in a draw. While Ferguson and Wright discussed the matter, the Atlantic players assumed the game was over and packed up their equipment and headed for the clubhouse. So did most of the fans, who started trickling out of the park. Umpire Charley Mills, who had called a fine game that neither team questioned, also thought the game was over, and was in a wagon near the exit when someone chased him down and told him that Wright, as was his prerogative, was demanding the game continue. Mills informed Ferguson that if he didn't get his team back on the field, he was going to award Cincinnati a forfeit. The milling fans were miffed and police had to quell the crowd. With order restored, the game resumed.

In 1869, the Red Stockings fielded the first totally professional team in history.

Neither team scored in the tenth inning, but the Red Stockings scored twice in the top of the eleventh to take a 7–5 lead. The Atlantics' famous rally began when Charles Smith hit a line single to left, then advanced to third on a wild pitch by Asa Brainard. The crowd became so loud and unruly that umpire Mills had to warn them to quiet down. The next batter, Joe Start, hit a long fly that landed on a dead stop on an incline behind right fielder Cal McVey. As McVey bent down to retrieve the ball, an exuberant fan jumped on his back. The crowd, which did not sympathize with the fan's actions, pulled him off McVey, but Start was standing on third by the time McVey got the ball in. John Chapman then grounded out, Start holding at third. Joe Ferguson, a switch-hitter, promptly hit a single to left, scoring Start with the tying run. The crowd again became so loud that Mills had to issue another warning. When order was restored, George Zettlein hit a hard smash to first baseman Charles Gould who bobbled it before getting off a throw to second baseman Charles Sweasy. Sweasy muffed the catch, allowing Ferguson to go to third, and then threw wildly in an attempt to catch Ferguson off base, which allowed Ferguson to come in with the winning run. With Sweasy's double error, Cincinnati's two-year unbeaten streak had come to an end.

After the defeat, Aaron Champion, president of the Red Stockings, is said to have cried like a child. Over the remainder of the 1870 season, the suddenly vulnerable Red Stockings lost five more games. The streak had been broken and the team's mythical status damaged. When Harry Wright presented the club's directors with the players' salary demands for 1871, they were shocked to see they sought roughly double what they had been making. The directors not only flatly refused to meet the demands, but published a circular presenting their reasons to their 500-plus members. Almost inexplicably, the directors then held a meeting at which the club was formally disbanded.

Before long, all the Red Stockings had new jobs with eastern teams, primarily Boston and Washington.

It was only many years later that the truth came out: The vote to disband the team had actually been a calculated bluff. When the players found new employment so quickly, the directors, rather than expose their mistake by fielding another professional team, decided to sponsor only amateur teams thereafter. And so the Cincinnati Red Stockings, one of the greatest teams ever assembled, the team that won more than 92 percent of its games (192–16–1), that routinely played before 10,000 or more fans when a few hundred was the norm, had suddenly evaporated—defeated by cost-conscious directors and a failed bluff.

BEER HERE

THE CINCINNATI REDS
National League
1876–80

When the National League began play in 1876, one of the charter members was Cincinnati. Originally called the Porkopolitans, a reference to team owner Josiah Keck's meatpacking business, the team soon took the Reds as its nickname in a thinly veiled attempt to capitalize on the fame of the fabled Cincinnati Red Stockings team of 1867–70, a legendary team with a national following that had been known for its playing ability, integrity, goodwill, and sportsmanship.

To ensure a continuation of the old Cincinnati baseball tradition, the 1876 Reds included two members of the great Red Stockings team, manager/first baseman Charlie Gould and second baseman Charlie Sweasy. But the comparison ended there. The Reds were simply dreadful, finishing the season in last place with a 9–56 record. Not only were victories hard to come by, but so were paying fans. Keck tried turning things around in 1877 by instituting Ladies Day promotions, letting women in for free in hopes of attracting more men. It failed, and so did the Reds after just seventeen games. With an embarrassing 3–14 start, few fans of either sex, and a huge amount of red ink, Keck folded the team just before a long road trip and gave all his players their unconditional release.

The NL was caught by surprise. The vacancy left the league with seven teams, a nightmare for scheduling. Cincinnati businessman J. Wayne Neff quickly assembled a group of seven other investors and offered to back a new Cincinnati team, but NL president William Hulbert put the brakes on that plan, citing Keck's failure to pay the league one hundred dollars for the team's

June dues. For several weeks there was much confusion; newspapers didn't know how to report the daily standings, so some of them listed standings with Cincinnati's record, some without, and some included both versions, side by side.

Adding to the confusion was a controversial move by Hulbert, who also owned the Chicago White Stockings. He sent his friend Lewis Meacham, sports editor of the *Chicago Tribune*, to Cincinnati to sign two of the former Reds, Jimmy Hallinan and Charley Jones, to Chicago contracts. Hallinan was cooling his heels in jail after a barroom brawl, so Meacham had to bail him out before he could sign him. This obvious conflict of interest on Hulbert's part ignited a firestorm. When the dust finally settled, Hulbert got to keep Hallinan, but Jones, the most popular of all the Reds, had to return to Cincinnati after playing two games with Chicago.

After almost three weeks in limbo, the Reds resumed play on July 3 under Neff's ownership. The NL officials tried to help the

1878 Cincinnati Reds stock certificate.

Reds' cash flow by reorganizing their schedule to give the team a fourteen-game home stand. It didn't matter; over the remainder of the season, the Reds were 12–28, for a final record of 15–42, and in the cellar once again.

By 1878, things were looking up for the Reds. Former Red Stocking and fan favorite Cal McVey returned to the team and became its manager/third baseman. Eventual superstar and Hall of Famer King Kelly was starting to blossom and five other Cincinnati hitters topped the .300 mark. Pitcher Will White (the first to wear glasses) went 30–21 with an excellent 1.79 ERA. The Reds also employed the first-ever left-handed pitcher, Bobby Mitchell. All this led to a surprising second-place finish for the Reds, just four games behind the Boston Red Caps. But the superb 1878 season proved to be the calm before the storm.

In 1879, Will White's brother and batterymate, Deacon, was promoted to manager, relegating McVey to first base duties, since Kelly had replaced McVey at the hot corner. Deacon became embroiled in controversy almost immediately. First, he appointed his brother-in-law as official team scorer, a position local sportswriter Oliver P. Caylor coveted. Angry at being passed over, Caylor began writing columns that questioned Deacon's managing abilities. Deacon's moves were soon being openly questioned by players and fans alike, leading to considerable clubhouse dissension. Second, Deacon signed infielder Ross Barnes, one of the game's biggest stars a few years before, but now clearly on the decline. That Deacon, Barnes, and McVey made $2,000 alienated the rest of the players, who made $800. Further complicating internal relations, McVey and Barnes both made no secret that they could run the team better than Deacon.

Deacon finally had enough of the sniping after only sixteen games and relinquished the manager's position to McVey, who promptly benched shortstop Mike Burke in favor of his old friend, Barnes. Burke was so angry at being benched that he started a fight with McVey on the field in the middle of a game. In his newspaper articles, Caylor supported Burke, further fanning the flames among teammates. Disgusted at the goings-on, Cincinnati fans began to stay away.

Owner Neff, painfully aware that his team was a far cry from the once proud and honorable Red Stockings team of a decade earlier, notified the league a week before the end of the season that he would be dissolving his team and giving all his players their unconditional release. NL owners were alarmed at the thought of a bunch of free agent players running around uncontrolled by the reserve system they had implemented that very year, so they quickly approved a replacement Cincinnati ownership group for the 1880 season headed by Justus Thorner, a Cincinnati brewer. Thorner, however, surprised (and offended) NL officials when he decided to release all but three of the players anyway, keeping only the White brothers and outfielder/pitcher Blondie Purcell.

As if the Reds didn't have enough of their own problems, some of the newspapers in other league cities began editorializing about the "wickedness" of Cincinnati because the Reds sold beer at their games and leased out their ballpark to amateur teams for Sunday games, both of which were against NL rules. The puritanical *Worcester Spy* was particularly harsh on the Reds and led the charge to have the Reds mend their ways or be booted out of the league.

Burke was so angry at being benched that he started a fight with McVey on the field in the middle of a game.

Thorner continued on where Neff left off, defying the league's rules against selling booze in the ballpark and renting out his facility for Sunday games. The NL looked the other way the whole season because it didn't want to deal with the scheduling problems resulting from an odd number of teams. But while the Reds were doing well financially, internally there was much bickering among board members, and Thorner was replaced in midseason as president by clothing manufacturer Nathan Menderson, who in turn was replaced by insurance executive John Kennett.

At a special league meeting held on October 6, just after the season ended, Kennett told league officials that Cincinnati was unlike the other cities in the league. He told them of the city's large population of German immigrants, whose tradition demanded Sunday entertainment that included beer drinking. His plea fell on deaf ears. NL president Hulbert drafted a pledge that required all teams to refrain from selling alcoholic beverages in their ballparks and not to allow their ballparks to be used for Sunday games. All the teams except Cincinnati signed the pledge. Two days later, the Cincinnati Reds were kicked out of the NL for refusing to sign the pledge and were replaced by the Detroit Wolverines. *(See Detroit Wolverines, page 115.)*

After the expulsion, one Cincinnati newspaper had an interesting take on the matter: "While the league is in the missionary field, they should turn their attention to Chicago and prohibit the admission to the Lake Front Grounds of the great number of prostitutes who patronize the game up there."

Justus Thorner, the team's first president in 1880, and influential sportswriter Oliver Caylor were infuriated over Cincinnati's expulsion. In 1882, the two of them were instrumental in both the creation of the American Association and bringing another major league team back to Cincinnati. Over the next decade, the AA would bleed the NL nearly to death with its Sunday games, ballpark beer sales, cheaper admission prices, and bidding wars for player services.

THEY SHALL BE RELEASED

THE CLEVELAND FOREST CITYS/BLUES
National League
1879–84

The New York Yankees are known for winning pennants. The Chicago Cubs are known for not winning them. The St. Louis Browns were famous for their futility, the Philadelphia Athletics for frugality. The Cleveland Blues were significant because they changed the way ballplayers were released and disposed of for the next one hundred years.

In 1879, National League president William Hulbert invited Cleveland to join the league after a successful 32–20 season as an independent team in 1878. Hulbert wanted to expand from six teams to eight and felt that Cleveland, with its population of 150,000, was ideal.

Originally called the Forest Citys when the team first came into the NL, Cleveland's move to the majors exposed its weaknesses, especially offensively. The team finished last in batting average at .223, and only the Troy Trojans had a worse record. Pitcher/manager Jim McCormick was a twenty-two-year-old workhorse with a 2.42 ERA, and his 20–40 record belied his potential. With the addition of other future stars like shortstop Jack Glasscock, outfielder Ned Hanlon, and second baseman Fred Dunlap, Cleveland improved dramatically in 1880 and finished the season in third place. In 1881, Cleveland slumped back to seventh place, but Dunlap had a great season, finishing with a .325 average (fifth in the NL), 156 total bases (second only to Chicago's Cap Anson), and 25 doubles (third). He was also fifth in singles and fourth in extra-base hits.

In 1882, the team got a new manager, team president J. Ford Evans, who ceded his presidential duties to C. H. Bulkley. They

also got new uniforms, which led to a new name. That year, the
NL mandated that each team wear a different color uniform—
Chicago was assigned white, Boston red, Buffalo gray, Detroit
gold, Providence light blue, Worcester brown, and Troy green,
while Cleveland was made to wear navy blue. The new uniforms
were so striking that the team changed its name from the Forest
Citys to the Blues.

Under Evans's one-season tenure, the Blues finished a respectable 42–40, good for fifth place, twelve games out. The season was remarkable for the game that took place on a very hot
and muggy day in Chicago on July 24. Evans decided to give
McCormick and his change pitcher, George Bradley, a rest, and
let reserve outfielder Dave Rowe pitch against the White Stockings. Rowe pitched a complete game—a completely horrible
game. He allowed 29 hits, 7 walks, and 35 runs, the last still a
record.

In 1883, under another new manager, Frank Bancroft, the
team had the best season it ever would—a 55–42 record was
good for a solid fourth place, just seven
and a half games behind the Boston

Hall of Famer Edward "Ned"
Hanlon spent his rookie
season as a member of the
Forest Citys in 1880 before
moving on to the Wolverines
in 1881 where he spent the
majority of his career.

Beaneaters. Heading into the 1884
season, things were looking up for the
Blues when disaster struck in the person of
Henry V. Lucas.

Lucas, who had been rebuffed in his attempt to get a St. Louis
franchise in the NL, formed his own new major league, the Union

Association, and gave himself the St. Louis franchise, the Maroons. While Cleveland was fortunate that neither the American Association nor the UA had a competing franchise in Cleveland, the Blues were hardest hit by player jumpings. The big money offered by Lucas was enough to convince Dunlap to break the reserve clause in his contract and sign with the Maroons. When Cleveland's other two popular stars, Glasscock and McCormick, along with catcher Fatty Briody, jumped to the UA's Cincinnati Outlaw Reds in August, it crippled the Blues' chances and devastated their fans. New manager Charlie Hackett tried to plug the holes with players from the recently disbanded Grand Rapids minor league club, but the fans weren't placated and attendance plummeted.

Facing severe financial difficulty, Blues president Bulkley appealed to NL president A. G. Mills for a $5,000 grant so the team could finish the season. While refusing to give Cleveland any money up front, Mills did convince the league's other seven owners to split their gate receipts fifty-fifty when the Blues came to town, but to accept the usual seventy-thirty split when they went to Cleveland. It wasn't enough.

In a move that shocked the baseball world, Bulkley, without consulting the other NL owners, sold his Cleveland franchise to Lucas of the rival UA for a paltry $2,500, receiving a $500 down payment. Lucas assumed the purchase price included all the player contracts, so he sat back and waited the required ten days (the rule at the time for players who were either released or victims of a disbanding team) before signing the players to new contracts. But, unbeknownst to Lucas, the Brooklyn Bridegrooms of the American Association hid seven former Blues players in hotel rooms where Lucas couldn't find them and, on the tenth day, signed all seven players to AA contracts.

Lucas was furious and threatened all-out war with the other two leagues over the actions of the Bridegrooms. Many owners in all three leagues sympathized with Lucas and knew that business as usual just couldn't go on the way it had been. Before the 1885 season began, a deal was worked out in which, among other things, the UA folded, but Lucas was given his long-coveted St. Louis NL franchise.

Later that season, in a secret meeting held in Saratoga, New York, between officials of the NL and AA, the National Agreement—the constitution that defined their existence and working relationship—was revised. The new rules provided that only teams in the same league could negotiate with a player in the first ten days after he was released or his club disbanded. After that, all teams were free to negotiate with such players. This led to the waiver system dictating how rival leagues could approach each other's players—which major league baseball has employed, with some fine-tuning, ever since.

In the final chapter of the Cleveland Blues story, Bulkley won a victory of sorts, but it was in the courtroom and not on the field. Lucas, angry over having lost the seven Blues players to the Bridegrooms, refused to pay Bulkley the remainder of the agreed-upon fee for his Cleveland franchise. Bulkley sued Lucas and won the remaining $2,000 owed him under their purchase agreement.

UNINTELLIGENT DESIGN

THE CLEVELAND SPIDERS
National League
1889–99

The National League's Cleveland Spiders of 1899 rank as the worst Major League Baseball team of all time, and not by chance. The team's owners, tractor magnate brothers Frank and Matthew Robison, had purchased the team in 1898. Though pleased with the team's 81–68 record that season, the owners were very disappointed in the team's attendance. The league at that time permitted ownership of more than one team, so when the opportunity came along to purchase the NL's popular St. Louis Browns, the Robison brothers leaped into action.

After acquiring the Browns, the Robison brothers tried to sell the Spiders to a group in Detroit, but the National League owners nixed the deal, citing Detroit's then meager population. The Robisons, who found no other buyers for their financial albatross in Cleveland, came up with another idea. Attendance in Cleveland was poor (in 1899 the Spiders averaged only 179 paying fans a game). St. Louis averaged over 2,000 a game. The Robisons decided to swap the best Cleveland players with the worst St. Louis players, thereby building a lucrative contender in St. Louis while relegating Cleveland to the ash heap of the national pastime.

The plan worked brilliantly, in no small part because in 1898 the Spiders were loaded with talent. Eventual Hall of Famers Cy Young, Bobby Wallace, and Jesse Burkett were all sent to St. Louis. Young, far and away the all-time leader in pitching wins with 511, had already won 241 with the Spiders, more than he would win with any other team. In 1899, Young pitched forty complete games for the Browns and won twenty-six of them, finishing second in the league in ERA at 2.58. Burkett, who hit over

.400 twice with the Spiders and was one of the best hitters of the nineteenth century, hit .396 for the rejuvenated Browns, good for second in the NL. He also finished in the top five in many other offensive categories. Bobby Wallace enjoyed his new St. Louis surroundings, too, finishing second in the NL in homers with twelve, one of only two hitters to finish in double figures, and fifth in RBIs with 108. Outfielder Emmet Heidrick, also sent over from Cleveland, hit .328 with fifty-five stolen bases, good for third in the league. The newly staffed St. Louis Browns finished fifth in the twelve-team league, 84–67, the first winning season for the popular Browns in eight years.

And the dismantled Spiders? Their final record of 20–134 is still the worst of any team in major league history, enough to make the 1962 New York Mets (40–120) look positively mediocre. They lost forty of their last forty-one games, and seventy of their last seventy-four. While the transplanted Wallace hit twelve homers for the Browns, the entire Spiders team managed to hit only twelve homers in 1899. No regular hit higher than .286. Their four main starting pitchers had records of 4–30, 4–22, 1–18, and 2–17, and the combined staff ERA was an astronomical 6.37. The team was so embarrassingly bad and drew so poorly at home that by June the owners moved all their home games to either neutral sites or to the visiting teams' home parks. Not only did this play havoc with the league's traveling schedule, but it infuriated the other owners, who felt the Robison brothers were making a mockery of the league. The Spiders' last game of the season, in Cincinnati, was the final straw for the other league owners. Cleveland drafted hotel cigar stand clerk Eddie Kolb to pitch their final league game for them, the only game Kolb would ever play in the major leagues. The Spiders lost a heartbreaker, 19–3.

Following the season, the National League contracted from twelve shaky teams to a more solid eight. The league was hurt not just by declining attendance in a lingering national depression, but was still reeling from the financial damage caused by the bidding wars for players with several rival leagues during the early 1890s. It would have been one of the nineteenth century's greatest surprises if the Spiders had not been among the victims.

After the 1899 season, the Spiders players chipped in to buy a gold locket for the team's traveling secretary. It was inscribed: "The only person who had the misfortune to watch all our games."

Hall of Fame pitcher John Clarkson won the last 41 of his 326 career victories as a member of the Spiders from 1892 to 1894.

OUT OF AMMUNITION

THE COLORADO SILVER BULLETS
Independent Professional Baseball
1994–97

The Silver Bullets opened their inaugural season with much pomp and ceremony on Mother's Day, 1994, against the independent Northern League's All-Star team. In a pregame statement to the press, manager Phil Niekro said, "I think we are going to surprise quite a few people with the ability of these athletes and the caliber of ball they can play."

Surprise, indeed. The Silver Bullets lost 19–0, and proceeded to lose their first six games by a combined score of 57–1. They lost twenty-two of their first twenty-three games and finished the 1994 season with a 6–38 record. The Prime Sports Network (now Fox Sports Net) was having second thoughts about their television deal with the team.

The biggest surprise, however, was not how bad they were, but that they existed in the first place. The Silver Bullets, owned by Whittle Communications of Knoxville, Tennessee, was the first all-women's professional team since the All-American Girls Professional Baseball League folded in 1954, leaving the Rockford Peaches, Fort Wayne Daisies, Kalamazoo Lassies, and all the other female teams benched forever. With a stated mission of providing a nurturing environment for top women athletes to learn and play professional baseball against existing *men's* teams and to gain the acceptance of women players by organized baseball, the Silver Bullets first sought and quickly received sponsorship from the Coors Brewing Company, from whose light beer the team took its nickname.

Hall of Fame pitcher Phil Niekro was named as manager, and he brought on board his brother Joe, also a former major league pitcher, as the team's pitching coach. Phil's son John doubled as the team's events coordinator and assistant coach. Shereen Samonds, named 1993 Female Executive of the Year by the National Association of Professional Baseball Leagues, was named general manager. In January and February of 1994, this brain trust organized a series of open tryout camps around the country, to which more than 1,300 women showed up in search of one of twenty-four roster spots. The Silver Bullets extended invitations to fifty-five women to attend a month-long spring training session in Orlando, and when spring training opened on March 5, forty-nine showed up. Among them were teachers, coaches, moms, students, and waitresses, all of whom put their lives on hold to pursue the unprecedented dream of playing professional baseball against men. On April 3, after five rounds of cuts and seven-days-a-week training, the final roster of twenty-four was chosen.

The Silver Bullets joined the six-team Northern League as an independent member. In addition to playing league games in Duluth, Minnesota; Sioux City, Iowa; Sioux Falls, South Dakota; Winnipeg, Manitoba; St. Paul, Minnesota; and Thunder Bay, Ontario, the Silver Bullets traveled around the country playing minor league and semi-pro teams, sometimes in major league stadiums like Candlestick Park, the Kingdome, and Mile High Stadium.

After their valiant but humbling first season, the Bullets did a little better in 1995, finishing 11–33. They improved a bit more, to 18–34, in 1996, but were embarrassed by a five-game series in Taiwan against several Taiwan Major League men's teams that November, during which they lost all five games by a combined score of 69–15.

The team posted its first winning season in 1997, going 23–22 against similar competition. They were even involved in their first all-out brawl, albeit with a team from an under-eighteen parks and recreation league. The brawl began when pitcher Greg Dominy hit Silver Bullet batter Kim Braatz-Voisard with a pitch, then laughed at her when she complained. As the reporter for the

Albany (Georgia) *Herald* wrote, "She was on him like a cat on a pork chop."

After the 1997 season, the team's fourth, Coors, which by then had spent $8 million as chief sponsor of the team, bit the Bullets and pulled out. Unable to secure a new sponsor for 1998, the Silver Bullets suspended operations until they could find new support. They couldn't, and the Silver Bullets were forced to fold, indefinitely suspending the dreams of many young women with a gift for baseball.

1994 Colorado Silver Bullets program.

SAINT JOAN

THE CONNECTICUT FALCONS
Professional Women's Softball Team
1976–79

Is it possible for one player to be so good that it destroys not only the team, but the entire league?

Yes it is, if your name is Joan Joyce.

How good a softball pitcher was Joyce? In 1961, Ted Williams came to Waterbury, Connecticut, to promote his charity, the Jimmy Fund. To spice up the event, the local club added nineteen-year-old Joyce and her 118 mph fastball to its roster, promising an exhibition between "the best hitter alive and the girl who could fire the ball past anyone." Twenty thousand fans crammed into Municipal Stadium, which was built to hold less than half that. The crowd lined the outfield, ten to twelve deep, so anxious were they to witness the great confrontation. After fifteen minutes in the batter's box, Williams managed only three foul balls. In 1966, the two met for a one-at-bat rematch. Williams took one pitch for a ball, then struck out on the next three. In 1978, Joyce struck out Hank Aaron in a similar exhibition.

Barred by gender from playing professional baseball, she dominated the world of women's softball. In 1954, at the age of twelve, Joyce began playing for the Raybestos Brakettes, the perennial national fast-pitch softball champions from Stratford, Connecticut. After stints at second base and in the outfield, she moved to the pitching mound, where she developed a unique slingshot pitching style that differed from the popular windmill style. She mastered five pitches, including a rising fastball that was almost impossible to hit.

By the mid-1970s, Joyce had attained legendary status within the fast-pitch softball community by establishing many eye-popping records. Among them: eighteen consecutive selections to the national all-star team; eight-time winner of the MVP Award in the National Tournament; most wins in a season (forty-two in 1974); eight no-hitters in National Tournament play; thirty-eight shutouts in one season; and most innings pitched in one game (twenty-nine in a 1968 game). In addition, she was a fifteen-time All-American, fourteen of them on the First Team. In 1974, Joyce pitched the Brakettes to the world championship, the first time an American team had won the event.

Joyce compiled a 750–42 career record with 150 no-hitters, thirty-three perfect games, and—get ready for this—an ERA of 0.09. (Did we mention that in college, Joyce was a four-time Women's Basketball Association All-American, played on the U.S. National Team in 1965, and set a National Tournament single-game scoring record in 1964 with 67 points?)

In 1976, Joyce was one of the cofounders of the International Professional Women's Softball Association, along with former professional golfer Janie Blaylock, tennis star Billie Jean King, sports entrepreneur Jim Jorgensen, and Dennis Murphy, founder of the World Hockey Association and cofounder of World Team Tennis. Joyce was the coach and part owner of the Connecticut

1976 pennant of the Buffalo Breskis, named after the team's star player, Cindy Breski, the leading rival of Joan Joyce's Connecticut Falcons.

Falcons, one of the league's ten teams. The other nine included the Buffalo Breskis (named after another star player of the era, Cindy Breski), Chicago Ravens, Michigan Travelers, Pennsylvania Liberties, Phoenix Bird, Santa Ana Lionettes, San Diego Sandpipers, San Jose Sunbirds, and Southern California Gems. The league's 120-game 1976 schedule required all teams to play sixty doubleheaders. Since most of the league's players were paid only between $1,000 and $3,000 for the season, most of the Falcons players moved to Waterbury and took jobs as teachers or office workers.

Joyce's Falcons dominated the league in all four years of its existence, finishing twenty-nine games ahead of second place in 1976. Over the next three years, the Falcons' success so demoralized every other team that, although the league suffered from the usual assortment of defects—insufficient financing, poor planning, inadequate facilities, and lack of fan interest—the Falcons' dominance played no small part in the league's eventual ruin. It was very similar to what happened to the National Association (1871–75), baseball's first professional league. Everyone knew the Boston Red Stockings were going to win anyway, so why bother to play? After the Connecticut Falcons romped to their fourth straight regular season title in 1979 and fourth straight playoff victory, the league folded.

As for Joyce, she became a member of the LPGA, a career that lasted nineteen years, made more amazing by the fact that she didn't even start playing golf until after college. She once had a round of eighteen holes in which she took only seventeen putts, a record for women *and* men!

A member of the National Softball Hall of Fame since 1983, Joan Joyce became head softball coach at Florida Atlantic University in 1994, creating the program from scratch. Not surprisingly, the FAU Owls have become one of the dominant softball programs in the country, and Joyce is still the coach, the only one the school's ever had.

BLACKBALLED

THE DALLAS TEXANS
National Football League
1952

There were a lot of assumptions about the Dallas Texans franchise, and they all turned out to be wrong.

Dallas's chance to become the first NFL team in the Deep South came about when another franchise failed, also on false assumptions. When Ted Collins's Boston Yanks joined the NFL in 1944, he assumed that the last large northeastern American city without a football team would be a natural home for professional football. Wrong. After five seasons of poor attendance and nothing close to a winning team, Collins relocated the team to New York and renamed them the Bulldogs. Surely, he reasoned, the largest city in the United States could support two NFL teams. Wrong again. After a pitiful 1–10–1 season, Collins figured that changing the team's name from the Yanks to the Bulldogs had somehow jinxed the team, so in 1950 he renamed them the Yanks again.

The new name didn't help much, as the New York Yanks went a combined 8–14–2 over the next two seasons and still didn't attract enough paying fans to keep the doors open. By the end of the 1951 season, Collins had had his fill of red ink, so he decided to sell the team and cut his losses. But Collins's assumption that it would be easy to sell an NFL franchise in New York proved wrong. With no buyer in sight, Collins disbanded the Yanks and turned the franchise rights back over to the NFL.

A few months later, the NFL announced that a search for a new owner had been successful. Texas millionaire Giles Miller had put together an investment group and purchased the rights to the vacant franchise, announcing that the team would be located in Dallas, Texas, the first professional sports team ever in the Lone Star state.

Miller assumed that an NFL team in Texas would be a natural fit, given the popularity of both high school and college football in the state. He also assumed that he would need a stadium commensurate with the large crowds that would be turning out, so he booked the 75,000-seat Cotton Bowl.

1952 Bowman Gum card of Dallas Texans head coach James Phelan.

JAMES M. PHELAN
Dallas Texans

Both assumptions proved wrong. The Texans' first game at the Cotton Bowl, a 24–6 loss to the New York Giants, attracted only 17,499 fans. It would be the largest crowd of the year, far smaller than nearly every college in Texas drew for their home games, and even smaller than some major high school games. Another assumption that proved wrong was that the hometown fans would cotton to the two African-Americans on Dallas's roster, George Taliaferro and Buddy Young, who also happened to be two of the best players on the team. But in the American South of 1952, it would have been surprising if fans *didn't* stay away from Texans games because of the presence of two black players. (When the NFL had voted 11–1 to approve the sale to Miller's group, the only nay vote belonged to Art Rooney of the Pittsburgh Steelers, who didn't believe the South was ready for an integrated football team and it would be doomed to fail.)

As Miller resisted local pressure to release the two black players from the team, the losses mounted and attendance continued to slide. After seven winless weeks, attendance was so bad he was unable to make the team's payroll, so he called it quits. He didn't even try to sell the team, but just turned it back over to the NFL, just as Collins had done the year before.

With a winless team dumped in its lap, the NFL was forced to scramble. The league decided to base the team out of a training facility in Hershey, Pennsylvania, though it would still be called the Dallas Texans. It also decided that Dallas would be a traveling team for the rest of the season. Four of its remaining five games would be scheduled at the opponents' home stadium while the fifth, against the Chicago Bears, would be held in a neutral site—Akron, Ohio's Rubber Bowl, home of the University of Akron Zips.

Following two routs by the Lions and Packers, the 0–9 Texans went to Akron to play the Bears in a Thanksgiving Day doubleheader. The special holiday affair featured a first game between two high school teams, for which the 31,000-seat stadium was nearly sold out. After it ended, the stadium all but emptied. Only about 3,000 fans remained for the NFL game, causing Texans coach Jimmy Phelan to remark, "Rather than introducing the players on the field, they should go into the stands and shake hands with each fan."

If the league was wrong in assuming that such a holiday doubleheader would attract a sizeable crowd, the Chicago Bears' George Halas was wrong in assuming the Texans didn't know how to play football. Halas overconfidently decided to start his entire second string, both offense and defense, in order to rest his first team, which had played four days before. After Dallas raced away to a 20–2 lead, Halas sent his first team into the game, but it was too late. A furious comeback by the Bears fell short, and Dallas won their first and only game of the season, 27–23.

After two more routs by the Eagles and Lions, the Texans' first and only season came to a merciful end. George Taliaferro was named to the NFL's Pro Bowl team and the NFL sold the rights to the available franchise to Carroll Rosenbloom, who used it to put a team in Baltimore called the Colts. Since only thirteen of the former Texans became Colts, the NFL did not consider the Colts an extension of the Dallas team. Instead, the Dallas Texans earned the distinction of being the last NFL team to fold.

CRAZY LIKE A FOX

THE DETROIT WOLVERINES
National League
1881–88

S ome franchises fall apart because of stupid owners. The Detroit Wolverines suffered a different fate: Their last owner was too shrewd.

Detroit mayor William G. Thompson had long felt the city deserved its own major league baseball team, and when he made official overtures to the National League in 1880, the league's owners agreed. As it happened, the league was fed up with its

1886 Detroit Wolverines.

renegade Cincinnati Reds franchise, which flouted league rules by playing non-league games on Sundays and selling beer in the ballpark. Because the Reds were unwilling to curtail either activity, which on top of everything else fostered gambling, National League owners simply banished the team before the 1881 season and replaced them with a newly created franchise, the Detroit Wolverines, which they awarded to Mayor Thompson.

The team, which Thompson ran from right out of the mayor's office in downtown Detroit, played its games at Recreation Park, an unfenced field so large that a baseball game could be held at the south end while a cricket match was played on the north end. During baseball games, the fans ringing the outfield would creep as close to the outfielders' backs as they dared, but other rules were observed and the Wolverines' first season was uneventful and profitable, with Thompson clearing $12,000 on his fourth-place team.

The Reformation did not last long. Detroit's second season, 1882, was filled with controversy. First, Thompson became suspicious of NL umpire Dick Higham and publicly accused him of consorting with gamblers. Higham protested loudly, demanding a hearing—foolishly, as it turned out. At the June 24 special hearing in Detroit, Thompson provided written proof of Higham's corruption and the umpire resigned on the spot. The Wolverines were also embroiled in three separate cases of player-jumping to American Association teams. The court battle over these three players, and the NL's dismissive attitude toward the AA regarding the cases, caused hard feelings that resulted in a prolonged war between the two leagues for years to come.

After Detroit finished fifth, Thompson sold the team in 1883 to Joseph H. Marsh. In June 1885, after the Wolverines had slid to seventh- and eighth-place finishes over the previous two seasons, John T. Brush, owner of the Western League's Indianapolis team, sent his manager, Bill Watkins, to Detroit to inquire about purchasing the team. When Watkins arrived, the Wolverines were entrenched in last place with a 7–32 record, but Marsh wasn't interested in selling. To the contrary, he offered Watkins the job of Wolverines' new manager. Watkins agreed and brought eight of his players with him, including outfielder Sam Thompson. The restocked Wolverines played nearly .500 ball (34–35) the rest of the way.

Before the end of the season, however, Marsh did sell—and new owner Frederick K. Stearns, who had made his millions in the pharmaceuticals business, promptly purchased another NL team, the Buffalo Bisons, merely in order to acquire its four best players: Dan Brouthers, Hardy Richardson, Jack Rowe, and Deacon White. The unconventional purchase created a storm of protest from other owners, who didn't have the cash to acquire star players in such a grandiose fashion. Stearns essentially told the other owners to mind their own business and the purchase was eventually upheld by the league's board of directors, even though Buffalo was forced to drop out of the NL.

But the newly acquired Buffalo players refused to report to the team at the end of the 1885 season because they didn't want to play in Detroit. Their reservations were overcome and the players finally reported to the Wolverines the following spring. The effect of "The Big Four" was immediate. The Wolverines shot to a second-place finish at 87–36, led by ace hurler "Lady" Baldwin, who notched forty-two wins, the most ever by a left-hander. The Wolverines lost the pennant by just two and a half games to the Chicago White Stockings, who finished with a record of 90–34. Detroit's .707 winning percentage still ranks as the best ever by a second-place team.

Meanwhile, the rest of the league's owners were upset with Detroit over the matter of the visitor's share of gate receipts. Under the standard arrangement, Detroit gave teams 30 percent of the gate, but the team profited disproportionately on the road, where they attracted huge crowds. To curb Detroit's income, and therefore extravagant spending, Boston owner Arthur Soden proposed that visitors get a flat fee of $100 instead of the 30 percent. Stearns opposed the flat fee concept and, in protest, even applied to the American Association for membership. A compromise was reached in which visitors would get $125 and half the receipts of games played on holidays. After Stearns again threatened to bolt to the AA, the next year the NL changed its policy again, this time giving the visitors 25 percent of the gate with a $150 guarantee.

By 1887, the Wolverines put it all together and won the NL pennant by three and a half games over the Philadelphia Quakers. Sam Thompson led the way with a .372 average, one of six Wolverines to top the .300 mark. He also had 203 hits, the first major leaguer ever to crack the 200-hit barrier. On the pitching side, Baldwin slipped to a 13–10 record, but Charlie Getzien's 29–13 season took up the slack.

After the season, Stearns challenged Chris Von Der Ahe of the St. Louis Browns, winners of the AA pennant for the third year in a row, to a fifteen-game series for the title of "world champions." Stearns's offer had four conditions: The winner would receive 75 percent of the gate; the winner would be given a huge pennant, costing at least $200, to fly at their ballpark; the games would use two umpires instead of one, a first; and all fifteen games were to be played regardless of the teams' standings. Von Der Ahe agreed.

The "World's Championship Series" (the fourth such postseason series undertaken) was played in ten different cities (Detroit, St. Louis, New York, Philadelphia, Boston, Washington, Baltimore, Chicago, Pittsburgh, and Brooklyn), so fans from around the two leagues could witness the two best teams in major league baseball. Detroit easily handled the Browns, winning ten of the fifteen games, the longest World Series ever held.

While Stearns was not a baseball man, he was a shrewd businessman. Knowing that his team would never have more value than right after winning the championship, he sold a large—but less than controlling—interest in the team to business acquaintance Charles W. Smith. In fact, the 1888 edition of the Wolverines was a letdown. Players were overweight, out of shape from a winter of partying as world's champs, and therefore injury-prone. The team's fan base eroded. The Wolverines were slogging along, barely above .500, when Stearns held a fire sale of the team's stars, scattering them to Boston, Pittsburgh, Philadelphia, and Indianapolis. Stearns then sold the remaining players and the rights to the NL franchise to streetcar tycoons Frank and Stanley Robison, owner of the AA's Cleveland Blues. The Robisons jumped on the purchase because it allowed them to shift their Cleveland team, which they renamed the Spiders, to the more lucrative NL, beginning with the 1889 season.

National League owners, who had never been enamored of the extravagant Wolverines, were happy to welcome Cleveland into the league, having come to the conclusion that Detroit didn't deserve to have a major league team after all. At least not for the time being.

A dozen years later, the brand-new American League awarded Detroit a franchise—the Tigers—that proved far more stable than the erratic Wolverines.

ROAD WARRIORS

THE DULUTH ESKIMOS
National Football League
1923–27

The NFL's Duluth Eskimos spent less time at home than any other team in professional sports history. Over the team's final two seasons, the Eskimos played thirty-eight consecutive road games, with one eight-day stretch of five games in five cities from St. Louis to New York—and this when commercial air travel was barely a gleam in the nation's eye.

When Duluth first formed its pro football team in 1923, it was a cooperative owned by the players, who split equally the expenses and gate receipts. The eleven-member team took the name Kelleys because Duluth's Kelley Hardware Store provided the uniforms. When the team members lost forty-four dollars each for the 1925 season, they asked the team's volunteer secretary-treasurer, Ole Haugsrud, to take over the team. He agreed, but insisted on paying the club one dollar to make the transaction legal.

Haugsrud felt the team needed a genuine star, and he had someone in mind: the all-purpose, two-way Ernie Nevers, a former high school classmate of his from Superior, Wisconsin. Nevers, a multisport star and one of the biggest names in sports in 1926, was an All-American who had just finished his college career at Stanford and was now pitching for the American League's St. Louis Browns.

At the same time, the NFL was experiencing a serious challenge from the new American Football League, founded by the legendary Red Grange and his manager, C. C. "Cash and Carry" Pyle. Haugsrud knew that Nevers was the only player who could challenge Grange as a box-office draw. However, Pyle announced that *he* had signed Nevers to a 1926 AFL contract, but when Haugsrud caught up with Nevers before a Browns game, he discovered his old high school buddy hadn't yet signed the contract because he was still deciding between careers in football and baseball. Nevers told him he would be willing to play for his old friend rather than Pyle, so long as Haugsrud equaled Pyle's offer. Haugsrud promptly sweetened the deal, offering Nevers a base salary of $15,000 plus a large percentage of the gate, and they changed the team's name to Ernie Nevers's Duluth Eskimos to capitalize on his name.

To fully exploit his drawing power, he and Haugsrud also decided to avoid as much as possible actually playing in Duluth, where the brutal weather and small stadium would be their biggest foes. After starting the 1926 season with two home warm-up games, the Eskimos hit the road—for two years. Besides playing thirteen NFL games in 1926, the Eskimos, in a season that lasted from October to February,

1926 program of game between Chicago Bears and Duluth Eskimos.

played sixteen more exhibition games, including ten on the West Coast, where Nevers was particularly popular.

As expected, the fans poured in to see the great Nevers. Every other pro team lined up to happily pay Duluth a $4,000 guarantee plus a cut of gate receipts over $8,000. The increased revenue allowed the Eskimos not only to pay the other players better (fifty dollars per game for a loss, sixty for a tie, and seventy-five for a win), but also to increase their roster to sixteen players.

They were well worth the price of admission; George Halas called them "the greatest football team ever put together." NFL president John Carr went further, saying Nevers and the Eskimos had "saved the NFL," and that, without them, Grange's AFL likely would have buried them. Impressed with their small roster size, famed sportswriter Grantland Rice called them the "Ironmen of the North."

The 1926 team finished the season with an overall record of 17–9–3, and 6–5–3 in the NFL, oftentimes playing in front of tens of thousands of spectators. Nevers led the way, passing, running, kicking, and punting, as well as playing defense. Besides Nevers, the Eskimos had two other eventual Hall of Famers, lineman Walt Kiesling and halfback Johnny "Blood" McNally, one of the most colorful men ever to put on the pads. Blood once raced a German shepherd on a seventy-five-dollar bet, and won. He also once hijacked a hotel elevator because the hotel restricted men to the odd-numbered floors and the women to even floors and he was in need of female companionship.

> George Halas called them "the greatest
> football team ever put together."

The Eskimos traveled in style, the first team ever to sport something besides a number on their uniforms; they had igloos emblazoned on their chests, coats, and luggage. Their hectic travel schedule often required them to improvise, including taking two showers after games, the first with their uniforms on to wash them. Haugsrud traveled with the team, often putting on a uniform during the pregame warm-ups, and practiced kicking field goals to make it look like the Eskimos had more players than they really did. Because he got to thinking himself pretty good, the Eskimos decided to let him get into a game. With the team leading the St. Louis Gunners 52–0 late in the game, Nevers brought Haugsrud in to kick a field goal. The wide-eyed team owner lined up and eyed the goalpost. But when the center hiked the ball to the holder, the whole line lay down and let the entire St. Louis team pile on Haugsrud. The owner got his revenge by pretending his arm had been broken in the pileup, putting it in a sling, and telling the players he couldn't sign their paychecks until his arm healed. It was two weeks before he ended the ruse.

Shortly thereafter, the Eskimos played two memorable games. They spent the night before the first of them, a big game against the Pottsville Maroons, in the local speakeasy, which happened to be located inside the fire department. An argument about the next day's game ensued, and then a fight broke out. Haugsrud ushered his players out of the joint, but the next day, when they arrived at the football field, the boys from the fire department were hosing down the field, turning it into a quagmire to slow the visiting Eskimos down. It didn't work. The Eskimos won when Nevers completed seventeen straight passes, three of them caught one-handed by Blood.

While that game may have been one of the muddiest ever, the next game, against Providence, was considered the crookedest of all time. After Blood caught a pass and was knocked out at the 5-yard line, the referees, clearly favoring Providence, called three consecutive 15-yard penalties on the Eskimos, pushing the ball out to the 50-yard line. Fed up with the refs' favoritism, the Eskimos took matters into their own hands on the next play. One Eskimo clotheslined the referee, knocking him out cold. Another Eskimo kicked the umpire in the teeth, disabling him. Blood then ran right over the field judge, knocking him out too. The lone remaining official took off running, blowing his whistle the whole way, ending the game in a scoreless tie.

By 1927, the AFL had folded (along with eleven of the NFL's twenty-two teams) and Red Grange moved to the NFL, becoming its big star. The other teams weren't as interested in booking games with the Eskimos, so Haugsrud was able to schedule only a nine-game season. The team did poorly, finishing 1–8, and Nevers decided to return to Stanford as an assistant coach to Pop Warner.

Having lost his drawing card, Haugsrud received permission from the NFL to suspend operations for the 1928 season. He also got an agreement from the league that if Minnesota ever got another NFL team, he would be given the option of owning it. When the Minnesota Vikings were created in 1961, the NFL allowed Haugsrud to purchase 10 percent of the team's stock for $60,000. By the time Haugsrud died in 1976, his shares were worth $2 million, a pretty fair return on his original one-dollar investment.

LOST

THE ELIZABETH RESOLUTES
National Association
1873

I n 1873, a Modoc Indian uprising was terrorizing white settlers in the American West. Back East, America's first professional sports league, the National Association, was in its third season and struggling with its own lawlessness, certainly compared to modern baseball's organization. Both topics consumed many pages of the *New York Times* that summer.

The National Association has been described as a league in which the players were more loaded than the bases, and for which gamblers knew tomorrow's results today. In any event, the league was dysfunctional by today's standards; the rules allowed teams to schedule their league games as the season progressed, allowing them to take time off whenever they wanted, and for whatever reason. It was also customary for most teams to take a month or so off in the heat of the summer to rest, tend to other business, or go barnstorming around the country. Some teams started in early April, some in late April. Some played four games in July, some played a dozen. Some teams played into November while others ended their season earlier. It was all a matter of choice and loose association. The National Association was created for the benefit of the players, not the team owners, so players chose which games to schedule—league or non-league—and did so according to their personal schedules and best chances to make money.

It's remarkable that, of the ten teams in the NA in 1873, six actually completed something resembling a full schedule. One of them that didn't was the now-forgotten Elizabeth (New Jersey) Resolutes, an established East Coast amateur team that decided to turn pro and join the National Association in 1873. *The New*

Unidentified player of the 1873 Elizabeth Resolutes.

York Times had been covering the team for several years, often writing glowingly of their prowess on the field. But the Resolutes were in for a surprise once they reached the big time.

The Resolutes opened the 1873 season with an April 28 home game against the Philadelphia White Stockings, itself a new NA team. The White Stockings had started their season with two impressive road wins earlier in the week over the Philadelphia Athletics and Harry Wright's Boston Red Stockings, the league's two powerhouses, but news traveled slowly in 1873 and the Resolutes hadn't yet heard of the White Stockings' shocking victories. Nor had the team's fans, who crammed the covered grandstand at Waverly Fairgrounds hoping to see their local boys succeed after making the jump to the pros. Unfortunately, the White Stockings mauled the Resolutes, 23–5, and, after losing its next game to the Baltimore Canaries, 8–3, on May 6, the Resolutes took a few weeks off from league play to regroup.

Feeling better about themselves, the Resolutes ill-advisedly scheduled their third and fourth league games against the White Stockings on May 20 and 26. The White Stockings, who were already 7–1 and on their way to a 27–3 start, were now the talk of the league, crushing everyone in their path, including the powerful Boston team. The Resolutes were improved, but still lost both games, 6–3 and 7–2. In between the games, the Resolutes traveled to Princeton to play the college team for a fifty-dollar appearance fee—and lost. The Resolutes proceeded to play eleven league games over the next month, losing all but a 12–9 road game against the Brooklyn Atlantics. They were now 1–14.

Watching the Resolutes' fortunes from Boston, Harry Wright saw a chance to fatten both his team's record and bank account. He wired the Resolutes, inviting them to Boston to play a July 4 doubleheader, one game in the morning and the other in the late afternoon, allowing Wright to charge two admissions for history's first day-night doubleheader. Between the games, nearby boat races would entertain the fans. The Resolutes, momentarily awaking from their slump behind the pitching of Hugh Campbell, surprised the powerful Red Stockings, 11–2. But the team immediately fell back into a stupor. Boston took its revenge in the nightcap, shellacking the Resolutes 32–3, scoring twenty-one of the runs in the ninth inning during an era when home teams batted in the bottom of the ninth, even when ahead.

After the Red Stockings again overwhelmed the Resolutes the next day, 13–2, the team returned home, its resolve crumbling. Over the last five weeks of their season, the Resolutes lost seven league games by a combined score of 133–25. Their greatest weakness—perhaps obviously—was their defense, which averaged nearly eleven errors a game. *The New York Times* now turned against the team, calling their play "pathetic" and "wretched" in an August 5 article, but hoping that ". . . we have seen the last of their miserable exhibitions."

Two days later, they would. On August 7, the Resolutes played their last NA game, losing 20–3 to the New York Mutuals. That was it for Hugh Campbell, the team's primary pitcher, who deserved better than his 2–16 record would indicate; although he did give up 213 runs in 165 innings, only 52 of them were earned, giving him an ERA of 2.84, sixth best in the league that year. However, he was so demoralized by his team's erratic defense that he and his catcher, John Farrow, jumped to an amateur team from Irvington, New York. It wasn't long before most of the other Resolutes deserted their sinking ship, scattering to various amateur and NA teams, closing the books forever on the first major league team to call New Jersey home.

HEARTLESS IN HARTFORD

THE HARTFORD DARK BLUES
National League
1876

The oldest, most stable professional sports league in the world is baseball's National League. But it wasn't always so. Though the league, which began play in 1876, has sixteen solid franchises today, many of the charter and early franchises have long since disappeared into the mists of sports history. Of these failed and forgotten teams, perhaps the strangest story belongs to the Hartford Dark Blues.

The impetus for creating the NL in 1876 was the monumentally dysfunctional National Association, baseball's first professional league, which lasted from 1871 to 1875. In the NA, the players were in control; gambling, drinking, rowdiness, and contract jumping were rampant. *(See Elizabeth Resolutes, page 125.)*

In an effort to end the madness, William Hulbert, owner of the NA's Chicago White Stockings, initiated a secret move to form a new league, one controlled by the owners, not the players. Besides desiring an end to the corruption and chaos, Hulbert sought to protect the new league's teams by placing only one team in each large city (the NA had two or three teams in some cities) and eliminating the small towns such as New Haven and Keokuk altogether.

After quietly securing the assurance of three other western teams (Louisville, Cincinnati, and St. Louis), Hulbert met with representatives of select eastern clubs (Philadelphia, New York, Boston, and Hartford) and came away with their commitment as well. The new venture, called the National League, spelled the death of the National Association.

When the NL began play in 1876, one of its charter members

was the Hartford Dark Blues, owned by Morgan G. Bulkeley (no relation to C. H. Bulkley, president of the Cleveland Blues), who sat on the board of directors of Aetna Insurance Company, the country's largest insurer. When the NL's owners held their first league meeting, they put the names of each team's owner in a hat. Bulkeley's name was drawn, so he became the first NL president. Although this lucky draw eventually earned Bulkeley a spot in the Baseball Hall of Fame, in reality he devoted little time to the position, resigning after just one year.

The Dark Blues played their home games at Hartford Base Ball Grounds, a wooden facility with a covered grandstand and a small press box on the roof directly behind home plate, similar to modern parks. It also had three apple trees in the outfield, one each in left, center, and right. (There is no record of the ground rules regarding the partaking of their fruit during lulls in the game.)

Hartford's manager/third baseman was baseball's first great switch-hitter, Bob Ferguson, whose nickname, "Death to Flying Things," was derived from his skill at snagging line drives at the hot corner. One of early baseball's most unquestionably honest men, Ferguson had been the captain or manager of nearly every

1875 Hartford Dark Blues.

team he played with during his fourteen-year career. After his playing career, Ferguson became an umpire, once using a bat to break a player's arm to end an argument. With a reputation for integrity and intelligence, it's no wonder he had been elected president of the NA by a majority of the players, though, ultimately, despite his spending four years in the top post, he had been unable to prevail over the unruly league's darker elements.

Other than outfielder Dick Higham, who led the team with a .327 average, the Dark Blues were a light-hitting bunch. The real stars were pitchers Tommy Bond and Candy Cummings. Cummings, one of the game's early great pitchers, and the player credited with inventing the curveball (an invention that secured him a place in the Hall of Fame), was the team's primary hurler in 1875 as he mentored the nineteen-year-old Bond in the art of pitching.

Apparently Cummings was a good teacher because in 1876 the two reversed roles, with Bond becoming the staff ace. Bond was 31–13 with a 1.68 ERA when the team suspended him for making the unbelievable public claim that Ferguson was throwing games. Bond's suspension opened the door for Cummings to again become the team's main hurler, and he didn't disappoint, going 16–8 with a 1.67 ERA and an amazing five shutouts in an era when whitewashings were quite rare. The potent one-two punch of Bond and Cummings wasn't enough to overcome the team's weak hitting, however, and the Dark Blues finished with a 47–21 record, good for third place, six games back of Chicago.

Only weeks after George Armstrong Custer and his troops were slaughtered at the Little Big Horn, George Washington Bradley of the St. Louis Brown Stockings scalped the Dark Blues at Sportsman's Park, 2–0, in the NL's first-ever no-hitter. Back at home, Bulkeley felt surrounded by enemies himself. Though he had put a winning team on the field, the Hartford fans failed to support the team.

Bulkeley attempted to increase attendance in a novel way. Since the NL had outlawed the sale of booze at the ballparks, Bulkeley was under the belief that many Hartford baseball fans were spending their afternoons in the local saloons rather than attending games, content to follow the team's progress in the afternoon papers. Bulkeley initiated a policy of not letting the newspapers print each day's game information until the following day, hoping to drive fans into the park. It didn't work. Maybe the fans were too drunk to care who won.

Ferguson became an umpire, once using a bat
to break a player's arm to end an argument.

As losses mounted, rumors began to surface that the Dark Blues were going to relocate to Brooklyn the next year. On August 14, Bulkeley held a press conference to announce that no such move was being contemplated. After the season was over, however, Bulkeley did indeed move the team to Brooklyn where it became officially known as the Hartford Dark Blues of Brooklyn (not the Brooklyn Dark Blues, as some record books indicate). Thus Bulkeley has the distinction of being the first team owner in baseball history to lie to his team's fans about moving the team for financial reasons.

Apparently the ability to tell a bold-faced lie to the public suited Bulkeley well, because after folding the team following the 1877 season, he went on to a career in politics, becoming a city councilman, mayor, governor, and U.S. senator.

BASEBRAWL

THE HOLLYWOOD STARS
Pacific Coast League
1926–35; 1938–57

Flashbulbs pop as Jayne Mansfield jiggles down the red carpet to the appreciative howls of scores of men. Elizabeth Taylor winks and blows kisses to the crowd. Academy Award winners mingle with local politicians and sports stars. Teenage girls swoon, then scream, "Frankie! Frankie! Over here!"

Where are we? At a Hollywood premiere? The Oscars? Nope. We're at a minor league baseball game, and it's the hottest ticket in Tinseltown.

The Hollywood Stars, called the Twinks by the local press, were members of the highly competitive Pacific Coast League from 1926 to 1957 with a two-year absence in 1936–37. The PCL, which produced such stars as Joe DiMaggio, Ted Williams, and Tony Lazzeri, was essentially a third major league. Even Babe Ruth, who played many exhibition games against PCL teams, once called the games in the league "as good as any in the majors."

PCL players typically collected salaries that were as good as, if not better than, most major leaguers'. And PCL teams had their own farm systems, just like the American and National leagues. League insiders often referred to the two major leagues as "the Eastern Leagues." And the Stars were innovators. They were the first professional team to fly (1928), the first to wear short pants (1950), the first to drag the infield after the fifth inning (hoping fans would rush to the concession stands), and the first to televise all their home games, in 1939.

Owner Bill Lane relocated his Salt Lake City team to Los Angeles after the 1925 season (in which Bees second baseman Tony Lazzeri hit sixty homers with 222 RBIs!). Lane, a former prospector who became rich after striking gold in the Yukon, was hoping his team would be "discovered" by local baseball fans after not faring well in Utah, far from the bright lights. Initially they were still called the Bees, but soon took on the unofficial name Sheiks in honor of several popular Rudy Valentino movies of the time. When local sportswriters insisted on calling them the Stars rather than the Sheiks and the fans picked it up, Lane eventually gave in and changed the name to please his customers.

They didn't actually play in Hollywood. They were miles away, sharing Wrigley Field with the Los Angeles Angels, the team that would quickly become their bitter rivals. *(See the Los Angeles Angels, page 153.)* Try as he might, Lane never could get the people of Los Angeles, let alone Hollywood, to accept this second PCL team, even though the Stars had won pennants in both 1929 and

c: 1940s Hollywood Stars pennant.

1930. After the 1935 season he moved the Stars to San Diego and renamed them the Padres.

In 1938, the PCL's San Francisco Mission Reds moved to Los Angeles and renamed themselves the Hollywood Stars. This venture failed after one season and the team was sold to attorney Victor Ford Collins and restaurateur Bob Cobb, who owned the famed Brown Derby, and for whom the Cobb salad is named. Realizing that the team really needed to be in Hollywood in order to win the support of Hollywood citizens, the new owners sold stock in the team to movie stars, movie moguls, and other Hollywood civic leaders.

The new stockholders included Gene Autry, who would later

purchase the Los Angeles Angels of the American League; William Frawley (Fred of *I Love Lucy* fame); movie mogul Cecil B. DeMille, who was the chairman of the board of the Stars; and auto magnate Frank Muller. They raised enough money to build their own ballpark in Hollywood, Gilmore Field, and in a shrewd strategic move located the new ballpark right next door to the CBS Studios. That way, when television actors and movie stars finished work for the day, they wouldn't have to go far to see a Stars game and generate some added publicity for them.

Gilmore Field "premiered" on May 2, 1939. There were lavish pregame festivities hosted by Jack Benny, Bing Crosby, Robert Taylor, Gary Cooper, and Al Jolson. Movie starlet (and co-owner) Gail Patrick threw out the first pitch to comedian Joe E. Brown. The Stars became immediately popular with the locals, though it might be said that the many celebrity owners had a larger following than the team.

In the 1940s and 1950s, it was quite common to walk through the stands and see the likes of Spencer Tracy, Milton Berle, Rosemary Clooney, George Burns, Gracie Allen, Jack Benny, Cyd Charisse, George Raft (who is said to have taken a different beautiful date to every game), and even gangsters Mickey Cohen and Bugsy Siegel. Jayne Mansfield, a frequent visitor, was named Miss Hollywood Stars in 1955. Elizabeth Taylor was even a bat girl for a time.

The many celebrity owners had a larger following than the team.

It was only a matter of time before Stars games became a magnet for aspiring starlets hoping to be "discovered" by Hollywood producers and directors. They were certainly discovered by many of the players, who, when the fans stood for the seventh-inning stretch, were known to scurry beneath the open bleachers for spectacular views of the local scenery.

Oh—and sometimes there was baseball, none of it more heated than the rivalry between the Hollywood Stars and the Los Angeles Angels. Almost every game had at least one fight, and the wildest brawl in all of baseball history took place between the Stars and Angels on August 2, 1953, and it was all televised. It was the sixth inning of the first game of a doubleheader when the first fight broke out after a hard slide into second base. The fight was quickly broken up, but reignited on the next play when the runner slid hard into third, badly spiking the third baseman. This time the fight involved all members of both teams and lasted more than thirty minutes. Los Angeles police chief William Parker was at home watching the game on television, and when the fight turned into a near riot, he dispatched fifty city police officers to quell the fracas. Even with the police on the scene, it took another half hour to restore order. Police were stationed in both dugouts and around the field, and only those players actually required to be on the field to play the game were allowed out of the dugouts. Numerous players were offered the chance to file criminal charges against other players, but all declined.

But, as popular as the Stars were, they suffered a sudden and surprising end. When the Brooklyn Dodgers and New York Giants decided to move to the West Coast together after the 1957 season, Dodgers owner Walter O'Malley bought the Los Angeles Angels and banished them to Spokane, Washington, exiling the Stars' main attraction. With so much fan attention now focused on the major league Dodgers, and the Angels gone, the Stars' owners knew it was time to put the team into turnaround. In December of 1957, the Stars were sold to Utah businessman Nick Morgan, who moved the team back to Salt Lake City, the original Stars' first home thirty-two years before, and renamed them the Bees.

BATTLE-TESTED

THE IOWA PRE-FLIGHT SEAHAWKS
NCAA Military College Football Team
1942–44

For a few special football franchises in the 1940s, survival was not linked to finances or fan interest, but nothing less than the fate of the world.

At Pearl Harbor on December 7, 1941, the Japanese changed life for countless professional and college athletes, who joined the military the following day. Some went to regular boot camps for training, while others, such as those training to be pilots and navigators for America's fighter and bomber squadrons, went to service colleges. Some of the toughest of these military schools were the pre-flight schools established by the U.S. Navy on campuses at the universities of Georgia, Iowa, and North Carolina, and Saint Mary's College in 1942. In addition to instruction in basic aerial navigation and communications, cadets were given three months of rigorous physical training before being sent to basic flight schools, advanced flight schools, and eventual assignment to the Pacific Fleet.

Top Navy brass felt college football was an ideal preparation for fighting and soon recruited major professional and college football coaches to coach service teams, which would play other service academies as well as established college football powers — although wartime travel restrictions kept all schools within their regions. The 1942 Iowa Pre-Flight team, under former Minnesota coach Bernie Bierman, faced a "suicide schedule" against teams such as Minnesota, Michigan, Notre Dame, Nebraska, Ohio State, and Missouri, but won seven out of ten.

In 1943, the first of two years in which service schools were included with regular colleges in the national rankings, former Missouri coach Don Faurot took over and led the Seahawks to a 9–1 record. After reeling off eight straight wins to start the season, including victories over Illinois, Ohio State, Iowa State, Missouri, Marquette, cross-campus rival Iowa, and two other service schools, the Seahawks squared off against Notre Dame in South Bend. The Irish prevailed, but barely, 14–13. Iowa Pre-Flight crushed Minnesota the next week, 32–0, but that lone, one-point loss to Notre Dame cost them the national title. The Seahawks finished second in the national polls.

In 1944, former Auburn coach Jack Meagher became the Seahawks' third coach in as many years. After losing the season opener to the powerful Michigan Wolverines, 12–7, Iowa Pre-Flight ran off ten straight wins, most of them lopsided affairs against major college teams, including a 47–27 pounding of the Tulsa Hurricanes, which had just come off two consecutive undefeated regular seasons, though losing the Sugar Bowl in both those years. Meagher led the Seahawks to a 10–1 record and sixth place in the final AP Poll.

Jim Tatum and Bud Wilkinson both cut their teeth as Seahawks assistant coaches, eventually becoming legends in their own right. Tatum won a national title with Maryland and never had a losing season. Wilkinson, meanwhile, went on to coach Oklahoma, where he set an NCAA record with forty-seven consecutive wins.

By late 1944, when it became clear to everyone that the war would soon be over, the Navy decided it no longer needed the pre-flight schools and put the unique football programs into mothballs, casualties of democracy's greatest victory.

MULE-HEADED

THE KANSAS CITY ATHLETICS
American League
1955–67

By the time the Athletics left Kansas City for Oakland after the 1967 season, few fans were shedding tears. Some, like U.S. senator Stuart Symington of Missouri, didn't mince words. About A's owner Charlie O. Finley, he declaimed, "He's one of the most disreputable characters ever to enter the American sports scene, and his impact on Kansas City is comparable to the atomic bomb on Nagasaki."

1966 Kansas City A's cap.

It didn't help that the Kansas City A's were losers, even if at times they were considered the lovable variety. From the time the A's—owned by Connie Mack and on the verge of bankruptcy, which forced their sale—relocated from Philadelphia to Kansas City in 1955, until they left for Oakland thirteen years later, the A's had a winning percentage of just .404 (829–1,224), the worst of any major league team in history that played as many seasons. In six of their thirteen seasons in Kansas City, the A's had the worst record in the American League, and not once did they have a winning season.

Many of those losing seasons can be attributed to their strange relationship with the New York Yankees and Arnold Johnson, which began before the A's were even in Kansas City. Several years earlier, Johnson, an executive with Chicago's Automatic Canteen Company of America, had purchased, as investments, both Yankee Stadium and Kansas City's Blues Stadium, home of the New York Yankee–affiliated minor league team. When the Philadelphia A's came up for sale, officials of Major League Baseball approached Johnson about buying the team and relocating it to Kansas City. At first Johnson declined, saying he wanted to be only a landlord, not a team owner. But after reflecting on it a while, Johnson changed his mind and on November 8, 1954, he bought Mack's team for $3.4 million and moved it to Missouri.

There were two votes against the sale, from Cleveland's Hank Greenberg and Washington's Clark Griffith, who both expressed reservations because of the relationship that had developed between Johnson and Yankee co-owners Del Webb and Dan Topping. When the A's moved to Kansas City, it meant the Yankees' minor league team based in Kansas City would have to move elsewhere. Under such a scenario, the Yankees would normally be due an indemnity payment from the A's for the loss and relocation of their minor league team.

Oddly, the Yankees waived the indemnity payment. This led to whispers of collusion between the two teams, especially in light of the fact that Johnson owned both stadiums. But the whispers turned to protests when time and again, the two teams engaged in trades that were suspiciously one-sided in favor of the Yankees. Many Kansas City stars ended up as Yankees, including Roger Maris, Clete Boyer, Ryne Duren, and Ralph Terry, while the A's got back players who were clearly over the hill, such as Johnny Sain, Ewell Blackwell, and Don Larsen.

Reporters began to joke that the A's were just a Yankee farm team. The front office personnel of other teams said the same thing, but they weren't joking. Then the league stepped in. When the Indians traded slugger Maris to the A's in midseason 1958, it warned the A's and Yankees that Maris had better not turn up on the Yankees' roster that year. He didn't. The two teams waited until the 1959 season was over before making the trade that sent Maris to New York, causing another uproar among all the other teams.

Everyone thought the chicanery was over when Johnson died of a heart attack during spring training of 1960 and his widow sold the team to Charlie O. Finley, an Indiana insurance executive. Finley, a miserly blowhard and wannabe tyrant, even confirmed as much with the first of his many legendary publicity stunts. He bought an old bus and painted "Yankee Shuttle" on the side, then had it burned, loudly declaring that the era of the Yankee Shuttle was over. Nonetheless, in Finley's first trade, he sent his team's best pitcher, Bud Daley (16–16 in 1960), to the Yankees for pitcher Art Ditmar (2–3) and little-used backup third baseman Deron Johnson, who was hitting .105 at the time.

Within a year, Finley alienated many of the team's fans. First, he eliminated delivery service for season-ticket purchases; then he ended telephone ticket sales altogether. And when he announced, after only one year, that he was fielding offers from potential buyers that would move the team to Dallas, Louisville, or Oakland, he incurred the wrath of almost everyone. Attendance plummeted 50 percent.

When Finley wasn't making fans cringe, he made them laugh. He changed the team mascot from a white elephant to a mule named Charlie O, and occasionally had his team arrive on the field by mule train. When Finley got tired of the local press's criticism, he liked to take a recently fed Charlie O with him to the press conferences, where the animal could express with bodily functions how the human Charlie O. felt about them.

Finley liked to take Charlie O to press conferences, where the animal could express how the human Charlie O. felt about them.

Finley was not simply feisty; he was an innovator, too. He hired Betty Caywood as the first full-time female color commentator for a baseball radio broadcast team. He used a mechanical rabbit to deliver fresh baseballs to the home-plate umpire. And, in one particularly popular promotion, Finley had his players autograph baseballs by the hundreds, and these baseballs would be used in play, so fans could catch an autographed home run or foul ball. He also broke from tradition when, in 1963, he dressed his players in tradition-defying, garish gold-and-green uniforms. Finley was also given to outrageous stunts, such as putting grazing sheep and other barnyard animals in the grassy areas beyond the outfield fences. And when the White Sox refused to let him take Charlie O with him onto their field, Finley rented a parking lot across the street from Comiskey Park and brought in a ten-piece band and six beautiful models to attract a crowd. Once he had his crowd, Finley denounced the White Sox for being "unfair to Charlie O. the man, Charlie O the mule, baseball, and muledom."

Eight managers during his eight years in Kansas City attested to Finley's difficult nature more than the team's lack of success. A group of players, led by Ken Harrelson and Lew Krausse, filed a petition against Finley for his cutbacks in food and clubhouse supplies as well as his "high-handedness." Finley was so angered over Harrelson's part in the petition that he gave him his outright release. The slugger signed on with Boston and became one of the AL's biggest stars.

By 1967, major league officials were as sick of Finley's tactics as were the people of Kansas City, so when he presented a viable plan to move to Oakland, the league happily agreed, mostly because the AL wanted to place a second team on the West Coast with the Angels so teams traveling west could play two series instead of one before flying back east.

Although many in town were relieved to see Finley on his way out, the sudden, though expected, loss of the A's didn't sit well with everyone. Kansas City's mayor threatened a lawsuit and Missouri's senators predictably called for an investigation into baseball's antitrust status. The AL sought to soften the loss of the A's by promising a new expansion team for the city by 1971. Local and state politicians said this wasn't good enough. When the AL offered to fast-track the new team to 1969, however, it was a compromise everyone could live with. After just one year without a team, Kansas City became home to the Royals, one of four expansion teams to begin play in 1969 along with the Seattle Pilots, San Diego Padres, and Montreal Expos.

The move to Oakland did nothing to soothe the cantankerous Finley. After putting a mini dynasty on the field in the early 1970s that won three consecutive World Series titles, Finley proceeded to either sell, trade, or let all of his big stars walk away to free agency. The A's went from dynasty to doormat in the same decade, and attendance dropped to less than 3,800 per game by 1979. When Finley asked for permission to sell the A's to Walter Haas, Jr., of the Levi Strauss Co. in 1980 for $12.7 million, the sale was approved by the other owners in record time.

EVERYTHING WAS UP-TO-DATE

THE KANSAS CITY MONARCHS
Negro National League
1920–65

Of all the teams that played in the various Negro Leagues, none won more pennants, had more star players, had more eventual Hall of Famers, had a better single-season record, drew bigger crowds, played more years, and made more money than the Kansas City Monarchs. The black equivalent of the New York Yankees, they also received the most respect from white teams and fans.

The Monarchs were formed in 1920 by owner J. L. Wilkinson, a white Kansas City businessman, when he combined the best talent of two teams, the All Nations barnstorming team and the 25th Infantry Wreckers, an all-black U.S. Army team. The team's big star was future Hall of Famer Bullet Rogan, the ace of the Monarchs' pitching staff, who played center field when he wasn't pitching. As the team's best hitter, he batted cleanup.

When Rube Foster, owner of the Chicago American Giants, formed the first Negro National League in 1920, Wilkinson entered his Monarchs as charter members. As the two best teams in the league, the Monarchs and American Giants became immediate rivals. Foster's Giants won the flag each year from 1920 to 1922, but in 1923 the Monarchs broke through for their first pennant and established the first of their two dynasty periods. After repeating as champs in 1924, the Monarchs played in the first Negro League World Series, facing off against the Hilldale (Pennsylvania)

Giants, winners of the Eastern Colored League. In a thrilling ten-game Series, the Monarchs took the title, five games to four with one tie.

The Monarchs ran away with the NNL pennant in 1924, so Foster implemented a split-season format in 1925, ostensibly to keep up fan interest, but in reality to give his Giants a shot at the pennant in case the Monarchs faltered in either half. They didn't, and Kansas City romped to its third straight pennant. But in a World Series rematch, Hilldale upset the Monarchs after they lost Rogan to an injury just prior to the Series.

Rogan took over as player/manager in 1926 and immediately began to build a strong pitching staff, something that would become a Monarch tradition. Over the next few years he added Chet Brewer, William Bell, Army Cooper, and future Hall of Famer Andy Cooper. He also traded for legendary Cuban outfielder Cristóbal Torriente. The Monarchs won the first-half pennant in 1926, but lost the best-of-nine playoffs to the Giants when Rogan pitched and lost both games of a Series-ending doubleheader.

By 1929, the Monarchs had put together the best single season in the history of the Negro Leagues, 62–17, and won their fourth NNL pennant. It would be the Monarchs' last bit of league glory for eight years as the NNL folded in 1930, the same year the Monarchs introduced portable lighting for night games, five years before the major leagues did.

Losing their league turned out to be a blessing in disguise for the Monarchs, who became the country's premier barnstorming team. With Andy Cooper now managing the team, the Monarchs toured the United States and Canada, often traveling with the House of David baseball team. The Monarchs possessed many more future Hall of Famers during this time, including pitcher Hilton Smith, shortstop/outfielder Willard Brown, outfielders Cool Papa Bell and Turkey Stearnes, and the legendary Satchel Paige, the first Negro League player elected to the Hall of Fame.

After six years of barnstorming, the Monarchs became charter members of the Negro American League in 1937, and Paige was largely responsible for helping the Monarchs win five NAL pennants in six years, failing only in 1938. Unfortunately for the Monarchs, the Colored World Series wasn't revived until 1942, though they did win that year in four straight over the powerful Homestead Grays of the second Negro National League, with Paige winning three of the games.

It was while with the Monarchs that the fireballing Paige achieved most of his fame and performed many of his legendary feats. As an advertising teaser to help lure large crowds, the Monarchs would often publicize that in a particular upcoming game Paige would guarantee to strike out the first nine men to face him, and more often than not he delivered. He would occasionally call in his entire outfield and have them sit behind him on the mound with the winning run on base while he proceeded to strike out the side. In another exhibition stunt, he would replace home plate with a chewing gum wrapper and bet anyone he could throw twenty consecutive strikes. He almost always won. And when Joe DiMaggio was on his way to the Yankees, he played one last exhibition game against the Monarchs, facing Paige. After

1925 Game 5 ticket to the Colored World Series between the Kansas City Monarchs and the Hilldale Giants.

collecting a single in four at bats, the Yankee scout who was accompanying DiMaggio wired the big club, DIMAGGIO EVERYTHING WE HOPED HE'D BE: HIT SATCH ONE FOR FOUR.

The Monarchs, like all baseball teams, lost many of their best players during the war years, but they managed to stay afloat through tough times. Kansas City didn't win another pennant until 1946, when it faced the Newark Eagles in the Colored World Series. The Monarchs were up, three games to one, when the Series shifted to Newark for the final two games. Kansas City lost both games, as Paige was nowhere to be found. It seems he left the team to negotiate a Caribbean winter league contract.

During Paige's later years with the Monarchs, his skills were clearly diminished, but he was still a great drawing card. In exhibition games with white major league teams, Paige's fame often helped draw crowds of 50,000 or more. During World War II, with DiMaggio and Ted Williams in the military, Paige was the highest paid baseball player in America, earning a $40,000 base salary plus a percentage of the gate receipts. Paige was so popular Wilkinson created a second Monarchs team called the Travelers, with Paige as the main attraction. To get Paige as many appearances as possible, Wilkinson purchased a Douglas DC-3 plane just to ferry Paige around to his many appearances, which were oftentimes only an inning or two. Because of Paige's clout, Wilkinson was able to insist that Paige and his teammates be allowed to eat and room where they wanted to, leaving it up to the local Chamber of Commerce to arrange and enforce the details. And if they couldn't guarantee that Paige could eat and sleep in the same town he was playing in, Wilkinson canceled the event.

When the major leagues started integrating in 1947, it was the beginning of the end for the Negro Leagues. The Monarchs lost Jackie Robinson, Elston Howard, Ernie Banks, and Hank Thompson, among others. The NNL folded first, in 1948, with several surviving teams moving to the NAL in 1949. By the early 1950s, Negro League baseball was a shadow of its former self, as most of the stars had been absorbed into the previously white major and minor leagues. When the Kansas City Athletics arrived from Philadelphia in 1955, the Monarchs became strictly a barnstorming team. Soon thereafter, Wilkinson sold the team to Ted Rasberry, who moved the Monarchs to Grand Rapids, Michigan, while keeping the name "Kansas City Monarchs." The NAL, the last of the Negro Leagues, officially disbanded in 1962, though the Monarchs remained in operation until 1965, when they folded after forty-six years, the longest tenure of any Negro League team.

SMALL BALL

THE KEOKUK WESTERNS
National Association
1875

E ven by 1875 standards, Keokuk, Iowa, was a small town. With a population of only 4,000, it's hard to imagine whatever possessed the National Association of Professional Baseball Players (NA) to establish a franchise in what amounted to little more than a riverbank settlement when compared to the league's other metropolitan centers like Philadelphia, Chicago, St. Louis, and Washington.

But Keokuk (named for Sauk Indian chief Keokuk) was bigger than met the eye. Though geographically isolated, Keokuk was economically strategic. Andrew Carnegie's new railroad bridge over the Mississippi River in 1871 connected Keokuk to the rest of the world and made it a major crossroads of rail activity. Unlike most Mississippi River towns that had to contend with a river that was then constantly changing its course, meandering in and out of its banks, and wreaking havoc with nearby land as well as steamboat routes, Keokuk had a deep, stable port. This helped the city become a bustling center for steamboats hauling passengers and cargo both north and south.

Keokuk had been important militarily, too, during the Civil War. Because the city was home to the College of Physicians and Surgeons, the federal government chose to locate a large military hospital in the town. Many soldiers from both the North and the South were treated (or died) at the hospital, and Keokuk became home to Iowa's only National Cemetery. Also, because Keokuk was the first major river port going north, many escaping slaves, or those freed after the war, chose to end their journey to freedom in Keokuk, helping to create a growing agricultural workforce in the region. Keokuk was also home to Orion Clemens, brother of Samuel Clemens, better known as Mark Twain. A one-time Mississippi River steamboat captain, Twain's many visits to Keokuk formed the inspiration for his book *Life on the Mississippi.*

While some of these factors may have played a part in Keokuk's promotion to big-league town, the more significant factor was Keokuk's position as a convenient halfway stopover point in that era for the league's nine eastern teams traveling between games against the Chicago White Stockings and the two St. Louis teams, the Red Stockings and Brown Stockings.

Keokuk's baseball team had been in existence for several years. Against a lineup of primarily amateur teams, Keokuk had put together a 23–9 record in 1874, the year before joining the National Association, and that was good enough for them to declare themselves the "Champions of Iowa." Four of their nine losses that season were competitive affairs against the Chicago White Stockings, so the Westerns felt they were competitive enough to join the National Association in 1875, which they did after scraping together the required twenty-dollar franchise fee.

The Westerns began league play on May 4 at home against Chicago in newly named Perry Park. Formerly known as Walter's Pasture, the field was carved out of a large

Outfielder Charley Jones, one of the most feared sluggers in the majors in the 1870s and 1880s.

cornfield (think *Field of Dreams*) and largely surrounded by a lagoon. Outfielders running down long drives had to be careful they didn't end up in the drink. Though Keokuk lost to the White Stockings, 15–1 in front of 680 fans, it would be the only truly embarrassing loss for the Westerns all season. The next day, only 147 fans showed up to watch Keokuk lose again to Chicago, 7–1. Leaving town with just sixty-eight dollars as their cut of the gate, the White Stockings vowed never to return.

The Westerns then entertained the St. Louis Red Stockings for a two-game series starting on May 6. Keokuk showed promise in the first game, drubbing the St. Louis nine, 15–2, but it would be the only NA game the hard luck Westerns would ever win. The team lost their next ten games, though six of the losses were by one or two runs. Twice they drew 1,000 fans into tiny Perry Park, but more typically drew between 150 and 500, hardly enough to operate a major league team, and certainly not enough to entice visiting teams to schedule games in Keokuk. Boston had been scheduled to play a three-game series in Keokuk from June 10 to 12, but after posting a 6–4 win on the 10th that made them little money, Boston gladly forfeited the next two games in order to get out of town early to play an extra game with Chicago.

The field was surrounded by a lagoon. Outfielders running down long drives had to be careful they didn't end up in the drink.

After a tough, rain-shortened 1–0 loss to the New York Mutuals at home on June 14, the Westerns were in a pickle. Word had spread among the eastern teams that there was no money to be made from a trip to Keokuk and it became virtually impossible for the Westerns to schedule league games at home. The team wired National Association president Bob Ferguson in Hartford, Connecticut (he was also the player/manager of the Hartford Dark Blues *and* a substitute league umpire!), advising him of their withdrawal from the league. The two forfeit wins were expunged from Keokuk's win total, leaving them with a 1–12 final record. Some of the better Western players scattered to other league teams.

For an expansion team from an out-of-the-way tiny town, the Keokuk Westerns had assembled a number of very good ballplayers on their roster, some of whom were the doomed team's legacy to baseball. The most prominent was rookie left fielder Charley Jones, who hooked up with Hartford after Keokuk's collapse and became one of the better sluggers in nineteenth-century baseball. In 1879 he led the National League in home runs, RBIs, and runs scored with the Boston Red Caps (who eventually became the Braves). In a twelve-year major league career, Jones hit .298 with more than one hundred triples. Another prominent Western was catcher/outfielder Billy Barnie, who joined the New York Mutuals after Keokuk folded and had four more mediocre seasons before putting in fourteen more as a manager, mostly with the Baltimore Orioles before their powerhouse days.

THE DEVIL'S PLAYGROUND

THE LOS ANGELES ANGELS
Pacific Coast League
1903–57

The Los Angeles Angels of the Pacific Coast League were one of the most storied franchises in minor league history. With legendary performances on the field, unrivaled attendance, and eleven pennants, the Angels are considered by most baseball historians to have been the most successful minor league team the game has ever seen. Which is why its sudden and unexpected demise at the hand of an unlikely perpetrator was all the more shocking.

The Angels were charter members of the PCL when it opened for business in 1903 and remained one of the league's mainstays throughout its history, winning fifteen pennants. They were so dominant during their later years that they were given the nickname "Yankees-West." The PCL, which had its own farm league system, was so good, in fact, that for decades it was considered a de facto major league, with many PCL players drawing higher salaries than their major league counterparts. Even Babe Ruth, who played many exhibition games against the Angels, said they were the equal of the majors.

The Angels, during their early years sometimes called the Seraphs (a six-winged angel and the name of the team during the nineteenth century while in the California League), played in 15,000-seat Washington Park in downtown L.A. from 1903 to 1925. When owner William K. Wrigley, the chewing gum magnate who also owned the Chicago Cubs at the same time, couldn't get the city of Los Angeles to expand the stadium's parking lots, in 1925 he built a new 21,000-seat ballpark south of downtown. He called it Wrigley Field, designing it largely after its major league namesake in Chicago. After Chicago's Wrigley covered its outfield walls with ivy, L.A.'s followed suit.

If the Cubs' home is known as the "friendly confines," L.A.'s version could have been known as the "movie-friendly confines"; Hollywood movie producers had a long love affair with Los Angeles's Wrigley Field, filming many classic baseball movies there, such as Gary Cooper's *Pride of the Yankees;* James Stewart's *The Stratton Story;* Ray Milland's *It Happens Every Spring* and *Rhubarb;* Joe E. Brown's *Alibi Ike;* Ronald Reagan's *The Winning Team;* Dan Dailey's *Pride of St. Louis;* Red Skelton's *Whistling in Brooklyn;* and the classic musical *Damn Yankees* with Gwen Verdon, Tab Hunter, and Ray Walston.

Wrigley Field also saw some incredible *athletic* performances. Some of baseball's greatest stars got their start in the PCL and routinely entertained Angels

1934 Zee-Nuts candy card of Jim Oglesby.

fans with their batting heroics, such as Ted Williams (San Diego Padres), Tony Lazzeri (Salt Lake City Bees), and Joe DiMaggio (San Francisco Seals), who had a sixty-one-game hitting streak in 1933. The hometown team had their share of legendary stars, not the least of which was Steve Bilko, who won the PCL Triple Crown in 1956, batting .360 with 55 home runs and 164 RBIs. Bilko played with the Angels from 1955 to 1957 and won the league's MVP Award all three years. When he was called up to the Cincinnati Reds in 1958, he actually had to take a pay cut. Another Angels star was Chuck Connors, who gave up a promising baseball career to become an actor, where he starred in the TV shows *The Rifleman* and *Branded.*

They also had some great teams. The 1934 edition is considered to be the greatest minor league team ever to take the field. The PCL used a split-season format in 1934 and the Angels dominated, winning both halves with a combined record of 137–50, nearly thirty games ahead of the Joe DiMaggio–led Seals. Since the Angels had no second-half champion to play against in the playoffs, the PCL decided to put together a fan-selected All-Star team from the league's other seven teams and let the Angels play them in a best-of-seven series. The Angels won, four games to two, with all six games being played in Wrigley Field.

The Angels were still flying high when they won their last PCL pennant in 1956, but earthly business dealings were about to ground them. Following the season, Wrigley sold the team to Walter O'Malley, owner of the Brooklyn Dodgers, for the astronomical sum of $3 million and the rights to the Dodgers' Texas League franchise, the Fort Worth Panthers. After the Angels' being a Chicago Cubs affiliate since 1921, fans and players were in shock.

But the biggest shock was yet to come. Their 1957 baseball season was disrupted by persistent rumors that the Dodgers were going to abandon Brooklyn for Los Angeles after the season. O'Malley denied them, proclaiming that the Dodgers were staying in Brooklyn and the Angels were going to stay in Los Angeles as part of the PCL. But as soon as the 1957 major league season ended, the fork-tongued O'Malley announced that Dem Bums were indeed moving to Tinseltown. And rather than have to worry about competing with the Angels and their fans, O'Malley quickly banished his new Angels team to Spokane, Washington, just about as far north as he could while still keeping them in the United States.

BAD MARRIAGE

THE LOS ANGELES RAMS
National Football League
1946–94

I f ever there was a city and a team that didn't deserve each other, it was Los Angeles, California, and the NFL's Rams. From fans who snubbed the Rams in favor of UCLA and USC, to city officials who continually refused to make needed improvements at L.A. Memorial Coliseum, the Rams were always up against it. Not that they did themselves any favors. On the field, the Rams should have been called the Los Angeles Chokes for all the playoff games they lost over the years. And they even had one owner who traded them for another NFL team.

The Rams came to Los Angeles in 1946 after spending their first ten years in Cleveland, which didn't always deserve them either. Even though the team won the NFL title in 1945, poor attendance forced Rams owner Dan Reeves to make the move. Concerned about inconvenient travel for their teams, the other owners begrudgingly approved the relocation, making the Rams the NFL's only team west of St. Louis.

When the Rams arrived in Los Angeles, hopes ran high and fanfare ran wild. The Rams were the defending NFL champs; their quarterback was a local boy, former UCLA standout Bob Waterfield; and the Rams stirred things up almost immediately when they signed Kenny Washington and Woody Strode, two former UCLA running backs who were the first African-Americans to play in the NFL since blacks were banned back in 1932. But hopes for a repeat championship soon faded, and the Rams managed only a 6–4–1 record in 1946.

The Rams were even more mediocre in 1947 (6–6) and 1948 (6–5–1); their biggest achievement was in the area of uniform design when one of their players, halfback Fred Gehrke, an industrial design artist during the off-season, designed the ram horns on the side of the team's helmet, making the Rams the first team in NFL history with a team insignia or logo on their helmets. In 1949, the Rams finally lived up to their promise, beginning the season with a six-game winning streak, then fumbled their way to an 8–2–2 finish, but did make the playoffs. In an NFL Championship game played in a driving rainstorm at the Coliseum, the Rams lost to the Philadelphia Eagles, 14–0 — the first of what would be many disappointing playoff losses.

1960 Los Angeles Rams program.

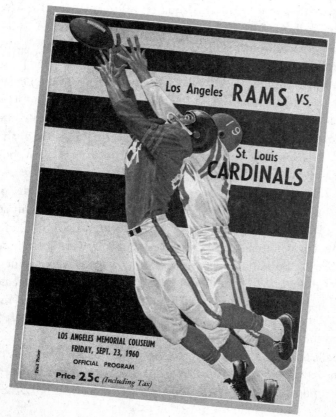

Los Angeles **RAMS** vs.

St. Louis
CARDINALS

LOS ANGELES MEMORIAL COLISEUM
FRIDAY, SEPT. 23, 1960
OFFICIAL PROGRAM
Price **25c** *(Including Tax)*

In 1950, the Rams became an offensive juggernaut, setting twenty-two records on their way to a 9–3 season. Receivers Elroy "Crazy Legs" Hirsch and Tom Fears led the way as the Rams scored 70 points in one game, 65 in another, and fewer than 30 only four times all year. In the NFL Championship game, though, the Rams upheld their young tradition of letting down their fans when they lost to Cleveland, 30–28, on a late Lou Groza field goal.

The only season in the Rams' forty-nine-year history in Los Angeles that didn't end in disappointment was 1951. Norm Van Brocklin took over at quarterback and the team's offensive explosion continued as the Rams scored 40 or more points in half their games while on their way to a 9–3 record. In a rematch of the 1950 title game, the Rams squared off against the Browns, this time in L.A. With the teams tied at 17–17 late in the game, Van Brocklin hit Tom Fears on a 73-yard bomb to win the game and the NFL Championship, 24–17.

In 1952, the Rams traded a record eleven players to the Dallas Texans to get placekicker and linebacker Les Richter, and won their last eight regular season games in a row to sneak into the postseason, but the Detroit Lions knocked the Rams out of the playoffs, from which they remained absent until 1955, when they reappeared in the NFL Championship game, once again against Cleveland and in the Coliseum. Rams fans went home disappointed again as the Browns routed L.A., 38–14. Fans remained largely disappointed for the next decade, during which the Rams had only one winning season (1958, 8–4), but they were starting to assemble the building blocks of a winning team. Deacon Jones, Merlin Olsen, Lamar Lundy, and Rosey Grier formed the "Fearsome Foursome," which would manhandle NFL offenses for more than ten years during the Pete Rozelle era, when the NFL became the preeminent sports league in the world.

The Rams ended their string of seven consecutive losing seasons in 1966 (8–6) behind new head coach George Allen, quarterback Roman Gabriel, and the Fearsome Foursome. In 1967, they finished 11–1–2, but were knocked out in the first round of the playoffs by Green Bay, 28–7. In 1969 it was the Minnesota Vikings who bounced the Rams from the playoffs. For the next three years, they didn't make the postseason.

During this period, owner Dan Reeves, who was suffering from Hodgkin's disease, confided to his friend Carroll Rosenbloom, owner of the Baltimore Colts, that if anything happened to him, he felt the Rams should be in Rosenbloom's hands. His wish was realized when, after Reeves died and Chicago businessman Robert Irsay bought the Rams, Irsay proceeded to trade the Rams to Rosenbloom for the Colts and $3 million, in one of the strangest deals in sports history.

From 1973 to 1979 the Rams won their division every year and made it to the NFC title game five times. True to their tradition of running out of gas, they lost four of the five NFC Championship games. In 1979, the one year they did win, they were beaten in the Super Bowl by the Steelers, 31–19, after leading 19–17 with twelve minutes to go. To make matters worse, the game was played in the Rose Bowl in Pasadena, making it essentially a home game for the Rams.

In 1980, unable to get the desired improvements to L.A. Memorial Coliseum, the Rams moved thirty miles south to Anaheim Stadium. It may have been a new venue, but it was the same old result in the playoffs: a 34–13 loss, this time to the Dallas Cowboys. For the remainder of the 1980s, the Rams made the playoffs six more times but were dumped in the first round five times and the NFC title game once, failing to earn a return trip to the Super Bowl. They also had to split local fan allegiance when the Oakland Raiders moved to Los Angeles for thirteen years beginning in 1982.

For the first five seasons of the 1990s, the Rams racked up a miserable 23–57 record and didn't come close to making the playoffs. Owner Georgia Rosenbloom Frontiere—who took over the team following her husband's death in 1979, then remarried—became fed up with the poor attendance and competition with the Raiders. After an aborted effort to move to Baltimore, she moved the team to St. Louis following the 1994 season. In a surprise move, the Raiders bolted back to Oakland following that same season, leaving the country's second largest population base and television market without an NFL team, and L.A.-area fans and city officials with just what they deserved.

MORAL GRAY AREA

THE LOUISVILLE GRAYS
National League
1876–77

When the National League opened its inaugural season in 1876 with a firm commitment to bring order out of the previous five years of chaos, otherwise known as the National Association, the Louisville Grays were among its charter members. By August of 1877, the Grays were among the league's elite teams, rushing headlong toward what everyone assumed would be their first pennant. Outfielder George Hall was among the league leaders in most offensive categories, while pitcher Jim Devlin, who pitched all but one of the Grays games during the 1876–1877 seasons, would be a thirty-five-game winner with an ERA of 2.25 and finish second in the league in strikeouts. Bill Craver was a steady shortstop and one of the National Association's stars during its final three years.

But a funny thing happened on the Grays' way to the pennant. In August, with the pennant within Louisville's grasp, Hall and Craver went into massive hitting slumps, and so did Devlin, the team's other best hitter. On the mound, Devlin suddenly couldn't find the strike zone. And all three players were making errors in the field so uncharacteristic that newspaper reporters started suggesting the three were in the tank. When team owner Charles Chase received an anonymous telegram accusing several of his players of game throwing, Chase ignored it . . . at first. But when the Grays began losing to clearly inferior teams like Cincinnati, Chase undertook an investigation. *Louisville Times* reporter John Haldeman, an amateur player of some ability and a man who deeply loved the national game, took matters further, publicly confronted Devlin and Hall, and accused them of throwing games. Over the last few weeks of the season, Louisville suffered a seven-game losing streak, including a series sweep at the hands of the rival Boston Red Caps, who went on to capture the pennant.

Following the regular season, the Grays, like most other teams, toured the country playing barnstorming exhibition games against local teams. The three Grays stars mysteriously regained their lost batting, pitching, and fielding prowess. Owner Chase, furious over his players' sudden return to form, was now convinced of their guilt and demanded that all his players voluntarily agree to a search of their personal telegram records at the city's local telegraph office. Any player who refused, he told them, would be kicked off the team. When Craver was the only one to disallow the search, Chase was as good as his word.

Haldeman was a patriot on a mission. After he found evidence that implicated Devlin, Hall, and part-time player Al Nichols, the

Outfielder Bill Crowley hit .282 as a rookie with the Louisville Grays in 1877.

CROWLEY, CATCHER, LACROSSE.

players ultimately confessed their part in the game-throwing. National League president William Hulbert banned the three from baseball for life, as well as Craver, although no evidence was ever turned up against him. As it turned out, Devlin had actually received only one hundred dollars to throw a midseason exhibition game, but was then blackmailed into throwing league games over the remainder of the season by Hall and Nichols, who pocketed all the money from the gamblers.

The ugly business affected the entire franchise. At the league's winter meeting following the season, the other owners found they no longer trusted the Louisville franchise and expelled the Grays from the league. (Louisville, a strong baseball town, wouldn't field another major league team until 1882, when the American Association opened play.) The fiasco spread even further when the St. Louis Brown Stockings, who had been counting heavily on signing Jim Devlin as their pitcher for 1878 (in an era when most teams had only one pitcher), were unable to come up with another suitable pitcher. Rather than field an uncompetitive team, the Brown Stockings simply decided to drop out of the National League.

Owner Chase demanded that his players agree to a search of their personal telegram records at the city's local telegraph office.

For many years, Jim Devlin and Bill Cramer repeatedly, and unsuccessfully, petitioned the National League for reinstatement. Ironically, both players became city police officers in their hometowns. Devlin served only a short time on the Philadelphia force before he died of tuberculosis in 1883 at the age of thirty-four. Cramer joined the department in Troy, New York, remaining there for the next quarter century until he died of heart disease at the age of fifty-seven.

NOWHERE MEN

THE MEMPHIS SOUTHMEN
World Football League
1974–75

When wealthy Canadian businessman John F. Bassett agreed to join the new World Football League as the majority owner of the Toronto Northmen franchise in 1974, he expected to battle the entrenched National Football League and its powerful owners. What he didn't expect was a fight to the death with his own countrymen and government.

His announcement that he was signing three of the NFL's biggest stars—Larry Csonka, Jim Kiick, and Paul Warfield (though the trio was still under contract with the Miami Dolphins and would have to wait until 1975 to play in the WFL)—only exacerbated the insult to Canada of inviting an American league franchise to compete with the Canadian Football League's Toronto Argonauts. Prime Minister Pierre Trudeau was so worried that he had his health minister, Marc Lalonde, introduce the Canadian Football Act, aimed at prohibiting any professional U.S. football team from playing in Canada. Trudeau even threatened economic sanctions against all of Bassett's holdings if he tried to proceed. And Bassett's holdings were nothing to sneeze at: He owned eleven newspapers, Canada's largest television station, a motion picture company, the WHA's Toronto Toros, the CFL's Toronto Argonauts (which he sold to raise money for his WFL franchise), and the Toronto franchise of World Team Tennis. He knew it was futile to fight the socialist government on so emotionally charged an issue. He cast an eye south of the border for a city to call home.

Down in Memphis, attorney Steve Arnold, a close friend of

WFL founder and commissioner Gary Davidson, had been granted a franchise for the WFL, but had been unable to obtain appropriate financing. When the well-funded Bassett inquired about the possibility of turning the Northmen into Memphis Southmen, the league readily agreed. He could easily have financed the new team himself, but understood the value of local involvement and took on limited partners such as country singer Charlie Rich, meat-packing magnate Nat Buring, and Avron Fogleman, owner of the American Basketball Association's Memphis Tams. After securing a five-year lease for Memphis's 50,000-seat Memorial Stadium, Bassett

1975 game ticket for Memphis Southmen.

hired legendary USC coach John McKay as head coach.

The fans, however—none bigger than Elvis Presley—disliked the name Southmen. Because the team logo depicted a grizzly bear backed by the sun, the fans, players, and coaches already referred to the team as the Grizzlies. Grizzlies or Southmen, in 1974 they finished 17–3, the WFL's best record, though they lost in the playoffs to the Florida Blazers, 18–15. By 1975, Csonka, Kiick, and Warfield had joined the team, though Memphis compiled only a 7–4 record before the league folded in midseason. The league's other owners, it turned out, weren't as well funded as Bassett.

Bassett refused to give up. He tried unsuccessfully to get the NFL to accept his Memphis franchise as an expansion team, even conducting a telethon in which he sold 40,000 deposits on season tickets if his attempt proved successful. It was not. The NFL acknowledged that the Memphis franchise had adequate funding, a first-rate front office, a sufficient fan base, and NFL-quality players, but the league's owners wanted to make a statement about competing with the NFL, and turned a deaf ear to Bassett's request.

The fans—none bigger than Elvis Presley—
disliked the name Southmen.

The Memphis fans also refused to give up, initiating a lawsuit (*Mid-South Grizzlies v. NFL*) meant to force the NFL to grant Memphis a franchise. The suit was not settled—in the NFL's favor—until 1984. To add insult to civic injury, when the NFL finally did expand to Tennessee in 1997, the former Houston Oilers stopped for only a year in Memphis before moving permanently to smaller Nashville. And the Northmen who had become Southmen ended up nowhere at all.

BRAVES' NEW WORLD

THE MILWAUKEE BRAVES
National League
1953–65

P erhaps no other major league baseball team has endured a more dysfunctional relationship with its fans than did the Milwaukee Braves during the 1965 season. Not only did hometown fans relish booing the team on the field, several fan and community groups sued the team in court, trying to prevent them from leaving Milwaukee for Atlanta as had been announced by their owner in October 1964. It was not a pleasant year to be a Brave or Braves fan.

The Braves had come to Milwaukee in 1953, leaving another contentious situation. They had spent the previous seventy-nine years in Boston, making them—along with the Chicago Cubs—one of the oldest continuous franchises in major league history. The problem for the Braves in Boston (besides the not-incidental fact that they finished at or near the bottom of the NL standings for fifty years) was the extreme popularity of the city's American League club, the Red Sox. The Red Sox had the fans, the media coverage, and most of the star players. After watching his team's attendance drop from 1.5 million in 1948 to a paltry 281,000 in 1952 (an average of just 3,653 per game), Braves owner Lou Perini agonized all winter about what to do. He had pending offers from Montreal, Denver, Toronto, Houston, and Dallas, when the city of Milwaukee unexpectedly jumped into the picture and began wooing the team.

Milwaukee city officials lobbied fiercely to attract the Braves, offering up their brand-new 35,000-seat County Stadium, built for their Triple-A team. This was enough to convince Perini to accept Milwaukee's offer during spring training of 1953, a move approved by the National League. But on March 7, 1953, Commissioner Ford Frick intervened and stopped the proposed franchise shift, claiming it was too close to the start of the season.

When Perini announced that the move to Milwaukee was off, Wisconsin state officials threatened to reopen the just-concluded congressional investigation into baseball's antitrust exemption if the team wasn't allowed to move to Milwaukee. Several days later, Frick backed down and allowed the move, which was announced publicly on March 13, a day that became known to Boston Braves fans as "Black Friday." The Braves' arrival in Milwaukee displaced the Triple-A team, which moved to Toledo, Ohio, without ever playing a single game in their new park.

1956 Milwaukee Braves jacket.

The payoff for Perini was immediate. The first-year attendance exceeded 1.8 million, nearly 400,000 more than their best season ever in Boston, and a new National League record. Over the next five years, the Braves averaged more than two million fans while winning two NL pennants and one World Series title. They also finished second five times between 1953 and 1960. The success of the new franchise was watched closely by other major league teams, particularly the Browns, Athletics, Dodgers, and Giants, all of whom moved to new cities shortly thereafter.

By 1961, however, the honeymoon was over. Attendance fell to 1.1 million. Perini saw the handwriting on the wall and in 1962 sold the team to an investment group headed by Bill Bartholomay. With the new, nearby Minnesota Twins franchise siphoning off fans from the upper Midwest, the slide continued. From 1962 through 1964, the Braves averaged only 816,000 fans.

Bartholomay didn't wait for things to get worse, announcing in October 1964 that the team would be moving to Atlanta for the 1965 season. He wanted to get the jump on the Kansas City A's, who were also considering a move to Atlanta, where a new 52,000-seat stadium was nearing completion in record time (fifty weeks) in order to lure both a major league baseball team and NFL team in time for the 1965 season.

Once Bartholomay announced the move to Atlanta, the citizens of Milwaukee went on the warpath. Various lawsuits attempting to prevent the team's relocation to Atlanta sped through the Wisconsin court system. Once again, the threat of reinvestigating Major League Baseball's antitrust exemption was raised. Ultimately, a judge ruled that the team had to remain in Wisconsin for the 1965 season because of various contractual obligations. Major League Baseball soothed the Milwaukee fans with the promise of a soon-to-be-announced expansion team for the city, which would turn out to be the American League Brewers, who arrived in 1970 after masquerading as the Seattle Pilots for one season.

Bitter over their team's future move to Atlanta, Milwaukee

fans soon voted with their feet, staying away in such droves that early in 1965 attendance plummeted to only a few thousand per game. But when the team caught fire and became serious pennant contenders in July, the fair-weather fans dropped their grievances and returned to the fold. By September 1, the Braves were just two games out of first place and the Milwaukee media fell in behind the lame-duck team and its pennant chase. This second honeymoon was short-lived, as the Los Angeles Dodgers reeled off fifteen wins in their last sixteen games to take the pennant.

The Braves may not have won the 1965 pennant on their way out of town, but, in addition to their legacy of big name stars such as Hank Aaron, Eddie Mathews, and Warren Spahn, they left behind a remarkable record of success. To this day, they are the only major league team in history to have played more than one season (they played thirteen in Milwaukee) and posted a winning record every year of their existence.

SHORT AND NOT SWEET

THE MILWAUKEE BREWERS
American League
1901

I n 1901, the city of Milwaukee, Wisconsin, had more German-speaking residents than English-speaking, and German-language newspapers than English, but its baseball team was ruled by Irish law—Murphy's Law, to be exact. Whatever could go wrong, did go wrong for the Milwaukee Brewers that season, and that's why they, along with the Seattle Pilots of 1969, are the only two American League teams ever to play just a single season.

The Brewers were members of the minor Western League from 1892 to 1899 when the league, under the direction of Ban

Johnson, changed its name to the American League for the 1900 season, although it remained a minor league. But Johnson's goal was the establishment of a major league to compete with the existing National League. When Johnson was re-buffed in his attempts to

Hall of Famer Hugh Duffy once hit .440 (the highest average in major league history) for Boston, before coming to Milwaukee.

get the NL to recognize his new AL as a fellow major league, he unilaterally declared it a major league beginning with the 1901 season. With a successful tradition on the field and at the gate, the Milwaukee Brewers were a natural choice to be one of the new league's charter members.

From Milwaukee's very first game as a major league team, Murphy was the team's biggest fan. On Opening Day in Detroit against the Tigers, the Brewers took an indestructible 13–4 lead heading into the bottom of the ninth. Oh, wait. Never mind. Detroit scored ten runs to win 14–13 — to this day the greatest ninth-inning comeback in major league history. On June 2 against the Boston Somersets (now the Red Sox), pitcher Bill Reidy allowed a record ten consecutive hits in the ninth inning of a 13–2 home loss.

Murphy's Law had some help in the person of Milwaukee's owner, Henry Killilea, who hadn't been as aggressive as the other AL teams in signing NL players. Of the AL's 185 players in 1901, 111 of them had jumped their NL contracts. While the other AL teams averaged about fifteen former NL players each, the Brewers had only a few. Criticized for this early on by his player/manager, Hugh Duffy, as well as by the fans, Killilea stated he simply didn't have the money.

And it didn't look like he was going to have more anytime soon. An average of only 2,015 paid per game showed up to watch a team on its way to a 48–89 season. Many fans were still angry over the loss of Connie Mack and Rube Waddell, two eventual Hall of Famers, before the 1901 season. Mack, the Brewers' manager, had left for a 25 percent stake in the Philadelphia Athletics and Waddell, the team's star pitcher, had jumped to the Pittsburgh Pirates.

Murphy's Law affected even the Brewers' ballpark, Lloyd Street Grounds. Not only was it much smaller than other league parks, but right field had a short but sharp incline just before the fence, so games there led the league in sprained ankles. Also, unlike every other major league field, which had outfield warning tracks before the fence to assist the outfielders, the Brewers' outfield fences had a series of dangerous wooden support beams that held the fence up. The beams were a major reason Milwaukee needed nine different outfielders to get through the 1901 season.

The surviving Brewers ended up last in the AL in batting, compiling a .261 average. Milwaukee was also near the bottom in ERA (4.06) and fielding (.934). Few stood out, including Duffy, who played the outfield every other day or so and hit .302, and the team's biggest star, first baseman John Anderson, who hit .330 with 99 RBIs and 35 stolen bases and was among the league leaders in many offensive categories.

Ban Johnson was itching to place an AL franchise in St. Louis to compete with the NL's Cardinals, and he saw a great opportunity to kill two birds with one stone. In August, Johnson, who had dictatorial control over the AL, encouraged Killilea to buy into the Boston franchise. After the season was over, Johnson pulled the plug on the Brewers and awarded a new franchise to oil magnate Ralph Orthwein of St. Louis, whose team became known as the St. Louis Browns.

Most history books report erroneously that the Brewers moved to St. Louis and became the Browns. Only six of the former Brewers came to St. Louis and became Browns, and of those, only three (Anderson, pitcher Bill Reidy, and catcher Billy Maloney) were regulars. The majority of the players stayed in Milwaukee and joined a new Western League, this time becoming the Milwaukee Creams. Back in the minors, Milwaukee was successful on and off the field, and the team remained a solid minor league franchise for the next fifty years.

As it turned out, Murphy and his law moved to St. Louis and became great fans of the Browns, but that's another story. (*See the St. Louis Browns, page 272*).

ONE-MAN BRAND

THE MINNEAPOLIS LAKERS
National Basketball League
National Basketball Association
1947–60

Dynasties are typically the result of well-balanced teams. The Pittsburgh Steelers of the 1970s had a potent offense led by Terry Bradshaw, Franco Harris, and Lynn Swann to go with their Steel Curtain defense. The Murderer's Row Yankees of Babe Ruth and Lou Gehrig had five pitchers on their staff with ERAs of 3.00 or below. When the Montreal Canadiens won five straight Stanley Cups from 1956 to 1960, they not only led the league in scoring all five years, but their goalie, Jacques Plante, allowed the fewest goals all five years. One dominant player seldom a great team makes. But professional basketball's first great dynasty, the Minneapolis Lakers, was largely the result of one man: a shy, nearsighted giant of that era, a time when very tall men were considered too awkward to play the game.

The Lakers were born in 1947 after playing one pitiful National Basketball League season in Detroit as the Gems, when they compiled a 4–40 record. Syd Hartman, a twenty-four-year-old sportswriter, acted as the front man for a Minnesota group that purchased the team for $15,000 and moved it to Minneapolis.

In one of Hartman's first player moves, he signed future Hall of Famer "Kangaroo Jim" Pollard, a Coast Guard veteran who had led the Oakland Bittners to the 1946 A.A.U. Championship and astonished fans with leaping dunk shots he launched from the free throw line. From the Chicago Stags, Hartman then purchased Tony Jaros and Don Carlson, two Minnesotans. He completed his preseason moves by hiring another future Hall of Famer, John Kundla, as the team's coach.

The biggest addition of all was yet to come. Four games into the 1947–48 NBL season, the rival twenty-four-team Professional Basketball League of America folded. The NBL held a dispersal draft, and in one of the luckiest draws in sports history, the Lakers were awarded 6'10" center George Mikan, formerly of the Chicago American Gears. After losing their first five games with Mikan in the lineup, the Lakers rebounded to finish 43–17, the best record in the NBL. They then went to the Chicago World Professional Basketball Tournament, where they defeated the famous all-black New York Rens in the title game. *(See the New York Rens, page 218.)* The Lakers capped off their rags-to-riches season by winning the NBL Championship, three games to one, over the Rochester Royals.

George Mikan bread label.

Before the 1948–49 season, the Lakers, Royals, and two other NBL teams jumped to the better-financed Basketball Association of America. The Lakers, with Mikan's league-best 28.3 scoring average leading the way, quickly became the BAA's best attraction. After going 44–16 during the regular season, the Lakers swept the Stags and Royals in the first two rounds of the playoffs before winning their second straight title, four games to two, over Red Auerbach's Washington Capitals.

Following the season, the NBL folded and the BAA absorbed six more of its teams, renaming itself the National Basketball Association. In 1949, the Lakers added another future Hall of Famer, power forward Vern Mikkelsen, to give Minneapolis the best front court in the league. Mikan was the league's top scorer again (27.4), and the Lakers won their third consecutive championship, their first in the NBA. During the 1950–51 season, the Lakers had the league's best record at 44–24, but, while Mikan (28.4) led the NBA in scoring once again, a late-season ankle injury slowed him down and contributed to the Lakers' second-round loss in the playoffs to their bitter rivals, the Rochester Royals.

An injury was the only way to keep Mikan from dominating the game. He was such a powerful force under the basket that, before the 1951–52 season, the NBA's rules committee voted to widen the foul lane from six feet to twelve. The move was not particularly effective; besides making better use of teammates who drove through the wider lane, Mikan added a solid jump shot to his arsenal of moves and became a more complete player. Mikan still finished second in scoring and led the Lakers to their fourth championship in five years, this time in seven games over the New York Knickerbockers. The 1952–53 NBA season was almost an instant replay of the year before. The Lakers had the best record in the NBA (48–22), Mikan was second in the league in scoring (20.6), and Minneapolis again defeated the Knicks for the NBA title, the team's fifth in six years, though this time it took only five games.

In anticipation of Mikan's eventual retirement, the Lakers added center Clyde Lovellette in 1953, and the rookie immediately began to spell big George, who slipped to fourth in the NBA in scoring (18.1). But the retooled Lakers again had the best record in the NBA (46–26) and won their sixth championship in seven years, this time a seven-game squeaker over the Syracuse Nationals.

An injury was the only way to keep Mikan
from dominating the game.

Before the 1954–55 season, Mikan, the premier player of the era, asked for a raise from his $12,000 annual salary, the same salary many other NBA players were making under the league's salary-cap system. When the Lakers refused, citing their cap limit, Mikan, who had once given professional basketball its first credibility, retired. The loss was felt immediately. The Lakers fell to 40–32, their worst record since joining the NBA. They were also knocked out of the playoffs in four games by the Fort Wayne Pistons.

For the rest of the 1950s, the Lakers finished under .500 every year, including particularly abysmal records in 1957–58 (19–53) and 1959–60 (25–50). With the dominating Mikan gone, attendance plummeted and financial losses mounted. With an eye on the Brooklyn Dodgers' wildly successful relocation to Los Angeles in 1958, in 1960 Lakers owner Bob Short followed suit and moved his team to L.A. in hopes of establishing another dynasty.

CHUTZPAH

THE MINNEAPOLIS MARINES
National Football League
1921–24

The Minneapolis Marines had the most unusual motive ever for joining the National Football League: They wanted to improve their play so they could be more competitive in their Minneapolis city league.

The Marines had a long history as one of the top amateur teams in the upper Midwest. Formed in 1905 by John Dunn and Val Ness, the Marines were composed primarily of working-class teenagers, most of whom had no high school or college football experience. They first played in the 115-pound weight class, and by 1907 had progressed to the 145-pound division. And though young, the Marines were a team ahead of their time, holding voluntary preseason training camps to get in top condition before the regular season started.

The Minneapolis area was a hotbed of football activity in the early 1900s, and the biggest prize was the city championship of the Independent Football League, usually fought over by the city's two best teams, the Marines and their biggest rival, the Beavers, who, unlike the Marines, had multiple players with college experience. Both teams' rosters included many who had played for their respective teams for years.

Whenever the Marines had a good winning streak going, it was almost always the Beavers who ended it. After one particular galling loss to the Beavers that ended a thirty-four-game winning streak in 1912, the coaching staff was convinced that the time had finally come to search for ex-college and former professional players. Among the more notable players they signed were Rube Ursella (who had a 22-year pro career), Bob Marshall (one of the first black players in professional football), Fred Chicken, Walt Buland, and Dewey Lyle. For the first time, Dunn also brought in some outside coaching help—Ossie Solem, a standout end with the Minnesota Gophers who later became a coach at Syracuse and then Iowa. Solem attempted to diversify their offense—the Marines had exclusively used the T formation for many years—by teaching them the Minnesota Shift and the single wing formations. But neither new and better educated players nor new and better offensive schemes made a difference as the Marines struggled to win like never before, and they fell from the league's elite teams for the next six years.

Things got even grimmer in 1918, when the entire season was wiped out because of the worldwide influenza epidemic. A number of the better Marines left the team and signed on with the professional Rock Island (Illinois) Independents, the closest pro

1928 broadside for game between Chicago Bears and Minneapolis Marines.

team to Minneapolis. After losing so many of their star players, the Marines went downhill in 1920, losing not just games but the kind of crowds they had enjoyed when they were the city's top amateur team.

Dunn's solution to the problem was at the very least counter-intuitive, and possibly insane as well: Since the Marines were struggling to compete on the independent-team level in the Minneapolis city league, he decided they needed to step up to the professional ranks. He reasoned that the Marines would rise to the level of their competition, and that the team's fans would return if they got to see the Marines play some of the top pro teams in the country.

This was all possible because, in 1921, all you had to do to join the NFL was hand over one hundred dollars to the league and—presto!—you were in the NFL. Each team could play as many or as few league games as they could get other teams to agree to, which is why some teams played twelve games and others only two or three. Next, Dunn booked his team into Nicollet Park, the home of the Minneapolis Millers minor league baseball team, a much larger stadium than any they had played in previously.

The Marines' first season in the NFL, under new coach and former Marines star Rube Ursella, was mixed. While they had a losing record at 1–3, they were competitive. In their four league games, the Marines lost 20–0 to the Chicago Cardinals, 7–6 to the Green Bay Packers, and 14–3 to the Rock Island Independents. Their lone win and only home game was a 28–0 pasting of the Columbus Panhandles, not one of the league's elite drawing-card teams.

The 1922 NFL season was more of the same: a new coach (Russell Tollefson) and a 1–3 record, caused mostly by a lack of offense. The Marines' only victory was a 13–6 game against Jim Thorpe's Oorang Indians, but then everybody was beating the Indians, and usually by bigger margins. The Marines were a little more competitive in their losses this year, losing 3–0 to the Cardinals, 14–6 to the Packers, and 17–0 to the Dayton Triangles.

Once again, the Marines got only one home NFL game, but at least it was against the Indians, and Thorpe's crew, with their unique halftime show, packed in the fans. In 1923, the Marines had the same tough defense, and the same weak offense, but yet another new coach, Harry Mehre. In a heavier schedule, the Marines went 2–5–2 and were shut out five times. Again, the two premier opponents on the schedule—the Packers and Cardinals—were away games.

All you had to do to join the NFL was hand over one hundred dollars and—*presto!*—you were in the NFL.

The 1924 season was the final straw for Dunn. With still another new head coach—Joe Brandy—leading the team, the Marines had their worst NFL season ever. They went 0–6 and were shut out their first four games. Dunn was again frustrated with the league's scheduling, which called for four road games (including the Cardinals and Packers) and two home games, both against the Duluth Kelleys, hardly an opponent that would fill Nicollet Park. But more than anything, Dunn was frustrated with a team that seemed to be going in reverse. Even their defense deteriorated; in the Marines' last two games of the season, they allowed 28 and 39 points, the most they had given up in four years of NFL play.

Dunn finally had to acknowledge that his plan had backfired. The Marines had been humbled, not helped, by their sojourn into football's professional ranks. Dunn withdrew his team from the NFL after the 1924 season and returned to independent play. Unfortunately, as if now cursed by their chutzpah, they never returned to their former dominance.

EXCUSEZ-MOI

THE MONTREAL EXPOS
National League
1969–2004

B efore the Montreal Expos ever played a game, they were dead in the water. They just didn't know it.

After being created in haste along with the San Diego Padres in response to the American League's equally hasty decision to expand to Seattle and Kansas City in 1969, the Expos (named after Expo 67, the name of the 1967 World's Fair) took up residence in flimsy Jarry Park Stadium, a facility that wasn't even up to minor league standards at the time. A hurried conversion added some uncovered bleacher seats along the left and right field lines as well as in left field. After an electric scoreboard was slapped together beyond the right field fence, the park was deemed ready, by a prodigious stretch of the imagination, for major league use.

Charles Bronfman, owner of the Seagram distilleries, paid $10 million for the Expos, and held the reins for the next twenty-two years. But Bronfman's ownership was the team's primary constant. Not only did he have eight different field managers during his tenure, but the front office was a revolving door of disgruntled personnel, culminating in the Dave Dombrowski affair. Dombrowski, the Expos' GM, quit his job with Montreal and took over baseball operations for the expansion Florida Marlins when they were first created in 1991. When Dombrowski's raids on Expos front office personnel got too excessive, National League president Bill White intervened and put a stop to the defections.

Nearly everyone who ever played for the Expos wanted out. Because Montreal is a French-speaking city, nearly every English,

Spanish, and Japanese-speaking player disliked playing there. Players also had to pay higher Canadian income taxes and suffer through cold, rainy, and even snowy weather at the beginning and end of every season. Nor did the players like Olympic Stadium—to which they moved in 1977—much better than Jarry Park Stadium: It was an oversize, unfinished, drafty monstrosity that was occasionally given to falling apart or catching fire. Even opposing players hated coming to Montreal because of the cultural differences, language barrier, and having to deal with the customs agents going in and out of our friendly neighbor to the north.

Although the Expos managed the best cumulative winning percentage in the National League from 1979 to 1983—and were

1982 Montreal Expos jersey.

hailed as the "Team of the '80s" on the brink of that decade—
they were seldom more than mediocre, making the playoffs only
once in the team's thirty-six-year history, and that was a fluke due
to the split-season format necessitated in 1981 by a lengthy midseason players strike. The Expos won the Eastern Division's second half by 1/2 game over the Cardinals, but, after beating the
Phillies in the National League Division Series, were dispatched
in the Championship Series by the Dodgers. The Expos' best season was 1994 when, behind Ken Hill's pitching (16–5) and Larry
Walker's hitting (.322, 19 homers, 86 RBIs), they had the best
record in all of baseball—74–40—before the rest of the season
and its postseason play (and part of the next) was wiped out because of another players' strike.

> Nearly everyone who ever played for the
> Expos wanted out.

The franchise's prolific farm system cranked out young stars,
but many left for free agency, and Expos fans were chronically
frustrated by the front office's inept player management. They
made many horrible trades and were simply awful at the annual
draft. From 1969 to 1973, for example, the most notable first-
round pick by the Expos was Jack Scalia, and he left baseball to
pursue a career in modeling. In December 1974, the Expos traded
Ken Singleton and Mike Torrez to Baltimore for Rich Coggins,
Bill Kirkpatrick, and Dave McNally. While Torrez became a
twenty-game winner and Singleton emerged as one of the most
feared sluggers in the American League, McNally retired without
playing a game for the Expos, Kirkpatrick never got out of the
minors, and Coggins collected only thirty-seven at bats for Montreal before he was injured and traded to the Yankees.

Bronfman eventually grew tired of the Expos' futility and in the mid-1980s openly announced the team was for sale, but found no takers for several years. In 1991, he finally sold out to a consortium of Montreal businessmen and the city of Montreal, led by one of his Seagram's executives, Claude Brochu. The team's fortunes only worsened under Brochu's watch and he sold the team in 1999 to a group of New York interests led by art dealer Jeffrey Loria.

Loria was full of undelivered promise. He had promised to build a new downtown stadium, but failed to deliver. He also failed to secure both television and English-speaking radio broadcast contracts. When Major League Baseball voted in 2001 to contract two teams, the Expos and Twins (it was later reversed by the courts), Loria made a deal to sell the Expos to MLB while he purchased the Florida Marlins.

Only when MLB took over the ownership reins did they take seriously all the franchise's problems, from its poor performance (eight last or next-to-last place finishes in the franchise's final ten years in Montreal) to poor attendance (they pulled in a million fans in only one season in the previous seven years). MLB quickly decided to move the team to Washington, D.C., but had to play three lame-duck years in Montreal until Washington's new stadium was completed. While waiting to move, MLB scheduled twenty-two Expos "home" games in 2003 and 2004 for Hiram Bithorn Stadium in San Juan, Puerto Rico. Though the seating capacity was only 18,000, the Expos drew better in San Juan than they did in Montreal.

And when the lights were finally turned out after the last Expos game in Olympic Stadium in 2004, not many in Montreal really cared.

ICE ON FIRE

THE MONTREAL WANDERERS
National Hockey Association
1917–18

The Montreal Wanderers, founded in 1903 as the darlings of the English-speaking citizens of French-controlled Montreal, did not choose their name idly. Their founding purpose was to wander around Canada playing challenge matches for the Stanley Cup in an era when any team could challenge the Stanley Cup holder at any time, and so long as the two teams agreed to the established format. This period in hockey history, now called the Challenge Cup era, often saw teams vying for the Stanley Cup three or four times a season—or, as was the case in 1908, five. (In 1914, Stanley Cup competition was normalized, becoming an annual affair featuring the winners of two leagues. Since 1926, the Stanley Cup trophy has been awarded only to the winner of the NHL's annual playoffs.)

Hall of Famer Art Ross, for whom the NHL's Art Ross Trophy is named.

ARTHUR ROSS

The Wanderers nearly won the Stanley Cup in their very first year, 1903, playing to a 5–5 tie in the first game with the legendary Ottawa Silver Seven. But when Montreal refused to play the overtime period with the same referee, and the two teams were unable to agree on a site for the second game, Ottawa was declared the winner and held on to the Cup. In 1906, the Wanderers ended Ottawa's eleven-Cup winning streak by outscoring them 12–10 in a two-game total-goals series—and the Wanderers would win nine more Stanley Cup challenges before the Challenge Cup era ended in March 1914.

During the Wanderers' run, in 1909, the first Canadian professional league, the Canadian Hockey Association, emerged to satisfy the sport's growing popularity. (Until then, professional hockey had consisted of individual pro teams traveling around willy-nilly, scheduling games as they went.) The Wanderers, however, were not invited to join because the league owners despised player/owner Jimmy Gardner, who, incensed at the league's rebuff, joined forces with millionaire Ambrose O'Brien, who was forming his own new pro league, the National Hockey Association. Between O'Brien's money and Gardner's vindictiveness, the NHA ran the ill-funded CHA out of business within a month. Gardner then had the last laugh on the other CHA owners when he agreed to absorb the now-defunct CHA into his NHA.

In the NHA's first season, the Wanderers romped to the title with an 11–1 record. They scored an amazing ninety-one goals in those twelve games, led by Ernie Russell's thirty-two. The team won the league's new prize, the O'Brien Trophy. The Wanderers then went on to defeat Berlin Dutchmen, 7–3, in a one-game Stanley Cup challenge.

After Gardner sold the Wanderers the next season and moved on to other ventures, the team largely struggled over the next six years. Their only successful season came in 1914–15, when they and the Ottawa Senators tied for first place with 14–6 records. But in a two-game, total-goals series, the Wanderers lost, 4–1, each team trading a shutout victory.

In 1917, a new opportunity presented itself. Personality clashes and infighting within the National Hockey Association—Toronto

Blueshirts owner Eddie Livingstone was a primary irritant—prompted some of the owners to form a new league. The National Hockey League would include four teams: the Montreal Canadiens, Ottawa Senators, Toronto Arenas, and the Wanderers. The Canadiens would represent Montreal's French-speaking citizens while the Wanderers would skate for the English-speaking fans.

The Wanderers opened the NHL's inaugural season in Toronto with a 10–9 victory over the Arenas, but their joy was brief. After five consecutive losses, the team was drowning in red ink. World War I robbed them of their best players, who joined Canada's war efforts in Europe. The other teams loaned them lesser players, but the fans wouldn't turn out to support a team of impostors.

Things went from bad to worse on January 2, 1918, when a mysterious fire destroyed Westmount Arena, home to both the Wanderers and the Canadiens. The fire, which started in the Wanderers' locker room, destroyed all the team's equipment. The Canadiens (and their equipment) happened to be out of town that night. When they returned to the charred arena, the Canadiens quickly made a deal to use Jubilee Rink for their home games and invited the Wanderers to share the building. They refused. When the city of Hamilton offered Wanderers' owner Sam Lichtenhein a new home if he relocated his team, he refused; Lichtenhein had lost $30,000 in the young season and he wasn't about to lose any more. Despite their long and noble history, the Wanderers ceased operations after only six games, never to skate again.

And the mysterious fire, for some peculiar reason, was never investigated.

FROZEN OUT

THE NEW YORK AMERICANS
National Hockey League
1925–42

The National Hockey League's New York Americans were used to being lied to. Lied to by other teams, promoters, arena owners, and other team owners. But after the NHL's board of governors lied to them, the Amerks became the only professional sports team in history to be lied right out of existence.

When the NHL was founded in 1917, it was strictly a Canadian league. In 1923, sports promoter Thomas Duggan purchased several options for U.S.-based NHL teams. After selling one of the options to Boston grocery store magnate Charles Adams for a promised 50 percent of that team's profits (he founded the Boston Bruins in 1924), Duggan partnered with New York's most celebrated bootlegger, Bill Dwyer, in establishing a franchise in New York called the Americans, playing off the popularity of baseball's Yankees.

The Americans wouldn't begin play until 1925, however, because they wanted to wait until the new Madison Square Garden facility opened. A cautious and savvy promoter, Duggan received assurances from the facility's owner that his would be the only hockey team allowed to play in the Garden.

By the summer of 1925, Duggan (the face of the franchise) and Dwyer (the real behind-the-scenes owner) had a team and a facility, but no players. An eighteen-month effort to stock their new team proved harder than anticipated. A number of players from various Canadian leagues gave verbal commitments, but reneged on their promises to sign on. After the team had signed only a few minor leaguers, Lady Luck arrived in the form of a players' strike by the Hamilton Tigers, the NHL's first.

The Tigers had finished in first place in 1924–25, a season in which the NHL had expanded its schedule from twenty-four games to thirty. But upon completion of the regular season and before the Stanley Cup playoffs, Hamilton's players refused to participate in the postseason unless they were paid $200 for the

1937 New York Americans jersey.

six extra regular season games. Hamilton's GM, Percy Thompson, rejected their demand and turned it over to the league.

The league also refused, demanding the Tigers report for their scheduled playoff series with fourth-place Ottawa. The players stood firm and were suspended and fined $200 each. When Dwyer heard about the standoff, he contacted Thompson and offered to buy out the contracts of all his striking players. Thompson accepted, selling the rights to his entire team for $75,000 plus the fines owed to the NHL. Dwyer was ecstatic over his player coup, and, not wanting a repeat performance by the players, he immediately doubled all their salaries. Overnight, the Americans had gone from a team of minor league scrubs to one that would finish first in North America's finest league.

The 1925–26 season was promising for the first-year Americans. They had the players from the NHL's best team the year before, a gleaming new arena, promotional expertise in the front office, and a lot of money at their disposal. Led by Yonkers native Billy Burch, a future Hall of Famer, the new team became popular, clad in eye-catching red, white, and blue stars-and-stripes uniforms. First dubbed the "Star Spangled Skaters," the Americans eventually became known as the Amerks.

And though the Amerks disappointed in their inaugural season, finishing in fifth place in the seven-team league with a record of 12–20–4, their fans filled the Garden for every game, 17,000 strong. The attendance was so surprisingly good that the Garden's owners went out and purchased a franchise of their own by the next season, the New York Rangers.

It was bad enough that the Garden's owners had broken their promise to Duggan and Dwyer, but they added insult to the Amerks' injury by getting the NHL to agree to allow the Rangers to schedule *both* teams' games as the Garden officials saw fit. Needless to say, the Rangers reserved the best dates—Friday nights, Saturdays, and Sundays, for their home games—leaving the weekday scraps for the Amerks. And if the circus or a dog show was in town, the Amerks were forced to play during the *day*.

The disaster was just in its early stages. While the Amerks struggled to a fourth-place finish in the much tougher Canadian Division in 1926–27, the expansion Rangers in their first year won not only the American Division, but the hearts of New York fans. In 1927–28, the Americans fell to last place while the Rangers won their first Stanley Cup, and in the process became the toast of the town. In 1929, the Amerks improved enough to make the playoffs for the first time, but were knocked out in the first round by you-know-who.

The attendance was so surprisingly good that the Garden's owners went out and purchased a franchise of their own by the next season—the New York Rangers.

By 1932, the Americans were an overmatched team suffering through another last-place season when they played Charles Adams's Bruins in Boston. Dwyer was steaming over Adams's having reneged on his promise to pay him 50 percent of his team's profits, so Dwyer instructed Americans coach Eddie Gerard to engage in a bit of mischief. During the game, the Amerks expressed their owner's displeasure by icing the puck sixty-one times (it was not prohibited then), an egregious display of delaying tactics and clock-killing. A furious Adams complained to the league and asked for a rule prohibiting icing. The league declined, so Adams vowed to get his revenge the next time the two teams played, which was at the Garden. True to his word, the Bruins iced the puck eighty-seven times, contributing to a scoreless tie that put some fans to sleep, drove others away, and eventually forced the NHL to enact a rule against icing.

By 1934, the Americans, still floundering in last place, were in deep financial trouble. The Great Depression was lingering and Prohibition was coming to an end, drying up bootlegger Dwyer's main source of income. He couldn't afford to sign high-priced free agents to strengthen the franchise, but he refused to sell his beloved Amerks. He tried merging his team with the Ottawa Senators, but the league rejected the attempt. In 1935, some of the Amerks complained to the league that they weren't being paid.

Dwyer finally put the team up for sale in 1936, but couldn't find a buyer. In 1937, he abandoned the team and the league took it over, passing it to coach Red Dutton, who immediately went out and signed talented veterans Ching Johnson, Hap Day, and Earl Robertson. They turned the team around, earning a rare appearance in the playoffs, where they knocked off the hated Rangers in the first round before losing to Chicago in the second. Impressed with how Dutton, who owned a large contracting business on the side, had turned the team around, the league sold him the team, which made the playoffs the next two years as well.

By 1939, however, the team's fortunes turned. The Amerks were decimated when many of their Canadian players left for military service. In 1940, Dutton watched helplessly as the hated Rangers won their third Stanley Cup. Desperate, he decided to move his team to Brooklyn for the 1941–42 season, hoping to create a new fan base. Though renamed the Brooklyn Americans and practicing in Brooklyn, the team still played its games at the Garden because Dutton couldn't find a proper arena. The arrangement alienated fans in both cities.

With America's entry into World War II, the Amerks were hit even harder by player losses and poor attendance. After selling off his best players for cash, Dutton asked for, and received, league approval to suspend operations until after the war. The NHL thought so highly of Dutton they named him league president in 1943, but in 1946 Dutton resigned as NHL president and prepared to resurrect the Amerks, arranging for the construction of a new $7 million arena in Brooklyn.

When Dutton met with the NHL's board of governors to lay out his plans, however, they informed him that the Garden's owners were opposed to a team in Brooklyn—and, despite the league's promise to Dutton four years earlier, that was that. Angry at another broken promise, Dutton stormed out of the meeting, cursing the Rangers and vowing they wouldn't win another Stanley Cup while he was alive.

And in the forty-one years Dutton continued breathing, they didn't.

INCOMPLETE

THE NEW YORK BRICKLEY GIANTS
American Professional Football Association
1921

When the New York Brickley Giants took the field in 1921, they were the first of seventeen different professional football teams to represent New York. None of them was conceived with so much riding on one football player, and no football player on whom so much was riding ever fell so far from grace.

The team was originally founded in 1919 by two-time All-American Charles Brickley and sponsored by Charles Stoneham's New York Giants baseball team. Stoneham owned both the baseball Giants and the Polo Grounds and he was looking for ways to make some money during the off-season. Although professional football was in its infancy—college football would remain the more popular game for decades—Stoneham felt there was a bright future for pro football, so he partnered with Brickley, a college football player who always seemed to be in the headlines.

An all-around athlete, Brickley played halfback and placekicked for the Harvard football team from 1911 to 1914. Considered to be the best placekicker of his day, Brickley once kicked five field goals in a 15–5 win over Yale, a time when the two schools were among the best football teams in America. He also set collegiate records (since broken) for most field goals in a season (13) and career (34). Brickley also finished in ninth place in the triple jump at the 1912 Olympics, at which he also participated in the baseball event that was being demonstrated at the Olympics that year. After graduating from Harvard, Brickley took a number of football coaching jobs with Virginia, Johns Hopkins, and Boston College before joining the Naval Reserve during World

War I. In 1919 he returned to civilian life and connected with Stoneham on the Brickley Giants project.

On October 5, 1919, Brickley held the team's first practice, just a week before the first scheduled game against the Massillon Tigers. But the game never took place. New York had recently passed a law that legalized Sunday baseball games and everyone naturally, but erroneously, assumed that football games were now legal as well. City officials scrubbed the game and the Brickley Giants were disbanded, reforming two years later after Sunday football was legalized. In 1921, Brickley was now backed by boxing promoter Billy Gibson, and together they were granted a franchise in the American Professional Football Association, which would change its name to the National Football League at the end of the season. There were no other former college players besides Brickley on the reformed Giants, although Brickley's brother George, who played five games as an outfielder with the Philadelphia A's in 1913, did make the team.

Brickley's Giants played only two league games that year to go along with a full schedule of exhibition matches, primarily against various semi-pro teams. The first league game took place on October 16 against the Buffalo All-Americans, and the Giants were routed, 55–0. After seven weeks of non-league games, the Giants played their second (and final) league game, this time against Jim Thorpe's Cleveland Tigers.

The Tigers prevailed, 17–0, in front of a disappointing Polo Grounds crowd of just 3,000. While Thorpe played a few downs to the glee of the fans, Brickley did not, even though there were many calls from the grandstand for him to do so. At halftime, however, Brickley and Thorpe entertained the crowd with a drop-kicking contest. They each made six of twelve attempts, but Brickley was declared the winner when he kicked one straight through the uprights from fifty yards while Thorpe missed his attempt.

After the 1921 season, the Giants were invited to return to the NFL in 1922, but decided against renewing their franchise for the required one-hundred-dollar fee. Having failed to capitalize on Brickley's once-famous name the way he had hoped, Gibson decided to downsize the operation, backing the Giants for one more year as a semi-pro team before folding. Perhaps Brickley was too many years removed from his college career or perhaps it was because he didn't spend much time on the field in 1921. In any event, Brickley never coached or played again; although he was offered the job of head coach at Northwestern University, he was unable to come to terms.

Brickley wasn't through making headlines. After leaving football, Brickley became a stockbroker, and he didn't play clean. In 1923 he was indicted, but not convicted, of engaging in illegal stock negotiations. In May of 1925, a jury found him not guilty of forgery and larceny. In March of 1928, Brickley was found guilty of four counts of larceny and bucketing orders from customers of his stock brokerage firm, and spent a short time in prison. In 1949, Brickley and his son were arrested after starting a fight in a Manhattan restaurant. Before his case came to trial, Brickley died of a heart attack at the age of fifty-eight.

PAY TO PELÉ

THE NEW YORK COSMOS
North American Soccer League
1971–84

The New York Cosmos franchise was a grand and lavish attempt to make soccer as popular in the United States as it was in the rest of the world. Founded by brothers Ahmet and Nesuhi Ertegun of Atlantic Records and Warner Communications president Steve Ross, the Cosmos were easily the strongest team in the North American Soccer League, both financially and on the field. The team took its name from a shortened version of "cosmopolitans," an affectionate term New Yorkers often use to describe themselves and their city, but which eventually took on a more global meaning for the franchise.

In the team's first home game, the Cosmos beat the Washington Darts 1–0 in front of just 3,746 fans sprinkled throughout cavernous Yankee Stadium. When the owners recovered from their overoptimism, they moved to the much smaller stadium at Hofstra University on Long Island for the 1972 season, where they would win the first of their five NASL titles. In 1974, the Cosmos moved again, this time to Downing Stadium on Randall's Island, where they finished 4–14–2, their only last-place finish.

From 1971 to 1974, home attendance averaged about 4,500 per game, hardly numbers to get excited about. The owners, knowing that they had to do something to create more fan interest or their young league was going to die on the vine, revved up their two-year effort to sign the greatest soccer player in the world, the legendary Pelé of Brazil. Pelé could give both the Cosmos and the league the spark they needed. In a not-so-subtle attempt to lure Pelé, the Cosmos redesigned their uniforms before the 1975 season to resemble the classic white jerseys and shorts of Pelé's Santos team. In an even less subtle move, the Cosmos offered Pelé $7 million for three years, a staggering salary for any athlete at the time. The plan worked, Pelé joined the team in midseason, and attendance jumped from 4,000 per game to overflow crowds of more than 20,000 after he arrived.

Figuring they were on to something, NASL owners decided to sign more name players from around the world. In 1976, the Cosmos added Italy's Giorgio Chinaglia, one of the most prolific goal scorers in the world (he scored 242 goals in 254 games for the Cosmos), and attendance shot up again, necessitating a move back to

1977 photo of the New York Cosmos' "Big 3," Giorgio Chinaglia, Pelé, and Franz Beckenbauer, three of the top players in the world.

Yankee Stadium. In 1977, the Cosmos added Franz Beckenbauer, who had led Germany to the World Cup title in 1974 and his Bayern Munich team to three consecutive European Cup championships afterward, then moved into brand-new Giants Stadium in New Jersey. Attendance rose again, averaging 34,000. On October 1, 1977, Pelé played his final game with the Cosmos, an exhibition against his former Brazilian team, Santos. He actually played one half for each team in front of 76,000 adoring fans and a worldwide television audience.

Over the next three years, the Cosmos continued to add world-class players from around the globe; at one point, sixteen different nationalities were represented on the roster. Attendance was staggering, averaging nearly 50,000 per game, with some games selling out all 78,000 seats. The fascination with the New York team, from both fans and the media, became known as "the Cosmos Phenomenon," something the rest of the league benefited from as well. Invariably, whenever the Cosmos came to town, every team in the league would enjoy its highest turnstile count of the year.

Never before or since has one sports team assembled such a vast array of international talent. The Cosmos of the mid-'70s to the early 1980s were popular around the world, and when the NASL regular season ended, the Cosmos routinely went on tour throughout Europe, Asia, and South America, playing exhibition matches in front of tremendous crowds, making headlines wherever they went.

The league's owners, however, had made two serious miscalculations: They tried to get Americans to accept a sport they didn't understand, and their overreliance on international superstars backfired. The NASL ended up with no recognizable American names, and while the Cosmos attracted incredible crowds for a few years, none of the other teams in the league had achieved anywhere near New York's success. The novelty of it all began to wear off in 1981, with attendance at Cosmos games dipping below 35,000, and averaging 28,000 in 1982.

Overexpansion during the league's few fat years eventually proved catastrophic. By 1984, the NASL was down to just five teams. For the Cosmos, the deep pockets of Warner Communications were history after the company was forced to sell off its assets—the Cosmos among them—after a failed hostile takeover bid by Rupert Murdoch a few years earlier. The dictatorial Chinaglia had retired and Beckenbauer had returned to Europe. The Cosmos were drawing fewer than 13,000 per game, not enough to break even, given escalating player salaries.

The league called it quits in late 1984. The Cosmos jettisoned some of their high-salaried stars and played one season in the Major Indoor Soccer League, but withdrew after thirty-three games because of poor attendance. After turning down offers to join several other soccer leagues, the Cosmos hung up their boots for good in 1985.

In 2006, *Once in a Lifetime,* a theatrically released feature-length documentary about the Cosmos, revisited the magic of the Cosmos phenomenon. Although many former Cosmos players were interviewed in the film, Pelé was conspicuously absent. Perhaps spoiled by his previous treatment by the Cosmos, he demanded $150,000 for an interview, a fee the producers refused to pay.

HALL OF FAME FACTORY

THE NEW YORK GIANTS
National League
1883–1957

The New York Giants never attained the dynastic status or glamorous aura of the New York Yankees, and even in their glory days may never have lived up to their potential. But although they last took the field in 1957, the *New York* Giants have still put more players in the Baseball Hall of Fame—fifty-five—than any other franchise throughout its *entire* history, including the vaunted Yankees, except for the Boston/Milwaukee/Atlanta Braves, who have had fifty-nine more years to accomplish the same feat. More astonishing, the New York Giants are the only team that had a future Hall of Famer in its lineup *every single year of its existence.*

Of course, they also had on their roster such characters as Charlie Faust, the human rabbit's foot, and Clint Hartung, whose descent from magnificence to mediocrity was breathtaking. But that story can wait.

The New York Giants, created in 1883 by tobacco merchant John Day and sports promoter Jim Mutrie, were invited into the National League along with the Philadelphia Phillies when the other owners decided to dissolve two small market teams, Worcester and Troy. Day also owned the New York Metropolitans of the American Association, who started play the same year.

Day's two teams played side by side on a field called the Polo Grounds that actually was a former polo grounds. The two ballfields were divided by a large canvas fence, which separated more than the teams. The NL team, called the Gothams for the team's first five years, played to a more upscale crowd who paid fifty cents admission for an alcohol-free event. The AA's Mets, managed at first by Mutrie before he moved over to the Giants, charged only twenty-five cents and served all the booze fans could handle—and, in many cases, *couldn't* handle.

The first Gothams/Giants of the 1880s were loaded with future Hall of Famers: first baseman Roger Connor (.317 career hitter, and baseball's home-run king until Babe Ruth eclipsed him); outfielder Jim O'Rourke (.311 career hitter in twenty-three seasons); jack-of-all-trades Buck Ewing (.303 career hitter, and considered by many baseball historians to be the best all-around player of the nineteenth century); pitcher/infielder John Ward (2,104 hits and 164 wins with a 2.10 ERA); and 300-game winners Mickey Welch (307–210, 2.71 ERA, seven seasons of twenty-five-plus wins) and Tim Keefe (342–225, 2.62 ERA, six seasons of thirty-plus wins).

In spite of his great pitching record, Welch got himself into some trouble with parents when too many New York public school children were overheard parroting his personal drinking jingle: "Pure elixir of malt and hops, beats all the drugs and all the drops." But much was forgiven when he combined with Keefe for sixty-one wins in 1888 and fifty-five wins in 1889 to help the Giants to their first two pennants. The Giants won the World Series both years, six games to four, over the St. Louis Browns in 1888 and six games to three over the Brooklyn Bridegrooms in 1889. Welch also became the first pinch-hitter in major league history in 1889, striking out.

Then there was another eventual Hall of Fame pitcher nicknamed "The Hoosier Thunderbolt." Amos Rusie combined an unhittable fastball (335-plus strikeouts in 1890 and 1891) with a genuine wild streak (200-plus walks for five straight years from 1890 to 1894), to win 233 games in eight seasons with the Giants. Thanks to Rusie, and the fear he inspired in batters, in 1893 the league moved the pitching rubber from 51' to its current distance of 60'6". Rusie had another distinction: He was involved in the worst trade in baseball history. In December of 1900, he was traded to the Cincinnati Reds to reacquire another future Hall of

Famer, Christy Mathewson, whom the Giants had lost to the Reds two weeks earlier in the 1900 Rule 5 Draft. Rusie, who hadn't pitched in the majors in two years, pitched just three games for the Reds before retiring with a dead arm, going 0–1 with an 8.59 ERA. Mathewson, on the other hand, won 372 games for the Giants over sixteen seasons, including four years in which he won thirty or more. Mathewson, who never pitched on Sunday because of a promise he made to his mother, had a minuscule career ERA of 2.13.

The Giants won five pennants during the Mathewson era, which was about the same time future Hall of Fame manager John McGraw was brought on board. After winning the pennant in 1904, however, the Giants refused to play the Boston Pilgrims, repeat winners in the American League, in the World Series. Giants owner John Brush and McGraw both felt the AL was an inferior league unworthy of recognition. They were also still carrying a grudge against AL president Ban Johnson over the belligerent, player-raiding manner in which he had established his league in 1901.

The New York Giants are the only team that has had a future Hall of Famer in its lineup *every single year of its existence.*

As a consequence of deciding not to play the 1904 World Series, the Giants were subjected to a year of abuse, being called chicken by teams in both leagues. The relentless teasing helped steel their resolve to set matters straight in 1905. The Giants took over first place on April 24 and never relinquished it, compiling a 105–48 record. In the 1905 World Series against Philadelphia, the Giants whipped Connie Mack's A's with the best pitching performance in the history of the Fall Classic. Mathewson shut out the

A's in Game 1, 3–0. Chief Bender returned the favor in Game 2, 3–0, beating the Giants' Joe McGinnity, a future Hall of Famer who won thirty-one games in 1903 and thirty-five games in 1904. Matty came back in Game 3 and pitched another shutout, 9–0. McGinnity bounced back with a 1–0 win in Game 4, and Mathewson closed it out with his third shutout of the Series, 2–0, to quiet the Giants' detractors.

Over the next fifteen years, the Giants endured nothing but frustration. First, they lost the 1908 pennant on the last day of the season after being forced to replay a game with the Cubs because of a baserunning mistake by the Giants' Fred Merkle, who failed to touch second base on the apparent winning run. Because

1888 Opening Day at Polo Grounds with the Philadelphia Phillies.

thousands of fans had run onto the field and darkness was setting in, the umpires decided not to continue the game. National League president Harry Pulliam ordered the game replayed at the end of the season if it had a bearing on the race. It most certainly did. The Cubs and Giants ended up tied at 98–55 and the Cubs won the replayed game, 4–2, and the pennant. McGraw was relentless in his criticism of Pulliam, and when Pulliam committed suicide the next summer, many people thought McGraw's vicious attacks had played a part.

One of the most unusual Giants arrived out of nowhere in 1911. His name was Charlie Faust. He showed up at the Polo Grounds one day and told McGraw that a fortune-teller had predicted that if he pitched for the team, the Giants would win the pennant. Faust couldn't hit, field, or pitch, but McGraw kept him around as a good luck charm. When the Giants took off on a long winning streak, the players started calling him "Victory" Faust, and he became one of the guys. With the pennant sewed up in the last week of the season, McGraw let Faust pitch twice, an inning each time. He gave up two hits and one run, and on the batting side he was 0-for-2, but he did steal two bases. After the season, he went on the vaudeville circuit to declaim about how he helped the Giants win the pennant. During losing streaks in both 1912 and 1913, McGraw brought Faust back, though he didn't let him play either year, and the Giants immediately began to win again on both occasions. McGraw decided against using Faust's lucky charms in 1914 and the strange young man disappeared. Months later he turned up in an Oregon mental institution, and in 1915 he died in a Washington asylum.

During the 1910s, the Giants added future Hall of Famers Rube Marquard (winner of nineteen straight games in 1912), George "High Pockets" Kelly, Bill McKechnie, Edd Roush, Ross Youngs (who hit .322 in a ten-year career cut short when he died at the age of thirty from Bright's disease), Waite Hoyt, and Frankie Frisch. Though this group helped the Giants win four NL pennants, they lost the World Series all four times. In 1916, the

Giants had an unusually frustrating season. They put together two of the longest winning streaks in history, twenty-six games and seventeen games, yet ended up in fourth place.

It wasn't until the next class of Hall of Famers joined the team in the first half of the 1920s that the Giants experienced post-season success. With the added help of Dave Bancroft, Casey Stengel, Travis Jackson, Hack Wilson, Bill Terry (.341 career hitter and the last to hit over .400 in the NL, at .401 in 1930), Hughie Jennings, Billy Southworth, and Freddie Lindstrom, the Giants won four more pennants during the 1920s, winning the World Series in 1921 and 1922.

The Giants had a staggering nine future Hall of Famers on the team in 1923 and ten in 1924 when they suffered one of the most unusual World Series defeats in history. With the Series against the Washington Senators tied at three games each, the two teams met in Washington's Griffith Stadium for Game 7. The Giants were leading, 3–1, in the bottom of the eighth when Washington's Bucky Harris slapped a ground ball to Giants third baseman Freddie Lindstrom, at eighteen years old the youngest ever to appear in the World Series. The ball hit a rock and bounced over Lindstrom's head, scoring two runs to tie the game. In the bottom of the twelfth, catcher Hank Gowdy dropped a foul pop that would have been the final out of the inning when he tripped over his mask with the winning run on base. Earl McNeely then hit a grounder to Lindstrom that, incredibly, hit another rock and bounced over Lindstrom's head, sending in the winning run.

More future Hall of Famers arrived in the last half of the 1920s—including Mel Ott (who retired as the NL's all-time home run leader in 1947 with 511), Rogers Hornsby, Burleigh Grimes, Carl Hubbell (who won twenty-four straight games in 1936–37), and Ray Schalk—but the Giants didn't win their next pennant until 1933, Bill Terry's first full year as manager after taking over from McGraw in midseason the year before. It was sweet revenge, though, a five-game win over the Senators. After two more pennants in 1936 and 1937, and losses to the Yankees in both

World Series, the Giants went through a long dry spell even though they added future Hall of Famers Gabby Hartnett, Johnny Mize, Ernie Lombardi, and Joe Medwick. It looked like the drought might come to an end in 1947 with the arrival of one of baseball's most hyped phenoms, Clint Hartung.

Hartung was an outfielder/pitcher who was hailed as the next Babe Ruth and Christy Mathewson all rolled into one. Nicknamed the Hondo Hurricane, he spent six years in the Polo Grounds bouncing back and forth between the outfield and the pitching mound. By the time his magnificently mediocre career was over, he'd accumulated all of 14 homers to go along with a .238 batting average. As a pitcher, he was 29–29 with a 5.02 ERA.

The Giants didn't win another pennant until 1951, but it provided the most significant moment in team history. After trailing the Brooklyn Dodgers by as many as thirteen and a half games in mid-August, the Giants, led by the last future Hall of Famer to join their roster, Leo Durocher, used a sixteen-game winning streak to get back in the race. When the regular season ended in a tie, the two bitter rivals squared off in a best-of-three playoff series. After splitting the first two games, the teams were tied, 1–1, in the seventh inning of the third game. Some sloppy fielding and a couple of hits gave the Dodgers a 4–1 lead that they carried into the bottom of the ninth. The Giants scored four runs, capped by Bobby Thomson's three-run homer known as "the Shot Heard 'Round the World." The Giants then lost the World Series (the first for rookies Mickey Mantle and Willie Mays, and the last for Joe DiMaggio) to the Yankees in six games, but for many Giants fans it was anticlimactic after beating the reviled Dodgers in the playoffs.

The Giants' last hurrah was a four-game sweep of Cleveland in the 1954 World Series, remembered mostly for "The Catch," Willie Mays's spectacular over-the-shoulder grab of Vic Wertz's smash to center in Game 1 that killed an Indians rally and set the stage for Dusty Rhodes's tenth-inning three-run homer. The Giants fell to third in 1955, when attendance fell off more than

300,000. They tumbled to sixth in both 1956 and 1957, and attendance fell another 200,000 each year. Alarmed by the huge drop in attendance and the decaying Harlem neighborhood of his Polo Grounds (in 1956, a sniper had even shot and killed a fan from across the street) and impressed by the huge crowds the Milwaukee Braves were drawing after relocating from Boston, Giants owner Horace Stoneham decided to move his team to Bloomington, Minnesota, where a new stadium had just been constructed for the minor league Minneapolis Millers.

When Stoneham confided his plan to his friend Walter O'Malley, owner of the Brooklyn Dodgers, O'Malley told Stoneham of his secret plan to move the Dodgers to Los Angeles. He then suggested that Stoneham investigate moving his team to the San Francisco area so that the rivalry between their two teams could be maintained. Stoneham canceled his planned move to Minnesota, and joined O'Malley in sunny California.

While the Giants had played nearly seventy years in the same decaying stadium in New York, once in California the enthusiastic new Bay Area fans built the team *two* new stadiums in just forty years, Candlestick Park and Pacific Bell Park (now called AT&T Park). But some things didn't change: the San Francisco Giants have continued to pad the Hall of Fame, adding eleven more players, and they won three more pennants, but lost the World Series each time.

DUST TO DUST

THE NEW YORK METROPOLITANS
American Association
1883–87

The New York Metropolitans of the American Association were the most controversial ball club of the nineteenth century. Once a respected team at the center of the baseball universe, by the time the team met its end in 1887, it was baseball carrion being picked over by buzzards. And no one really cared.

Seven years earlier, the Mets had an important role in baseball history when they played the first professional game ever in New York City. All previous professional New York teams, including those in the National Association and the National League, had played in Brooklyn, a separate city until 1899. Owned by tobacco merchant John B. Day, and managed by Jim Mutrie, the Mets were formed in 1880 as an independent minor league club. After success on the field and at the box office, especially in their exhibition games against NL clubs, in 1881 Day's club joined the Eastern Championship Association and won the pennant, averaging 3,000 fans per game.

In 1882, the Mets were offered a place in the newly created AA, but, after meeting secretly with NL president William Hulbert, Mutrie announced that the Mets would remain an independent team.

Publicly, Mutrie and Day announced they turned down the offer to join the new major league because they didn't want to give up their lucrative exhibition games with all the NL teams—which totaled sixty games in 1882. Secretly, there was another reason. By 1883, the Mets were being courted by both the AA and NL. Day's plan was to form another team and put one in each league, a practice that was both legal and fairly common in the nineteenth century. When the NL contracted the Troy Trojans, Day purchased the contracts of seven Trojans, assigning four of them to his new NL team, the Gothams, and three to the Mets. He filled out his Gotham roster by purchasing the contracts of a dozen other minor and major league players.

The Mets and Gothams shared the Polo Grounds in 1883, sometimes playing their games side by side at the same time. While the NL's Gothams got to play on the main part of the field, the AA's Mets had to play on a makeshift field carved out of the remainder. Day hung a large canvas curtain between the fields, although fans sitting high enough in the stands could actually watch both games. When the AA objected to this second-class treatment, Day moved the Mets in 1884 to some newly leveled ground near the East River and 108th Street, calling it Metropolitan Park. The field stank—literally—because it had been built over a covered garbage dump. Pitcher Jack Lynch memorably said of the Mets' new field, "A player may go down for a grounder and come up with six months of malaria." After the AA again complained of the Mets' playing field, league games were moved back to the second-class section of the Polo Grounds in July.

> The field stank—literally—because it had been built over a covered garbage dump.

The less-than-ideal playing conditions didn't stop the Mets from winning the AA pennant. Led by Dave Orr's batting (.354) and the pitching of aces Lynch and Tim Keefe (who each won thirty-seven games), the Mets moved to the top of the standings in June and never relinquished it, finishing with a record of 75–32, six and a half games ahead of the Columbus Buckeyes. By August, when it was clear that the Mets would likely win the AA and the

Providence Grays the NL flag, Mutrie proposed a postseason series between the two teams, to be called the World's Championship Series. Providence accepted, the two leagues finalized the details of a best-of-five match, and the first officially sanctioned World's Series was born.

Day had high hopes for his team in the 1884 World's Series, knowing a victory would give both his Mets and the entire AA added prestige and credibility. Day's hopes, however, were dashed when the Grays swept them in three straight. Charles "Ol' Hoss" Radbourn was the winning pitcher in all three games, 6–0, 3–1, and 12–2.

Furious over the embarrassing defeats, Day took out his anger on the Mets. Before the 1885 season began, he transferred several of the Mets' star players, including Keefe, to his fifth-place NL team, the Gothams, which had changed its name to the Giants. Once the season got under way, Day scheduled Mets games for early in the morning when few people were able to watch them. He also promoted the Giants heavily while doing next to nothing for the Mets, particularly since he was allowed to charge fifty cents admission to Giants games while being limited to twenty-five cents by the AA for his Mets.

Utility player Elmer Foster hit .184 for the Mets in 1886, his only year with the team.

The transfer of the better Mets to the Giants and the continued second-class treatment of the Mets so angered AA officials that they sought to have the Mets kicked out of the league. Unable to get enough votes to expel the Mets, the AA settled on a $500 fine for Day and a suspension and lesser fine for Mutrie, who many in the AA felt was just a spy for the NL.

Mutrie's status as a traitor to his own team was enhanced when it was discovered that, besides his open contract as manager of the Mets, Mutrie had a secret contract with the Giants. He provided the AA's schedule well in advance of publication, giving Day and other NL owners sufficient time to alter their schedules in a favorable manner. Unfazed by his suspension, Mutrie simply moved his gear to the Giants' clubhouse and became *their* manager.

The depleted Mets fell to seventh place in 1885. After the season, the league forced Day to sell the team to someone who would treat them better, who turned out to be Erastus Wiman, owner of Staten Island Amusement Company, which promoted concerts, circuses, fountain displays, and Buffalo Bill's Wild West Show. Wiman also owned a ferry that transported passengers between Manhattan and Staten Island for the Baltimore and Ohio Railroad. His compensation from the railroad was pegged to the number of passengers his ferry carried, so he saw the ownership of a major league baseball team on Staten Island as a boost to business.

When Wiman announced that he was moving the Mets' games to the St. George Cricket Grounds on Staten Island beginning in 1886, the AA was highly suspicious that Wiman was actually fronting Day, who was moving the team so his Giants could have Manhattan all to themselves. The AA promptly expelled the Mets and distributed the players around the league. Wiman received a court injunction to stop the AA's actions. The judge sided with Wiman and the AA was forced to give back the team and retract its player moves.

While Wiman did see a small increase in his ferry business,

many former Mets fans refused to make the ferry ride and switched their allegiance to the Giants. After the Mets finished seventh in 1886 and 1887, Wiman, who lost $30,000 in the ordeal, sold his damaged goods to Charles Byrne, owner of the AA's Brooklyn Bridegrooms. Byrne kept five of the best players for himself, and gave all the others their unconditional release, and returned the rights to the franchise to the AA, which in turn granted a new franchise to Joseph Heim of Kansas City, previous owner of the NL's Kansas City Cowboys in 1886.

And the skeleton that had once been the New York Metropolitans eventually turned to dust.

MUTUALLY UNSATISFACTORY

THE NEW YORK MUTUALS
National League
1876

The New York Mutuals, who began play in 1857 as one of the important amateur clubs in early baseball history, were one of the first teams to prove that, while winning isn't everything, it can sure be a lucrative thing.

The team's original members came from the ranks of New York's Mutual Hook and Ladder Company Number One—hence their name—and by 1864 the team was charging ten cents admission to its games. This worked out so well that it caught the eye of Tammany Hall's notorious William "Boss" Tweed, who eventually took over the team. Once in control, Tweed raised the price of admission to twenty-five cents for most games, fifty cents for big games. Because a winning team drew more fans, Tweed secretly paid "ringers" to play for the Mutuals by giving them highly paid no-show city jobs, usually in the morgue. Besides raking in several thousand dollars from every Mutuals home game, Tweed made even more money by betting on the team. Gambling on baseball was both common and open in the 1860s, as was "hippodroming," a fancy term for game-fixing. This was accomplished in the usual fashion, by players of one team throwing the game to the other team (though sometimes players on both teams were in on the scheme).

After the massively corrupt Tweed was hauled away in handcuffs in 1871, control of the team shifted to William Cammeyer, owner of Brooklyn's Union Grounds, the ballpark the Mutuals called home. Initially, Cammeyer let the Mutuals play in his park rent-free while he kept the gate. Eventually, however, he agreed to the team's demand for a split of the receipts. In 1871, the Mutuals became charter members of baseball's first professional league, the National Association, which was controlled by the players, not the owners. The hippodroming at Unions Grounds continued.

Five years later, William Hulbert, the owner of the National Association's Chicago franchise, founded a new—and hopefully cleaner—league, the National League, with the owners, rather than the players, in control. After quietly securing seven solid franchises before the 1876 season, but none from New York, Hul-

Pitcher Bobby Mathews won 166 games in his major league career, including 21 with the Mutuals in 1876.

bert gave in and invited the Mutuals to join his new National League. He felt a problematic New York team was better than no New York team.

He was wrong. Union Grounds continued to be the center of baseball's gambling and game-fixing. Newspapers railed against the evils of gambling on league games by fans and players alike, and several Mutuals were openly accused in print of throwing games. Over the course of the season, the constant reports of game-fixing in the *New York Times, Clipper,* and *Spirit of the Times* eroded attendance, and the crowds eventually became so small that the team lost money for the first time in its twenty-year existence.

The team was awash in red ink by September, when owner Cammeyer decided to cancel the Mutuals' last western swing of the year. Such unilateral decisions were common in the National Association, but Hulbert's National League was supposed to be different. He insisted the Mutuals make their scheduled western trip, and, along with St. Louis Brown Stockings president Charles Fowle, offered Cammeyer a guarantee of $400 to make the trip to St. Louis and Chicago. Cammeyer refused. When he skipped the National League's winter meeting in December, the Mutuals were unanimously voted out of the league, upon which the team disbanded.

It had been a swift decline. Although the team had pulled off the first triple play in major league history, it came in a 28–3 loss to Hartford. Considered one of the league's best teams before the season started, the Mutuals finished with a disappointing 21–35 record, suggesting that the "hippodroming" had played an important role in the team's fortunes.

To make up for revenue lost when the Mutuals disbanded, Cammeyer recruited the Hartford Dark Blues to play at his Union Grounds in 1877. But that franchise folded after a single season, and New York, the nation's largest city, would not get another major league team until 1883.

COLOR MEN

THE NEW YORK RENS
Professional Basketball
1923–49

They once won eighty-eight straight games, the all-time record for a professional basketball team, twice as many as the second-best Celtics' forty-four-game streak. Their career winning percentage of .860 is second to none. They won the World Basketball Tournament in 1939. They had one season in which their record was 112–8. Their entire team was elected to the Basketball Hall of Fame in the same year. But they were repeatedly denied admission to professional leagues, let alone the hotels and restaurants of their choice.

The New York Renaissance was an all-black professional basketball team created in 1923 by Bob Douglas, the "Father of Black Basketball." Douglas owned and managed two amateur all-black teams in Harlem called the Spartan Braves and Spartan Hornets. From 1919 to 1923, the Braves and Hornets played against other New York City–area teams, both black and white. Douglas tired of the amateur game and decided to take it to the next level, but he didn't have a court he could call home.

Douglas solved his dilemma when he made a deal with William Roach, a real estate developer who owned Harlem's newly opened Renaissance Ballroom and Casino. Douglas combined the Braves and Hornets into one team and agreed to change the name of his team to the Renaissance in exchange for Roach's permission to play its home games in his facility's ballroom. It was a win-win situation that gave Roach's dance hall region-wide advertising. For the "Rens," it provided a central Harlem location with a spacious floor and large balcony seating. A typical game day at the Renaissance began with an afternoon dance followed by an early evening Rens game followed by a big band dance in the late evening. The Renaissance Ballroom, advertised as "New York's Prettiest Dance Hall," was at the epicenter of the Harlem Renaissance in the 1920s, and the Rens' basketball prowess was yet another form of black self-expression.

The Rens played a furious schedule, sometimes as many as 120 games a year, mostly on the road, sometimes playing one game during the day and a second one later that night in another city. Douglas's team attracted the best athletes of the era, including four players who also played in baseball's Negro Leagues: Frank "Strangler" Forbes; Clarence "Fats" Jenkins; James "Pappy" Ricks; and Leon Monde; and one, George Crowe, who later had a nine-year career in the National League.

The Rens took on all comers—black, white, amateur, college, or pro—including the best professional white teams of the era, such as the all-Jewish Philadelphia SPHAs (for South Philadelphia Hebrew Association) and the Indianapolis Kautskys. Hall of Fame coach John Wooden, who played with the Kautskys in the 1930s, said, "To this day, I have never seen a team play better *team* basketball. The way they handled and passed the ball was just amazing to me then, and I believe it would be today."

At least five of their games included race riots
between black and white fans.

The hottest games, though, were those against the Original Celtics (also called the New York Celtics and Brooklyn Celtics, but no connection to today's Boston Celtics), the best white professional team of the 1920s. With the Celtics led by future Hall of Famer Joe Lapchick, basketball's first dominant big man, the hotly contested Celtics-Rens games often drew 15,000 fans. And if the Rens happened to beat the Celtics, Douglas always made sure to give each player an extra twenty-five or fifty dollars, depending on his gate receipts.

Although at least five of their games included race riots between black and white fans, the players' numerous battles led to a genuine, mutual respect that extended off the court. Bucking the racial prejudices of the times, Lapchick and the other Original Celtics would often go to dinner with Rens players after their games. But the occasional social mixings were exceptions to the overwhelming institutional barriers for African-Americans. In 1925, the Rens applied for, but were denied, membership in the American Basketball League. In solidarity, the Celtics, who were offered a place in the ABL, refused. A year later they were forced to relent when ABL founder George Marshall's organized league-wide boycott against playing the Celtics took its toll.

The Rens simply persisted in their pursuit of acceptance. In 1937, they tried again, this time with the National Basketball League, but were again denied admission because they were black. And in 1946, Lapchick, now the coach of the New York Knicks, tried to get the Basketball Association of America (forerunner of the NBA) to admit the Rens, but they, too, denied them admission because of their race.

Finally, in 1948, the Rens were admitted to the NBL as the Dayton Rens, replacing the Detroit Vagabonds. Their record was an uncharacteristic 14–16, earning them last place in the Eastern Division. Ironically, once mainstream professional basketball accepted black players into the fold, it spelled the end for all-black teams like the Rens. In 1949, Abe Saperstein, owner of the Harlem Globetrotters, purchased the Rens and included them on his Trotters Tour, using them in preliminary games. It lasted only one year before Saperstein disbanded the Rens permanently.

WOMAN'S WORK

THE NEWARK EAGLES
Negro National League
1936–48

Playing in the Negro Leagues meant second-class transportation, third-rate hotels, and fourth-rate paychecks. Luckily for the Newark Eagles, they had a compassionate, yet tenacious owner, Effa Manley, whose unique methods and pioneering vision helped Eagles players gain an unparalleled measure of dignity, respect, and fairness in a world where separate was anything but equal. It was uncommon enough that Manley was a woman, but astonishing that she was white—and assumed to be half-black or a light-skinned black. Her dogged pursuit of fairness in a racially segregated world helped secure her election as the only woman in the Baseball Hall of Fame, but, ironically, it led to the demise of her team.

Abe Manley was a black Newark businessman who, some say, made his fortune through successful real estate investments. Others say his money came from racketeering and numbers running. Either way, he loved baseball. In 1932, he met Effa— twenty-four years his junior and an even bigger baseball fan than himself—at a New York Yankees game, and three years later they married. Together they formed the Brooklyn Eagles in 1935, a Negro League team that played its games at Ebbets Field. Because the Eagles took a big back seat to the Dodgers, the Manleys went looking for a new home. They purchased a second team, the Newark Dodgers, a black semi-pro team, and combined them into one team based out of Newark called the Eagles.

In Newark they shared the comfortable and spacious Ruppert Stadium with a white minor league team, the Newark Bears. In 1936, the Eagles joined the Negro National League, and from the beginning, Abe turned over the day-to-day operation of the team to his wife, who did it all: scheduled games; arranged transportation, lodging, and ballpark labor; purchased equipment; designed all the advertising and promotional campaigns; and policed the team's dress and behavior codes.

Effa was even good at schmoozing local VIPs. When the Eagles played their home opener in 1936, 185 VIPs were on hand, including New York mayor Fiorello La Guardia, who threw out the first pitch. She also arranged for a band to play the National Anthem before each game and music between innings. She hired Jocko Maxwell, considered to be the first black sportscaster, to be the Eagles' public address announcer.

Effa was comfortable in the black community. After her mother Bertha became pregnant out of wedlock by her white employer, Bertha married a black man, divorced him and married another black man. Since both black men already had children from previous marriages, Effa was raised in a household full of black siblings. Living in the black community exposed Effa to a side of racism and prejudice that white people didn't ordinarily see, and once she became a baseball owner she used her team to help educate whites about racism and to promote equality. As an example of what she and blacks everywhere were up against, in 1939 the Eagles hosted a promotion called "Anti-Lynching Day" at Ruppert Stadium. As treasurer of the local chapter of the NAACP, she once organized a boycott of Harlem businesses that refused to hire blacks.

Sometimes, however, Effa got a little too close to her players. Her occasional dalliances with Eagles players were well known, even to her husband. At the ballpark, she would sometimes sit in the dugout, giving the bunt sign (or taking it off) to Eagles batters by hiking her skirt up and crossing or uncrossing her legs. One of Effa's well-known paramours was Terris McDuffie, a pitcher Effa liked to show off to her social club. McDuffie, who wore fancy clothes, diamond rings, and gold watches, was a "pretty boy" who fancied himself a great lover. But during a lover's quarrel at Pennsylvania Station, he knocked Effa down and kicked her. When word of what happened reached her husband, Abe traded McDuffie to the New York Black Yankees for two broken bats and a pair of old sliding pants.

Most of the time, though, the Manleys were known for taking care of their players. They were the godparents to Larry Doby's first child. They loaned Monte Irvin the money for a down payment on his first house. They financed former player Lennie Pearson's first tavern after he retired. Concerned about their players' well-being during the off-season, the Manleys sponsored a team in the Puerto Rican winter leagues to give them some income.

Effa's Eagles, more than any other team—black or white—made an effort to connect to the community. Effa made sure that the Eagles offered ballpark fare second to none, but she also encouraged fans to bring their own food, and many did, especially on Sundays, which became popular social events in Ruppert Stadium. Effa didn't start the Sunday games until two o'clock, which gave fans plenty of time to get to the ballpark after church. Since bleacher seats were just forty cents, whole families could afford to come. Thousands of black Newark residents came dressed to the nines, men in suits and ties, women in flowery hats and dresses, many carrying large picnic baskets.

Eagles fans had a reputation for being somewhat rabid—fans would jump and yell like it was New Year's every time an Eagle hit a home run—so

Effa Manley at work.

Effa hired undercover security personnel to roam the stands looking for excessive drinking, gambling, and other problems. She also convinced the city of Newark to post a judge inside the ballpark so that miscreants could be dealt with quickly!

At the center of all the hoopla was a fine baseball team. Over the years players like Larry Doby (the first black to play in the American League), Leon Day, Monte Irvin, Ray Dandridge, and Willie Wells (all Hall of Famers), and Don Newcombe (1956 winner of both the NL MVP Award and MLB Cy Young Award) all wore Eagle uniforms. The Eagles were either second or third every year from their inception in 1936 to 1945. But in 1946, the Eagles put it all together and won their only Negro National League pennant, winning both halves of the split season with a combined winning percentage of .746, ending a run of nine consecutive pennants by the Homestead Grays.

She would sometimes sit in the dugout,
giving batters signs by hiking her skirt up
and crossing or uncrossing her legs.

The championship team was led by returning war veterans Doby (second base) and Irvin (shortstop), who formed a potent double-play combination, but Hall of Fame manager Biz Mackey's lineup also included Lennie Pearson at first and outfielders Johnny Davis and Bob Harvey, and pitchers Leon Day (who pitched a no-hitter on Opening Day), Max Manning, and Rufus Lewis. To make sure they were all well rested when they traveled, Effa purchased a $15,000 air-conditioned Clipper Bus, extravagant for the Negro Leagues.

When the Eagles met Satchel Paige's Kansas City Monarchs, champions of the Negro American League, in the 1946 Colored World Series, it was a thrilling seven-game affair. The Monarchs won Game 1 at New York's Polo Grounds, 2–1, beating Day. The Eagles evened it up in Game 2 in their home stadium, 7–4, on a home run by Doby. Games 3 and 4 moved to Kansas City's Blues Stadium. The Monarchs routed Newark in the third game, 15–5. Newark returned the beating in Game 4 by a score of 8–1, routing Paige for a second time. The Monarchs won Game 5 in Chicago's Comiskey Park, handing Manning only his second loss of the season, 5–1. With Kansas City up three games to two, the World Series shifted to Ruppert Stadium. Leon Day was knocked around for five runs in the first inning, but the Eagles came back to win, 9–7, setting up the deciding seventh game. Trailing 2–1 in the bottom of the eighth, the Eagles scored two runs on a Johnny Davis double and won, 3–2, copping the only pennant in their thirteen-year history.

The Eagles' pennant came at a price: Major League Baseball was ready to integrate (Jackie Robinson was already playing in Montreal) and the 1946 Colored World Series attracted an inordinate number of major league scouts. It wasn't long before Newcombe, Irvin, and Doby were lost to the major leagues. Having lost Newcombe to the Dodgers without compensation, an angry Effa conducted a letter-writing campaign to Brooklyn's Branch Rickey and other major league officials, demanding that they respect the rights and contracts of and between Negro League owners and players. Her efforts eventually led to an agreement in which Negro League team owners were compensated when they lost players, and all contracts were mutually respected.

But Effa's victory in this issue only helped speed up the disintegration of the Negro Leagues as the player exodus, at first a trickle, turned to a flood. The loss of so many star players to the major leagues caused attendance in Newark to plummet from 120,000 in 1946 (twenty-eight games) to just 57,000 in 1948. No longer able to turn a profit, Effa sold the team to Dr. W. H. Young, a black dentist from Memphis. When the Negro National League folded following the 1948 season, Young moved the team to Houston as a barnstorming club, but in mid-1949, after heavy losses, he folded the team.

As for Effa, she passed away in 1981, but not before publishing *Negro Baseball . . . Before Integration,* a book listing seventy-three players she felt belonged in the Hall of Fame. She also wrote many letters to *The Sporting News,* seeking recognition of the Negro Leagues and their players. Largely through her efforts, the Hall of Fame enshrined eleven Negro League players in 1973, and many more since. The Hall added a Negro League exhibit to its library in 1985, and finally, in 2006, Effa Manley herself was enshrined in Cooperstown.

SLICK

THE NEWARK PEPPERS
Federal League
1915

B y 1900, the National League had learned over the previous thirty-five years in battles with the American Association, the Players' League, and the Union Association, how financially devastating it could be when upstart major leagues attempted to horn in on their business. In 1901, when the American League became the latest major league to jump on the bandwagon, the National League figured it was wiser to negotiate away its differences with the new league rather than try to bury it in a costly war. The two leagues would not be challenged again until the Federal League of 1914–15 became the last serious attempt by any new major league to force its way onto the major league scene.

Once again, conciliation ruled and the Federal League began play in eight cities, from Buffalo to Kansas City. When an Oklahoma oil tycoon with a bright future named Harry F. Sinclair learned that a new major league was being formed, he saw a chance to make some money and publicly expressed an interest. Federal League president James Gilmore heard of Sinclair's interest but, knowing nothing about him, asked Philip Ball, owner of the Federal League's St. Louis Terriers, for an opinion. Ball wired Gilmore: "Rockefeller has half the money in the world, Sinclair the other half."

That was good enough for Gilmore, who, anxious to take advantage of Sinclair's deep pockets, eventually arranged for the oil tycoon to purchase the league's 1914 champions, the Indianapolis Hoosiers, who had won the FL flag with a record of 88–65, but didn't draw well at the gate. Gilmore convinced Sinclair of the need for an FL team in the New York City metro area to compete with the NL's New York Giants and Brooklyn Robins, as well as the AL's New York Yankees. Another New York–area team would also provide a natural league rival for the FL's Brooklyn Tip-Tops. Gilmore then told Sinclair that while a New York team was every FL executive's wish, it would need a proper stadium in which to play. Sinclair easily solved this problem by quickly going out and purchasing property in Harrison, New Jersey, on the outskirts of Newark and about seven miles on the New Jersey side of the Hudson River. He funded the construction of a brand-new 20,000-seat stadium that would soon be the envy of every major league owner.

Before the 1915 season, the other FL owners quickly approved the transfer of the Indianapolis franchise to Newark, where Sinclair nicknamed the team "the Peppers" in honor of the spirit and spice Sinclair saw his team injecting into the New York City baseball scene. (With the move, the Indianapolis Hoosiers gained the distinction of being the only major league franchise ever to play just one season and win the league.) Sinclair, who acted deci-

1915 Newark
Peppers program.

sively and traveled first-class, wasted no time in trying to secure the top manager in the game, John McGraw of the Giants, a man he knew could give instant credibility to both the Peppers and the Federal League. McGraw, however, not only turned down Sinclair's $100,000 offer, an astronomical amount in 1915, but became a bitter opponent of the Federal League's encroachment on his Giants' territory. Unable to sign McGraw, Sinclair retained Bill Phillips, the same manager who had led the Hoosiers the year before. Phillips was replaced in midseason by the team's third baseman (and rookie pilot) Bill McKechnie, who would eventually be elected to the Hall of Fame as a manager.

After going 3–2 in a season-opening road trip, the Peppers christened their new home park on April 16 with a game against the Baltimore Terrapins. More than 26,000 fans overflowed Harrison Field. Thousands more were turned away. Although the Peppers lost, 6–2, it was an encouraging start. After five weeks, Newark was a very respectable 19–12, and just a half game out of first—and this even though the Peppers' big star from the year before, outfielder Benny Kauff, who had led the FL in nine offensive categories, had jumped to the Brooklyn Tip-Tops for 1915.

However, while the Peppers were fully prepared to do battle with the AL and NL franchises in the New York City area, Sinclair had underestimated his minor league rivals, the International League's Newark Indians, owned by Charlie Ebbets of Brooklyn. The Indians, an established local favorite with lower admission prices, cut into the Peppers' business. But the Indians suffered more, and on July 2 they moved to Harrisburg, Pennsylvania. In an effort to attract the Indians' former fans, Sinclair tried a variety of measures, including bicycle races to supplement his baseball games, to no avail. He threatened to move the team if local officials didn't extend the trolley line across the Passaic River to Harrison Field. In August, Sinclair experimented with reduced ticket prices, including ten cents for the bleachers and twenty-five cents for pavilion seats. Nearly 20,000 fans showed up, causing most other FL teams to follow suit.

Newark would finish the 1915 season in fifth place with a record of 80–72, led by outfielders Vin Campbell (.310) and Edd Roush (.298), the latter of whom would go on to a Hall of Fame career with the Cincinnati Reds. On the pitching side, the Peppers were first in the FL in ERA at 2.60, led by Big Ed Reulbach, the former longtime Cub, who went 21–10 with a 2.33 ERA. Nonetheless, as the summer wore on, baseball officials everywhere came to the conclusion that three major leagues was one too many. When peace negotiations between the leagues were finally undertaken, Harry Sinclair, with his immense wealth, played a major role. A deal to fold the newcomer, the Federal League, was hammered out, in which Sinclair, proving the rich get richer, was given a hefty payout ($100,000), the only FL owner to turn a profit from the two-year league.

He was also given control over Newark's FL player contracts, which he then sold to AL and NL teams. Once the Federal League had folded, Sinclair toyed with the idea of buying the New York Giants, if for no other reason than to get back at John McGraw for his vocal opposition to the Peppers' arrival in the first place.

McGraw not only turned down Sinclair's $100,000 offer—an astronomical amount in 1915—but became a bitter opponent of the Federal League's encroachment on his Giants' territory.

Eventually, though, Sinclair decided to return to the oil business in Texas and Oklahoma, a business for which time would prove he had a better knack. Until, that is, he was arrested in 1922 for bribing Secretary of the Interior Albert B. Fall and others in order to secure government oil leases in an affair that became known as the Teapot Dome Scandal. Although acquitted of conspiracy, he was found guilty of contempt of Congress and sentenced to three months in jail.

Peppers first baseman Rupert Mills was more of a stickler for details. He already had signed his Newark contract for 1916 to the tune of $3,000 before the league (and team) folded, and refused to take a buyout (he was offered $600), as had all other FL players still under contract. No, darn it, he signed for $3,000 and that's exactly what he was going to get. So, Peppers president Patrick Powers demanded that Mills work out for seven hours every day to keep in playing shape. Mills showed up all by himself at Harrison Field for sixty-five straight days, working out as required, the only player still active in the FL in 1916. In July, Mills finally ended the silliness by signing a contract with Harrisburg of the New York State League.

HOT DOGS AND REAL DOGS

THE OORANG INDIANS
National Football League
1922–23

LaRue, Ohio, is the smallest city ever to host a major American sports team. It's not even close. LaRue was so small—population 700—that it didn't even have a football field.

But that didn't stop it from becoming the home of the National Football League's Oorang Indians for two years.

The Oorang Indians were the brainchild of Walter Lingo, Airedale dog breeder and owner of Lingo's Oorang Kennels in LaRue. His kennel had an international reputation, and he often invited famous friends and other guests—Ty Cobb and Tris Speaker; boxer Jack Dempsey; actor Gary Cooper; and Olympic sprinter Charles Paddock—to join him in hunting excursions with his Airedales. One frequent hunting guest who became a close friend was Jim Thorpe, dubbed "the greatest athlete in the world" by Sweden's King Gustav V after Thorpe won gold medals in both the decathlon and pentathlon in the 1912 Olympics.

In 1922, during one of their many possum-hunting expeditions, Lingo and Thorpe hatched an idea to promote Lingo's Oorang Kennels. They would create a football team comprised entirely of American Indians that would travel around the country, playing football and promoting the Airedale breed and Lingo's Kennels. Thorpe, who served as the NFL's first president in 1920–21, suggested that Lingo try to secure an NFL team for his purpose.

Lingo did buy the rights to an NFL team to be based out of LaRue, paying the league's one-hundred-dollar franchise fee, which was 5 percent of his advertising budget and fifty dollars less than he charged for one of his Airedales. Once Lingo had the franchise, he hired Thorpe as the team's coach and GM, and set him the task of putting together their all-Indian team.

Thorpe recruited Indians from a variety of tribes, including the Cherokee, Chippewa, Mission, Mohawk, Mohican, Pomo, Sac and Fox (Thorpe's tribe), Winnebago, and Wyandot. Lingo hired the Indians as full-time employees of Oorang Kennels, and they tended to kennel duties when not playing football. On October 1, 1922, Joe Little Twig, Eagle Feather, Baptiste Thunder, Ted Buffalo, Gray Horse, Xavier Downwind, Arrowhead, Joe Guyon (who would be elected along with Thorpe to the Hall of Fame), and the other Indians played their inaugural NFL game in Dayton against the Triangles. Oorang lost, 36–0, but it didn't matter much to them. Lingo had made it clear to all the Indian players that the main purpose behind their games was to promote his kennel business.

At halftime, rather than go into the locker room and discuss second-half strategy, the Indians put on a halftime show orchestrated by Lingo, the first halftime show in football history not featuring a marching band. The spectacle included Indian dances, tomahawk and knife-throwing demonstrations, rifle shooting, and target-shooting exhibitions in which the Airedales retrieved the targets. They also had a skit in which the Airedales would tree a real bear and then one of the Indians, Long-Time-Sleep, would wrestle the bear. Thorpe would cap the halftime activities by kicking a bunch of drop-kick field goals from the 50-yard line. Before, during, and after the game, Lingo and his players would mingle with the fans, showing off the abilities of the Airedales and making sales when they could.

The Indians finished with a 3–6 record in 1922, a record that would be disappointing for most teams, but not Oorang. They were playing to big crowds everywhere they went, and their halftime show, which resembled Buffalo Bill's Wild West Show, was more popular than the game. And no one was happier than Lingo, an owner who always insisted on the best for his players. The Indians traveled first-class all the way, eating at the finest restaurants and staying in the best hotels, and were tended to by the same trainers and dietitians Lingo sent along to take care of the dogs.

For the two seasons the Oorang Indians were in the NFL, the players made the best money of their lives. They worked hard, played hard, and partied hard. One time they descended upon a Chicago bar just before closing time and when the bartender in-

Oorang's Jim Thorpe, one of the greatest athletes of all time.

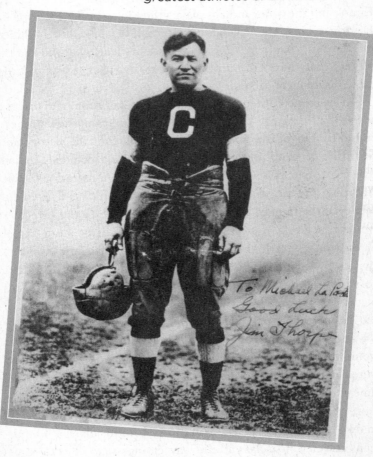

formed them he was closing, they simply hog-tied him and put him in a phone booth. After turning the phone booth upside down and chaining it shut, they proceeded to serve themselves until the next morning.

By 1923, the Oorang Indians' act had grown stale. Fans knew they wouldn't see a good football game (Oorang finished 1–9 and was shut out six times in its first eight games) and the halftime activities never changed, so attendance fell off dramatically. With his team's novelty gone and his revenues fading, Lingo folded the team after the season.

The Indians put on the first halftime show in football history not featuring a marching band.

Over the next five years, Thorpe played for five different NFL teams in as many years and Lingo's kennel business thrived. But when the stock market crashed in 1929, so did the kennels. Lingo eventually established a new business, Oorang Dog Biscuits, while his wife revived the kennels, which remained in operation until Walter Lingo's death in 1969.

BIPOLAR

THE PHILADELPHIA ATHLETICS
American League
1901–54

More than any other team in baseball history, the Philadelphia Athletics' fortunes were directly tied to owner Connie Mack's financial roller coaster. The dizzying fifty-four-year ride inevitably required that Mack periodically sell off his star players just to survive.

From the time of the American League's inception in 1901 until the end of the Babe Ruth era in New York (1934), no team—including the Yankees—won more AL pennants than Philadelphia's nine. But Mack's A's also finished in the cellar seven times during that same period, and eighteen times during the team's fifty-four-year existence. The reason the A's were so good in the good years was Mack's uncanny ability to assess the potential of

1913 World Champion Philadelphia A's.

COLLINS   DAN MURPHY   SCHANG   COOMBS   CONNIE MACK   ED. MURPHY   McINNES   BAKER

LAPP   BENDER   ORR   OLDRING   PLANK   BARRY   BUSH   STRUNK

PHILADELPHIA AMERICAN LEAGUE CHAMPIONS 1913

future star players and get them under contract before anyone else did. And the reason the A's were so bad for so many years was because Mack later was forced to sell off every one of those same stars in order to pay the club's bills.

It could be argued that had the Philadelphia A's attracted the same number of paying fans that the Yankees did, the A's would have been baseball's dynasty team instead, because the talent that came and went on the A's roster was clearly superior to that of the Yankees, particularly when it came to pitching.

When Ban Johnson renamed his minor Western League the American League in 1900 and declared it a major league in 1901, he intended the AL to be a direct competitor of the National League. Johnson wanted an AL club to compete in as many NL cities as possible, so he created the Philadelphia Athletics and re-cruited Connie Mack of the Western League's Milwaukee franchise to run the operation. He gave Mack $50,000 in seed money and a 25 percent stake in the ownership. Ben Shibe, a partner of sporting goods manufacturer A. J. Reach, owned 50 percent, while two newspapermen, Frank Hough (sports editor of the *Philadelphia Inquirer*) and Sam Jones (of Philadelphia's AP bureau) owned the rest.

Mack used $35,000 of the seed money to construct Columbia Park, his new 12,000-seat single-deck ballpark. He also used some of it to lure three players away from their contracts with the crosstown Phillies: star second baseman Napoleon Lajoie and pitchers Chick Fraser and Bill Bernhard. The move paid immedi-ate dividends: The Lajoie-led A's drew over 10,000 for their home opener while the Lajoie-less Phillies drew only 779 for theirs. And the financial virtues of a winning team were evident: The A's fin-ished a respectable fourth in 1901, drawing 206,000 fans, but when they won the AL pennant in 1902, their attendance more than doubled to 420,000.

But 1902 was not without its difficulties. Phillies owner John Rogers was incensed about losing the three ballplayers, especially Lajoie, who in 1901 won the AL's Triple Crown with a .426 average, 14 homers, and 125 RBIs. He also led the league in doubles (48), hits (232), and runs scored (145). And Fraser won twenty-two games while Bernhard chipped in with seventeen. Rogers took the matter to court, and although he wasn't able to force the three to return to the Phillies, he did win an injunction that prevented any of them from playing in the state of Pennsylvania for anyone but the Phillies.

However, by the time the court's ruling came down, Mack had lured away two more Phillies in 1902—Elmer Flick and Bill Duggleby. Fearful of retaliation, though, Duggleby and Fraser jumped back to the Phillies. Then Mack lost Lajoie, Flick (both eventual Hall of Famers), and Bernhard to Cleveland in a deal brokered by Ban Johnson. In another deal not well known, the A's also lost rookie pitcher Christy Mathewson, who had jumped from the New York Giants to the A's over the winter, but, after second thoughts, jumped back to the Giants.

By 1910, the A's were no longer a good team.
They were a great team.

To restock his pitching staff, Mack promoted Rube Waddell from the minors to join Eddie Plank, and the two future Hall of Famers helped the A's to their first pennant in 1902. In 1903, Mack brought up Chief Bender, a graduate of Pennsylvania's Carlisle Indian School. Although all three hurlers were twenty-game winners in 1903, and attendance improved again, the A's fell to second, but two years later, behind the overpowering pitching staff led by Waddell (27–10) and Plank (24–12), the team won its second pennant and first World Series berth (the modern World Series didn't start until 1903). In the Series, the A's were outpitched by Christy Mathewson, who tossed three shutouts as the Giants won in five games. The A's topped 554,000 at the gate.

Before the A's won their next pennant in 1910, three other rookie phenoms joined the team: Eddie Collins in 1906, Frank "Home Run" Baker in 1908, and "Shoeless" Joe Jackson in 1909. Mack also unveiled a new stadium, Shibe Park, the first completely steel and concrete stadium. Buoyed by the new ballpark and Jackson's late-season arrival (though he didn't stay long), attendance rose to a record 675,000 in 1909.

By 1910, the A's were no longer a good team—they were a great team. The addition of pitcher Jack Coombs (31–9) helped the A's to their first 100-win season (102–48), fourteen and a half games ahead of the Yankees. In the World Series, they knocked off the Cubs in five games. By 1913, the A's had the makings of a dynasty, winning their third pennant in four years, and others were taking note. Yankee owner Frank Farrell offered Mack the managerial reins of his team. Mack, however, accepted Shibe's counteroffer of an additional 25 percent stake in the A's.

But something unexpected happened in 1914, and it wasn't the team's fourth pennant in five years. Even though the A's romped to the AL title by an eight-and-a-half-game margin over the Red Sox, the attendance *declined* by 225,000 from 1913. The only possible explanation was that the city had become complacent about the team's success. As if on cue, the A's lost the World Series in four straight to the Miracle Braves. Moreover, the new Federal League had opened for business, forcing Mack and other owners to pay much higher salaries just to keep players from defecting.

Mack's financial situation was serious. In order to alleviate the red ink, Mack sold Collins to the White Sox for $50,000. He let Plank and Bender go on waivers. He couldn't meet Baker's higher salary demand, so Baker sat out a year before Mack eventually sold him to the Yankees for $37,500. Mack also had to turn down the chance to purchase Babe Ruth from the International League's Orioles because he didn't have the cash.

By May of 1915, as the A's flirted with the unaccustomed American League cellar, Mack continued his fire sale, sending future Hall of Famer Herb Pennock to the Red Sox for the waiver price; shortstop Jack Barry went to the Red Sox for $8,000; Eddie Murphy to the White Sox for $13,000; and Bob Shawkey to the Yankees for $18,000. The gutting was complete, and the A's completed their descent into the cellar, finishing fifty-eight and a half games behind Boston with attendance of just 146,000. To fill out his team, Mack brought in collegians, semi-pros, amateurs, and even high schoolers.

By the mid-1920s, the A's rose to prominence again when many of Mack's young players turned into the stars he expected they'd be. With the help of a large bank loan, Mack signed Al Simmons, Mickey Cochrane, Jimmie Foxx, Lefty Grove, Tris Speaker, Zach Wheat, and even Ty Cobb (who got his 4,000th career hit with the A's). From 1929 to 1931, the A's romped to three more AL pennants and two World Series titles, winning more than 100 games every year. Strangely, there was a recurrence of fan malaise. Philadelphia's attendance went from 839,000 in 1929, to 722,000 in 1930, to 627,000 in 1931. When the A's finished second in 1932 with a 94–60 record, the attendance plummeted to 405,000.

Mack had once again filled his team with high-priced superstars (the highest payroll in baseball up to that time), and the fans had once again abandoned them at the height of their glory. When Mack's bank called in his $400,000 loan, Mack was forced to undertake another major fire sale. He sold Simmons and two others to the White Sox for $150,000 to retire part of the debt. The next season he sold Cochrane to Detroit for $100,000; Grove and two others to the Red Sox for $150,000; and George Earnshaw to the White Sox for $20,000. And finally, when Jimmie Foxx balked at having his salary cut by $6,000 after leading the AL in home runs in three of the four previous seasons, Mack sold him and two others to Boston for $225,000.

From 1933 to 1954, the A's got out of the second division only twice, and that was just to fourth place. Attendance was as bad as the team's performance, forcing Mack to penny-pinch any way he could. In 1935, he lost a lawsuit to have people barred from watching from their apartment rooftops across the street from Shibe Park, so he had a twenty-two-foot high corrugated iron fence installed on the top of his outfield wall. In 1946, Mack refused to compensate returning veterans who were unable to make the roster, as he was required to do under the Veterans Act.

By 1954, with the A's once again in the cellar, Mack was deeply in debt again. This time, Mack, who had managed the team for fifty years and was at least partial owner for fifty-four, didn't have a collection of star players he could sell to bail himself out. Instead, he got off the roller coaster altogether, selling the team to vending-machine magnate Arnold Johnson, who moved the franchise to Kansas City.

NOT AS POPULAR AS THE SONG

THE PHILADELPHIA FREEDOMS
World Team Tennis
1974

T he early 1970s was a period of intense activity in the area of equal rights for women, from the successful passage of Title IX to the proposed Equal Rights Amendment's ultimately unsuccessful campaign to be ratified by three-quarters of the states. However, few events encapsulated the struggle like "The Battle of the Sexes" in 1973, one of the most publicized events in sports history, in which twenty-nine-year-old Billie Jean King thrashed Bobby Riggs, a former number one male player in the world, on national television.

Riggs was a publicity hound of the first order and enjoyed spouting off about how women tennis players couldn't compete against men, even "fifty-five-year-old has-beens" like himself. Riggs challenged King, but she turned him down. Riggs then finagled thirty-year-old Margaret Court, the number one woman player in the world, into a Mother's Day match in 1973. After Riggs handled her easily, 6–2, 6–1, King finally accepted Riggs's challenge and took revenge on behalf of women everywhere by beating him in straight sets, 6–4, 6–3, 6–3. That single exhibition match, with its extensive media coverage, probably promoted the equality of the sexes more than all the pro-ERA politicians running around the country at the time.

It also helped to jump-start the groundbreaking co-ed professional tennis league, World Team Tennis, that was founded the same year and began play in May 1974 with sixteen teams. The league used a multicolored court and played a forty-four-match season. Teams of six players—three men and three women—played five one-set, no-ad matches: men's and women's singles, men's and women's doubles, and mixed doubles, with equal weight given to the scoring of all matches. One point was

Advertising poster for Billie Jean King's "Battle of the Sexes" match against Bobby Riggs.

awarded for each game won within the matches, with most total points accumulated in all the matches deciding the winner.

Major tennis stars who have played in the WTT over the years include Rod Laver, Björn Borg, Chris Evert, Jimmy Connors, and John McEnroe. Billie Jean King, a thirty-nine-time Grand Slam title winner, starred for the Philadelphia Freedoms. It was at a promotional party for the WTT in 1974 that she met rock star Elton John, who admitted to King that he had idolized her for many years, largely because of her public stand on gay rights. The two quickly became friends, and when King had a tracksuit custom made for John as a gift, John reciprocated by promising to write a song for her. Months went by and King forgot about John's promise, only to be surprised when he appeared, portable stereo in hand, in her dressing room during a break in a match in Denver. John played her his newly recorded song, "Philadelphia Freedom." She loved it and so did just about everyone else. The song rose to number one on the charts and quickly became the theme song for King's WTT team.

The Freedoms finished the 1974 season with the best record in the league, but did not prove as popular as the song. Despite on-court success (although the Denver Racquets upset them in the league championship match, 55–45) and a number one hit song, the Freedoms lasted just one year in Philadelphia before moving to Boston and merging with the Lobsters. Philadelphia was not alone in its financial troubles; six WTT teams folded outright after the 1974 season while two other franchises relocated to new cities. The league's owners had seriously miscalculated their expected revenue, both from television and attendance, a fatal error given the high salaries they were paying to King and others.

Elton John admitted to King that he had idolized her for many years, largely because of her public stand on gay rights.

The league suffered numerous franchise shifts and failures over the next few years before suspending operations following the 1978 season. After a two-year hiatus, the league, renamed Team Tennis, began play again in 1981 and remains in operation to this day, though in 1992 it again took the original name of World Team Tennis. After retiring as a player, Billie Jean King became commissioner of the WTT in 1984, a position she held until 2001, the same year that a new Philadelphia franchise, again called the Freedoms, joined the league.

BROTHERLY INEPTITUDE

THE PHILADELPHIA QUAKERS
National Hockey League
1930–31

When the National Hockey League's Pittsburgh Pirates relocated to Philadelphia following the 1929–30 season, they were seeking redemption on a number of fronts. In Pittsburgh, they left behind the league's poorest attendance, the worst record in league history (5–36–3), and the most unsuitable arena in the NHL, a forty-year-old converted trolley barn. The team had New York City bootlegger Bill Dwyer for an owner, ex-boxer Benny Leonard (who knew nothing about hockey) as its GM and front man, and the lamest bunch of players that ever laced up skates. But a change in cities and names was going to transform all that.

Dwyer, who also owned the NHL's New York Americans under a different front man (sports promoter Thomas Duggan), liked the idea of moving the team to Philadelphia, not only because of its larger fan base, but also because it would be closer to his New York bootlegging operation. The choice of "Quakers" as the team's new nickname was strategic. The Quaker religion had a heavy following in and around the Philadelphia area. Besides, Dwyer knew Philadelphia sports fans tended to be on the rabid side, which fit right in with an old Quaker joke that the Holy Trinity consists of the fatherhood of God, the brotherhood of man, and the neighborhood of Philadelphia.

The move to Philadelphia was intended to be a temporary one, only as long as it took Dwyer to build an adequate arena back in Pittsburgh to replace the pitiful Duquesne Gardens the team had called home its first five years in the league. But the Great Depression had hit Dwyer's illegal booze-running business just as hard as any legitimate business, and the money to build a new arena never materialized. There was also no money with which to sign a few good players to improve the team's fortunes on the ice.

Dwyer tried to make the best of a bad situation by constantly pushing his front man Leonard, a very popular and successful former lightweight boxer, in front of the local reporters for interviews during the preseason. Unfortunately, Leonard's hockey expertise and command of the English language were both, to put it mildly, limited. "I will spare no expense," said Leonard, "to give the fans what they want. We have other deals in mind which will be consumed if the men we have now fail to deliver. I want to produce a winning club, and if I don't, it won't be my fault." He promised the press and the fans that the Quakers would be fighters, and he was going to train them himself.

The Quakers did live up to their reputation as fighters, racking up penalty minutes during the season. Victories were another matter. In the team's first game at Philadelphia Arena, a facility not much better than the one they had left in Pittsburgh, 5,000 fans showed up to watch the visiting New York Rangers shut out the Quakers, 3–0. One *New York Herald Tribune* writer, Stanley Woodward, wrote discreetly, "The Philadelphia crowd of 4,000 to 5,000 began to make 'caustic remarks.'" Most fans left before the game was over. Fewer than 2,000 showed up for the next one.

The Quakers wouldn't record a victory until their sixth game of the season, a 2–1 shocker over the Toronto Maple Leafs, who had come into the game with five consecutive shutouts. But that would be the last win for six weeks. The Quakers set an NHL record by losing their next fifteen straight games, falling to 1–19–1. (It would be forty-four years before the Washington Capitals would eclipse the Quakers' dubious streak, losing seventeen straight in 1974–75.) Attendance declined so badly that the Philadelphia Arrows, a minor league hockey team that shared the Arena, outdrew them.

The Quakers didn't collect their second win of the year until January 10, a 4–3 overtime game against the Montreal Canadiens, and then got only two more victories the rest of the season. Dwyer and Leonard (who owned a small piece of the team) were dismayed, to say the least, that the team had actually surpassed its ineptitude of the year before by finishing at 4–36–4. The Quakers' winning percentage (.136) was the worst in the NHL's first fifty-seven years, and to this day is still second worst, trailing only the Washington Capitals of 1974–75 (.131).

By the end of the season, nobody wanted the one-year blunders in Philadelphia. The fans despised them, opposing teams didn't want to travel all the way to Philly for a lousy share of the gate, and Dwyer and Leonard wanted to move. But they had nowhere to go. Before the 1931 season began, Leonard got permission from the league's board of governors to suspend operations until a suitable new city could be found. After a year of searching, during which Leonard had made a poor showing in a boxing comeback in an attempt to recoup some of the money he had lost on the Quakers, he repeated his request and was again granted permission to sit out for another year.

> By the end of the season, nobody wanted the
> one-year blunders in Philadelphia.

This same scenario was repeated for five years until finally, with the Depression worsening and the end of Prohibition drastically cutting into Dwyer's cash flow, the team was officially disbanded. So sour was the taste left in everyone's mouth from the NHL's failed Philadelphia experiment, the city would not get another chance for a team until the Flyers arrived in 1967, when the NHL expanded from six teams to twelve.

ANGER MISMANAGEMENT

THE PITTSBURGH IRONMEN
Basketball Association of America
1946–47

Perhaps no team in the history of professional basketball was less hallowed than the Pittsburgh Ironmen of the Basketball Association of America, a league that began play in 1946 and merged in 1949 with the National Basketball League (which had started play in 1937) to form the youngest of the four major professional sports leagues in America today.

In its inaugural season, the BAA named Pittsburgh one of its charter members, despite the fact that two earlier NBL franchises had failed there. Pittsburgh Ironmen owner John Harris apparently didn't appreciate the planning needed to run a professional sports franchise and didn't pick his head coach, the fiery Paul Birch, until only four weeks remained before the start of the season. Short on time and way behind the rest of the teams in the league in preparation, Birch staffed his team largely with former local college players, largely from Duquesne, Pitt, and Youngstown.

Whereas the older NBL located its franchises mostly in small market cities, the BAA went after bigger game. The driving force behind the strategy was a consortium of big city hockey arena owners who wanted to maximize the profits from their arenas by adding basketball games to their hockey schedules. Much like today, but with far less sophisticated technology, whenever a BAA game was scheduled, a makeshift floor was placed right on top of the ice. Invariably, however, the ice would melt and water would seep up onto the basketball floor, creating many opportunities for traveling, if not also wading.

The Ironmen's first home game at Duquesne Gardens in 1946

was so wet that at halftime the players threatened to walk off the court, which would leave the owner no choice but to forfeit. Fortunately, Coach Birch talked them out of their mutiny by explaining that the team would likely be kicked out of the league and they'd all lose their paychecks. Many of the Ironmen players later admitted that they wished they had walked away that first game and ended their professional basketball careers, because they had no idea that Birch would be a far greater impediment to success than slick floors.

Paul Birch was his era's Bobby Knight, routinely screaming at and demeaning his players on the court, throwing basketballs at players' heads during practice, and throwing punches at their heads as well during games. At halftime, Birch was known to throw chairs at his players in the locker room. Birch once told a showering player if he got out of the shower before Birch left the locker room, he'd kick him off the team. The player remained in the shower for nearly two hours before the coast was clear.

Paul Birch was his era's Bobby Knight, routinely screaming at and demeaning his players on the court.

Birch's aggression was hardly confined to his own charges. When he occasionally punched out an opposing player on the road, the crowd would invariably threaten to riot, often littering the floor with debris and stopping play. One time, when a crowd threatened to beat Birch, his players refused to help him. On more than one occasion, he punched out referees and opposing coaches. The league's commissioner fined Birch often, and probably without reservation, because fining players and coaches was the only way the commissioner made his salary in the league's early days.

Unable to take Birch's abuse any longer, several Ironmen quit during the season, leaving the team shorthanded. Because of foul trouble, the depleted Pittsburgh team was once forced to finish a game with only four players. One of the Ironmen, Red Mihalik, played only seven games before quitting to become a referee, a position in which he was so instrumental in enforcing civility on the court that he made the NBA Hall of Fame as a referee.

Another player was so alienated by Birch's behavior that he quit playing forever during Pittsburgh's only season, vowing to make his name as a better example of a coach. A few months after the season ended, the wife of the disgruntled Press Maravich gave birth to future phenom and NBA great Pete, whom Press would eventually coach at Louisiana State University.

Birch even took out his hostility on the league. Lack of preparation time meant he had to settle for a team considerably smaller than most BAA teams. To compensate, Birch employed a zone defense that slowed down the game more effectively than puddles. The fans hated it, the league didn't like it and ruled against it, but Birch persisted. Over the last half of the season, Birch played an irritating cat-and-mouse game with both officials and league honchos. By season's end, everyone had had their fill of Birch.

Pittsburgh finished the schedule with a dismal 15–45 record and it was no surprise that nobody—neither owner, coaches, players, fans, nor league officials—expressed the slightest interest in a second Pittsburgh Ironmen season.

HOME ALONE

THE PITTSBURGH PIPERS/CONDORS
American Basketball Association
1967–68, 1969–72

T he Pittsburgh Pipers apparently hadn't heard the adage, "You can't go home again." They tried it—the only major sports franchise to abandon a city and play somewhere else for a year, only to return to it—and, boy, was that a mistake. When the American Basketball Association began play in

1968 Connie Hawkins warm-up jacket.

1967, the Pittsburgh Pipers were charter members of the eleven-team league. Coached by Vince Cazzetta, the Pipers optimistically played their home games in the Pittsburgh Civic Arena, a facility they shared with the NHL's Penguins, who also began play in 1967. The 17,500-seat Civic Arena dwarfed the Pipers' 3,200 per game average—although it turned out that was quite a respectable number for an ABA team that first season.

Six of the twenty-one different players on the roster that year saw most of the court time. The big attraction was acrobatic Connie Hawkins, a 6'8" center/forward who had been kicked out of the University of Iowa under a cloud of suspicion surrounding a point-shaving scandal. Although never charged, he was suspended anyway for failing to notify school officials of the scandal that he knew was taking place. Banned from the NBA as well, Hawkins played for the Harlem Globetrotters before the ABA started up and gave him his chance. Hawkins averaged 26.8 points and 13.5 rebounds a game and was named the league's Most Valuable Player. The supporting cast included Charlie Williams (20.8 points a game), who had been set to play for the NBA Seattle SuperSonics when he was banned after it was revealed that he had failed to report a bribe while in college; Chico Vaughn (19.9); Art Heyman (20.1); Ira Harge (9.1); and Trooper Washington (11.6).

After Pittsburgh stumbled its way to an 11–12 start, Heyman joined the team and sparked the Pipers to a fifteen-game winning streak, and eighteen out of nineteen. After a 9–8 stretch, the Pipers reeled off a twelve-game winning streak to take their division. In the playoffs, the Pipers swept the Indiana Pacers in three games, then defeated the Minnesota Muskies four games to one. In the ABA Championship, the Doug Moe–led Western Division champion New Orleans Buccaneers provided a bigger challenge, sending the series to a seventh game, where so many Pittsburgh fans—12,000 of them—descended on the Civic Arena that the game's start had to be delayed an hour. The Pipers were more prepared than the box office and prevailed, 122–113, to become the ABA's first champions.

And then the weirdness really began. Before the Pipers and their fans even had a chance to bask in the glory of their new title, it was announced that the Pipers had been sold to Minneapolis attorney Bill Erickson and were moving to Minnesota for the 1968–69 season, where they would replace the Muskies, who had done so poorly that their owner moved them to Miami for the 1968–69 season, renaming them The Floridians. Apparently Erickson felt the Pipers could succeed where the Muskies had not.

The Pipers got out of the gate fast with an 18–7 record in 1968, then disaster struck. The team's four biggest stars, Hawkins, Williams, Vaughn, and Heyman, all suffered serious injuries and the losses started to mount, although by the time of the ABA All-Star Game in Louisville on January 28, 1969, the Pipers were still a respectable 26–19 and their new coach, Jim Harding, was chosen to coach the East team. At the All-Star Game banquet, however, all hell broke loose. Harding, who had been constantly criticized by Pipers chairman Gabe Rubin for running his players into the ground, finally lost it and physically assaulted him at the banquet. As *Basketball Weekly* magazine described it, ". . . Harding was punching Rubin and Rubin was scratching and clawing at Harding." Harding was fired that same night.

Pipers GM Vern Mikkelsen, former star of the George Mikan–era Minneapolis Lakers, took over as coach for a short while until new coach Gus Young was named. It didn't help. With a month to go in the season, the financially strapped Pipers were so desperate they lowered the price of all seats to two dollars. It didn't work. The Pipers continued to lose, finishing the season on a 4–15 note, barely qualifying for the playoffs. As fate would have it, the Pipers played the Floridians, their reincarnated predecessors in Minnesota, and were knocked out in the first round.

After losing more than $400,000 on the season, rumors circulated that the Pipers were moving to New Jersey. Instead, Erickson surprised everyone by moving the Pipers back to Pittsburgh for the 1969–70 season. It was the triumph of hope over experience. Most former Pipers fans, angry over the team's having left in the first place, refused to turn out for the returning team. In any event, Connie Hawkins wasn't around, having finally been accepted into the NBA and playing for the Phoenix Suns, and the team was pathetic, losing one game 177–135, and finishing 29–55 and well out of the playoffs.

Erickson had the bright idea that what the team needed was a name change to something more intimidating, but the team now known as the Condors in 1970–71 still stank, losing thirty-one of its last thirty-seven games and dropping to 25–59.

The financially strapped Pipers were so desperate they lowered the price of all seats to two dollars.

How bad did it get before it was all over? The only media coverage Pittsburgh could get was an occasional game on a UHF station. Fred Cranwell, Pipers PR man at the time, had sold twenty-five ad spots during one game against the Carolina Cougars, but when the game was nearly over only twenty-two of them had run. The game was tied with seconds to go and one of the Cougars was about to go to the free throw line. During a time-out, Cranwell rushed down to the court and burst into Carolina coach Bones McKinney's huddle, hinting that an overtime game would be good for the entire ABA. Though McKinney said nothing to Cranwell, and never admitted to it later, the Cougar player did miss both free throws and the game went into overtime, Carolina eventually prevailing by two points. However, the Pittsburgh Condors didn't have to worry much longer about advertisers. After the 1971–72 season, the team at last joined the long list of franchises never to be heard from again.

SPARTAN EXISTENCE

THE PORTSMOUTH SPARTANS
National Football League
1930–33

The mid-America region of Ohio, Kentucky, and West Virginia was a football hotbed in the 1920s and 1930s, teeming with professional and semi-pro teams—few better than the Spartans of Portsmouth, Ohio, formed in 1929. The purple-and-gold-clad Purple Herd performed so well against the other top independent teams (even beating the heralded Ironton Tanks twice) that the Green Bay Packers sponsored the Spartans for membership into the NFL in 1930.

After a respectable beginning in 1930 when they finished 5–6–3, the Spartans turned it up a notch in 1931 by going 11-3, playing in front of overflow crowds at home. Several weeks before the end of the season, the Spartans and Green Bay Packers entered into a tentative agreement to play an additional game in Portsmouth after the regular season ended as a sort of "championship" game. But when the Packers finished 12–2, one game ahead of Portsmouth, Green Bay president L. H. Joanness unilaterally decided there would be no playoff game, enraging Spartan owner Harry Snyder, who had already sold tickets for the game and traveled all the way to Chicago to discuss the details of this distant ancestor of the Super Bowl. Snyder filed a protest with the league, but the NFL sided with the Packers, citing rules allowing either team to cancel a tentatively scheduled game at any time.

The *Ironton* (Ohio) *Evening Tribune* had a field day with Green Bay's refusal to participate in the playoff game. PACKERS KEEP TITLE SAFE BY QUITTING! blared the headline. CHAMPS RUN AWAY FROM DECIDING GAME, and PACKERS REFUSE TO MEET SPARTANS said the same paper in other editions. Since the Spartans couldn't get the Packers to meet them on the gridiron, they scheduled a game with the Columbus Taxicabs, a respected independent team. Their 101–7 thrashing of the unhailed and unheralded Taxicabs only whetted the Spartans' taste for revenge.

When the Spartans took the field in 1932, they were on a mission. In the season's third game, the Spartans traveled to Green Bay for the first of two games between them. A victory would vindicate them for the previous season's snubbing at the hands of the Packers' owner. But the wound was only opened wider when Green Bay prevailed, 15–10, amidst taunts from Packers players and fans. When the two teams met again on December 4, this time in Portsmouth, they each—along with the Chicago Bears— had suffered only one loss on the season. Portsmouth coach Potsy Clark was so convinced that his team was better than Green Bay that he bragged to the press that he needed only eleven players to beat the Packers. And that's just what happened. In a game that became famous as the "iron man game," Clark played the same eleven players on both offense and defense for the entire game, not once making a substitution. When the final gun sounded, the Spartans had whipped the Pack, 19–0. And while Clark, Snyder, the Spartans, and their fans all finally had a measure of revenge, there was still one matter that needed settling: the NFL title. Because the Bears won their last game too, Portsmouth and Chicago had finished the season in a tie.

Since the NFL's inception in 1920, the league winner had always been decided by best overall won-lost record. But because of all the negative press over the previous year's postseason flap, and this year's dead-heat tie, the NFL decided to schedule an official playoff game—the league's first ever—for Wrigley Field in Chicago on December 18.

The weather, unfortunately, took its revenge on both teams, as one of the coldest winters on record roared into Chicago. Below-zero windchill, deep snow, and blizzardlike conditions made playing outdoors impossible, and so, on short notice, the league took the unusual step of moving the title game indoors to Chicago Stadium.

The indoor field had to be modified—in a preview of Arena Football decades later. The field was shortened from 100 yards to just 60, and made 10 yards narrower. The field's sidelines butted right up against the walls for the seats, necessitating the invention of hash marks, 10 yards from the sideline, to keep the spectators safer from the mayhem. Any play that ended outside the hash marks would be brought back to the hash mark for the next play. The goal posts were moved from the end lines to the goal lines.

Chicago won the game, 9–0, on a safety and a two-yard pass from Bronko Nagurski to Red Grange. The Spartans protested the touchdown, claiming it had been thrown from less than five yards behind the line of scrimmage—that was the rule at the time—but the play stood.

Action shot of 1932 NFL title game between Chicago Bears and Portsmouth Spartans.

The NFL's first playoff game was a huge success, with historical consequences as well. Hash marks were here to stay. The argument over the Nagurski-Grange touchdown led the NFL to change its rules, allowing a forward pass to be made from anywhere behind the line of scrimmage, thereby opening up the offensive game. The NFL, which heretofore had played by collegiate rules, threw out the college rulebook after the 1932 season and drafted their own in 1933. Finally, the excitement generated by the playoff game convinced the league's owners to schedule a regular title game, prompting the creation of an Eastern and a Western Conference to supply the contestants.

For the Portsmouth Spartans, however, it was all downhill. Despite the loyal fan base that packed Universal Stadium for every home game, the team had been losing money every time it stepped on the field. Portsmouth was the smallest city in the NFL at the time, and Universal Stadium (a high school field that held just 8,200 fans) just wasn't big enough to cover payroll and operating expenses, let alone generate a profit.

An emergency meeting of the forty-four stockholders was called. The eighteen who attended offered to double their investments, but for most of them that meant merely raising their stake from $100 to $200, far short of the $17,000 that was needed. So, following a fourth straight red-ink season in 1933, the Spartans were sold to wealthy radio station executive George A. Richards, who moved the team to Detroit with its 25,000-seat University of Detroit Stadium, completing the NFL's push to eliminate all of its small market cities except Green Bay.

Richards called his team the Lions after the monarch of the jungle because he expected his team to be king of the NFL. It obliged one year later, in 1935, when, still stocked with former Spartans, the Lions won the NFL Championship, something that had eluded them during their four seasons in Portsmouth.

INTERCEPTED

THE POTTSVILLE MAROONS
National Football League
1925–28

When professional football was in its infancy in the 1920s, college football was king, which is understandable since the college game had more than a fifty-year head start on the pros. So when the NFL champion Pottsville Maroons upset the heavily favored Notre Dame All-Stars and its famous Four Horsemen, putting the NFL on the football map, the fledgling league must have been grateful, right?

Nope. For trying to cash in on their success, the NFL stripped them of their title and punted them out of football.

The Pottsville (Pennsylvania) Eleven football team got its start in 1920, playing as an independent team until 1924, when it joined the Anthracite League, a circuit made up of teams from coal-mining towns. Most team members worked for the Yorkville Hose Company, but the team's sponsors beefed up the squad with professional ringers like Carl Beck, Benny Boynton, and Stan Cofall. If large crowds and a winning record are any indication, the combination of professional players and hometown boys was a successful mix.

1925 Pottsville Maroons NFL Championship commemorative ring made in the early 1960s and given to surviving players at a team reunion.

In 1924, when Dr. John Striegel, a local surgeon, purchased the Eleven for $1,500, he ordered new uniforms from Joe Zacko, owner of the local sporting goods store, telling him that he didn't care what color the new jerseys were. When twenty-five maroon jerseys arrived, the Pottsville Eleven had a new nickname. The Maroons further strengthened their lineup in 1924 with the addition of three players from the 1923 NFL champion Canton Bulldogs—Larry Conover, Harry Robb, and future Hall of Famer Wilbur "Pete" Henry. The Bulldogs sued to get Henry back, but a Pennsylvania judge dismissed the suit. The Maroons won the Anthracite League title that year with a 6–0–1 record, and after the league season, Pottsville issued challenges to the NFL's two best teams, the champion Cleveland Bulldogs and the Frankford Yellow Jackets (who played in that northeastern section of Philadelphia), but both declined. The NFL's Rochester Jeffersons did accept a challenge, and defeated the Maroons, 10–7, handing Pottsville its only loss of a 12–1–1 season in which it outscored its opponents 288–17 with twelve shutouts.

Having proved themselves, the Maroons joined the NFL in 1925 and quickly proved to be a popular addition. Because Pottsville was so close to Philadelphia, visiting teams were able to double their gate receipts by playing a Saturday game in Philly against the Yellow Jackets and a Sunday game against the Maroons, who were willing to ignore Pennsylvania's blue laws against Sunday sporting events. Pottsville added more former standout college players in 1925, including Walter French, Jack Ernst, Charlie Berry, and Eddie Doyle, who would sadly become the first American killed in World War II's North Africa landings. Berry was a two-sport star who signed pro contracts in both football and baseball (Philadelphia A's).

As the 1925 season wound down, it was obvious that the NFL champion would be either Pottsville or the Chicago Cardinals. A December 6 game between the two in Chicago's Comiskey Park would decide the matter. In a game played in heavy snow, the Maroons prevailed, 21–7, giving them a league record of 10–2–0 to the Cardinals' 9–2–1, and the NFL championship. Dr. Striegel decided to cash in on his new title by scheduling several more games, including one for the following Saturday in Philadelphia's Shibe Park against the Notre Dame All-Star team featuring the famous Four Horsemen.

Dr. Striegel badly needed the exhibition game against Notre Dame because home games at tiny Minersville Park had been insufficient to meet his soaring payroll. But the Frankford Yellow Jackets protested to NFL president Joseph Carr that the Maroons' game with Notre Dame violated Frankford's territorial rights to the city of Philadelphia. Carr upheld the protest and warned Striegel that if the Maroons played the game they would be suspended from the NFL, stripped of their title, and fined up to $5,000.

Whether Striegel thought Carr was bluffing or believed that his payday for the Notre Dame game would outweigh a $5,000 fine, he decided to play the game anyway, figuring he could win the matter in court if he had to.

The game with the Notre Dame All-Stars lived up to its billing. More than 10,000 fans made their way into Shibe Park to watch the classic battle with many of the game's greatest names involved. Notre Dame led 7–6 at halftime, the margin a result of a Maroons missed extra point. As Striegel led his team out of the locker room after the half, he was given a telegram from Carr informing him that he was fining the Maroons $500, suspending them from the league, and stripping them of the title they had won the week before. According to the *Philadelphia Record,* the players were ordered to return their championship medallions. The bad news fired up the Maroons, who held the Irish scoreless the rest of the way while Charlie Berry kicked a 30-yard field goal with less than a minute left to give Pottsville the upset victory over the nation's best team. With the win, the NFL finally got the recognition and credibility it had been seeking.

Pottsville's suspension didn't last long, however. In 1926, Red Grange's new American Football League was courting every professional team in the country, including the Maroons. Fearing a defection of the league's best teams, the NFL reinstated the Maroons for the 1926 season. Pottsville finished third in the twenty-two-team league with a 10–2–1 record, but after they floundered the next two seasons (5–8–0 in 1927 and 2–8–0 in 1928), Striegel sold the team to a group from New England who moved the team to Boston (and renamed it the Bulldogs), where they played one final NFL season before folding.

The 1925 NFL title that was stripped from the Maroons has been the subject of controversy ever since. It wasn't until 1933 that the Chicago Cardinals even claimed to be the rightful title-holder. In 1967, the NFL created a special committee to investigate the situation. When the committee brought its findings in front of an owners' meeting, the owners voted 12–2 to leave the title with the Cardinals, who were then playing in St. Louis. At the behest of Pennsylvania governor Ed Rendell, another investigation was undertaken in 2003, this time resulting in a 30–2 vote to let the Cardinals, now playing in Phoenix, keep the title. The vote so infuriated Rendell that he sent the NFL an angry letter, concluding it with, "I . . . wish that every NFL franchise except the Eagles and Steelers lose large quantities of money."

A 2008 comparative study by *USA Today* statistician Jeff Sagarin determined that Pottsville was the better team, and a movie in development based on David Fleming's book *Breaker Boys: The NFL's Greatest Team and the Stolen 1925 Championship,* will no doubt strengthen the case.

FLATTENED BY THE DEPRESSION

THE PROVIDENCE STEAM ROLLER
National Football League
1925–31

B y winning the National Football League title in 1928, the
Providence Steam Roller earned an enduring distinction as
the last team not now in the NFL to win the title. Like
many other NFL teams of the day, Providence was a small
market city and the franchise had financial challenges. But their
greatest challenge was on the field; they played their home games
at their 10,000-seat Cyclodome, an outdoor facility built for bicycle racing.

The Cyclodome had room for only five-yard end zones.
Worse, they were hemmed in by the sharply banked wooden
racetrack, which did little to encourage passing attacks in the red
zone. Temporary bleacher seating ran right up to the sidelines,
maximizing the small arena's attendance, but also involving spectators in many ferocious tackles in which the play wasn't whistled
dead until the mayhem ended up in the third row.

The Steam Roller, which had been playing organized ball
since 1916, didn't join the NFL until 1925, finishing with a respectable record every year of its seven-year professional existence. Its all-time won-lost record was 41–32–11, a winning
percentage of .562. Its worst finish was 4–6–2 in 1929, the year
after it won the NFL title with an 8–1–2 record.

The Steam Roller set a number of firsts in NFL history.
Besides being the first NFL team to play in a bicycle stadium,
Providence hosted the first night game in league history on No-

vember 6, 1929, when they entertained the Chicago Cardinals.
The game was originally to have been played on Sunday, November 3, but a heavy rain flooded the Cyclodome. Since neither team
wanted to lose a paycheck, the makeup game was hastily scheduled
for nearby Kinsley Park Stadium. The owners brought in temporary floodlighting (a local paper reported that "the monster floodlights were just as good as daylight for the players") and painted

*1931 broadside of game between
Providence Steam Roller and Green
Bay Packers.*

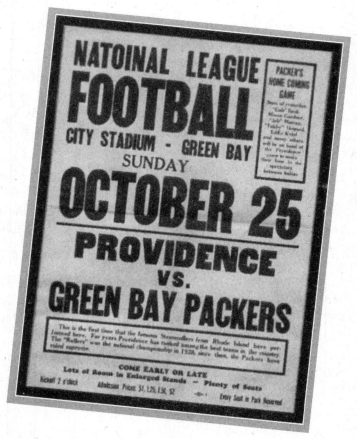

the ball white. Although Providence lost 16–0, the game was a huge success, with 6,000 paying customers pouring through the turnstiles to witness the historic affair. The following year flood-lights were installed at the Cyclodome.

Though night football did not catch on immediately around the NFL, the team ownership was quick to make sure they didn't lose any money on it. According to Tony Latone's 1930 player con-tract, one of the few early contracts that survives today (on dis-play at the NFL Hall of Fame in Canton, Ohio), he was to be paid $125 for all daylight games and 60 percent of that amount for "floodlight" games. Team owner Pearce Johnson later confirmed with league historians that the team needed to reduce player salaries to help offset the cost of the floodlights.

Another Steam Roller first turned out to be a really bad idea. Beginning with a Tuesday game against Staten Island on Novem-ber 5, Providence played four league games in six days (including the historic night game), and quickly proved the folly of their iron man scheduling by losing three and tying one, including back-to-back home and road losses to the Frankford (Pennsylva-nia) Yellow Jackets, 7–0 and 7–6, on November 9 and 10.

In 1931, steamrolled by the Great Depression, the franchise suspended operations after a respectable 4–4–3 record on the field. When things hadn't improved by 1933, the team officially ceased operations. The popular Steam Roller name was brought out of mothballs, however, by original owner Pearce Johnson in-termittently until 1964 as the name of his various semi-pro, inde-pendent, and minor league football teams. And in 1988, an Arena Football team from Providence called the New England Steam-rollers took the field, honoring the original Steam Roller team by wearing their colors of orange, black, and white.

PEACHY

THE ROCKFORD PEACHES
All-American Girls Professional Baseball League
1943–54

By 1943, executives of Major League Baseball were worried that baseball operations were going to be suspended until after the war. The reasons included wartime travel restrictions, rationing of needed resources such as gasoline, a general refocusing of American society on an all-out effort to win the

1944 team photo of the Rockford Peaches.

war . . . and the shortage of men who could hit major league pitching. Even though President Franklin Roosevelt had given the major leagues his blessing to continue operations, most teams were suffering severe attendance drops. Moreover, by 1943 many minor leagues had already ceased operations due to the loss of players through enlistment or the draft.

Philip K. Wrigley, millionaire chewing-gum magnate and owner of the Chicago Cubs, convened a special committee headed by his assistant Ken Sells to come up with ideas for how the Cubs might create additional revenue to replace that lost due to the war. The committee recommended a girls' softball league, with teams placed in all major league cities. Of all the major league executives, only Wrigley and Branch Rickey of the Brooklyn Dodgers liked the idea and formed the league themselves as a nonprofit organization.

The league combined various aspects of softball and baseball to create a unique game that constantly evolved over the early years. They started by using 12" softballs and underhand pitching, but eventually went to hardballs and overhand pitching. In a departure from softball, the league used nine players instead of ten (eliminating the rover), and increased the distance of the pitching rubber and base paths to that used in baseball in order to liven up the offense. The new league also allowed runners to lead off and steal bases, something not allowed in regular softball.

The league was initially called the All-American Girls Softball League, but in midseason the name was changed to All-American Girls Baseball League. When reporters gave them grief in print for calling it a "baseball" league while using a softball, the league's directors changed the name again, this time to the All-American Girls Professional Ball League—before reverting to using "Baseball" again two years later when the softball was finally replaced with a baseball. The league underwent several more name changes over the next few years, but, ironically, the name it's known by today, the All-American Girls Professional Baseball League, wasn't actually adopted until 1988, thirty-four years after the league's last pitch was thrown, when renewed interest in the former league prompted the change for marketing purposes.

Once the league was created, dozens of major cities around the country hosted tryouts. From thousands of aspiring women, 280 were invited to the final tryout in Chicago's Wrigley Field, from which sixty finalists were chosen to stock four teams. The original intention had been to play in major league ballparks, but the league scaled back to four small cities within a short drive of each other: Racine and Kenosha, Wisconsin; South Bend, Indiana; and Rockford, Illinois. The league owned all four teams, with Wrigley paying half of all teams' operating expenses. Selected host directors of the four teams paid the other half, with the proceeds split between them and Wrigley.

When the Rockford Peaches took the field in 1943, some of the girls were no more than fifteen years old. They did, however, earn very grown-up salaries for the times, forty-five to eighty-five dollars per week, with a few stars making even more. This was more than most of the girls' parents could make at a skilled trade in 1943.

The league doubled as a kind of finishing school for the women, all of whom were expected to maintain high moral standards and rules of conduct. Each team had a chaperone. Wrigley contracted with the Helena Rubinstein Beauty Salon to work with the players after practice during spring training. All were required to attend evening charm school classes, where they were instructed in personal hygiene, wardrobe, and feminine mannerisms. The league, which seemed as interested in a healthy, attractive, "All-American" image as it was in baseball, made sure all girls had beauty kits and knew how to use them. Before each game, the two teams would line up along the first and third base lines, forming a "V" for victory in support of the war effort. Many games were used to raise money for the Red Cross and other patriotic causes. After the games, the girls would do their part to help the war effort, visiting wounded soldiers at Army hospitals.

On the field, the league handpicked each of the teams to

achieve competitive balance, then manipulated the team rosters to maintain that balance. Midseason "trades" were common. At the gate, the league of four very competitive teams was successful. But by the end of the second season, in 1944, when Wrigley realized that the war would not cause major league operations to cease, he lost interest in the AAGPBL. He sold his interests to the individual four directors, who changed the league's direction. They expanded to more cities (Fort Wayne and Grand Rapids in 1945, Muskegon and Peoria in 1946), eliminated the nightly charm school sessions, and the rules were changed to allow, first, sidearm pitching (1946) and then overhand pitching (1948). Junior "minor league" teams were created for girls fourteen and older, and two new rookie training teams, the Colleens and the Sallies, traveled the country in an effort to recruit new talent, even playing exhibitions in Yankee Stadium and Washington's Griffith Park.

Wrigley contracted with the Helena Rubinstein Beauty Salon to work with the players after practice.

But expansion and decentralization had some unfortunate consequences. First, expansion thinned the talent pool, making the AAGPBL product less special. Second, exhibition games were played in major league cities such as Milwaukee and Chicago with the hopes of eventually moving into larger markets, but the games were met with little public interest and low attendance. Decentralization left advertising and promotion up to each team's owner, and those in financial trouble were unable to promote their team. There was no longer parity on the field, which led to one-sided, boring games.

By 1954, however, the jig was up. The end of World War II had meant a grateful return to normal life, and that concept of nor-

'malcy didn't include girls playing baseball. The league responded after the war by making a total switch to traditional, regulation baseball, which meant using a hardball, 90-foot base paths, a 60'6" pitching distance, and deeper outfield fences. By the early 1950s, this made it difficult for the league to find enough skilled players. Declining revenue meant the league could no longer afford to support its traveling promotional teams, the Colleens and the Sallies, and one by one the teams dropped out. In the end, the league was losing fan interest to another female sport, this one featuring a much lower standard of etiquette. It was called roller derby. *(See the Bay City Bombers, page 34.)*

When the league finally folded following the 1954 season, more than 600 women had played, none more impressive than the Rockford Peaches' Dorothy Kamenshek, a two-time batting champion who had been named to the All-Star team all seven years that a team was selected. In nearly 4,000 at bats, she struck out just eighty-one times. Former New York Yankee Wally Pipp once called Kamenshek the most accomplished player he had ever seen, of either sex. She was even recruited by a men's team out of Fort Lauderdale, Florida, but turned them down because she felt their offer was just a publicity stunt. The Peaches, one of only two teams to play the entire twelve-year history of the AAGPBL, were the class of the league, making the playoffs eight times and winning four league titles. It was no accident that when director Penny Marshall made her 1992 movie, *A League of Their Own,* with Tom Hanks and Geena Davis, the Peaches took the league's historical starring role.

MEET ME IN BALTIMORE

THE ST. LOUIS BROWNS
American League
1902–53

Lawsuits, losses, and loony promotions are the lasting legacy of the St. Louis Browns. During the fifty-two years the Browns were in the American League, no other AL team lost as many games, filed as many strange lawsuits, or engaged in as many wild promotions as did the Brownies, as they were affectionately called by their long-suffering fans.

The Browns were not one of the AL's charter teams in 1901. St. Louis did not get its team until 1902 when AL president Ban Johnson summarily relocated the last-place Milwaukee Brewers to St. Louis to challenge the NL's Cardinals in the country's fourth largest market. Ralph Orthwein immediately raided the Cardinals of their best players, including future Hall of Famers Jesse Burkett and Bobby Wallace.

1953 St. Louis Browns sleeve patch, featuring the popular impish elf.

Orthwein's piracy led to a series of failed lawsuits by the Cardinals, who sought injunctions to keep the players. The protracted court battles convinced Orthwein that major league baseball was not for him, and he sold the team to Robert Hedges, a Cincinnati carriage maker, for $30,000. Hedges's thirteen-year tenure produced only one first-division finish and four last-place ones, including three straight years from 1910 to 1912 in which the Browns lost more than one hundred games. Financially, however, Hedges made a killing when he sold the team for a $765,000 profit, even after spending a considerable sum in 1908 on a complete overhaul of Sportsman's Park.

One of baseball's more interesting scandals occurred during Hedges's ownership—the tainted batting title race of 1910. With his team firmly entrenched in the cellar, Browns manager Jack O'Connor took it upon himself to decide the AL batting championship. On the last day of the season, Cleveland's Napoleon Lajoie and Detroit's Ty Cobb were locked in a tight race for the batting title. Cobb, with what he thought was a comfortable lead, sat out the final day in order to protect his lead. Lajoie collected eight hits that day—seven on bunt singles to third—in the season-ending doubleheader because O'Connor ordered his rookie third baseman, Red Corriden, to play extra deep, almost on the outfield grass. When Ban Johnson found out what the Browns had done, he expelled O'Connor. Corriden was banished to the minors. O'Connor, who still had one year left on his contract, sued the Browns for his remaining year's salary and won.

One of Hedges's best moves was to bring in University of Michigan coach Branch Rickey as manager in 1914. After two years in the dugout, Rickey moved up to general manager. His greatest claim to Browns fame was the surreptitious signing of George Sisler, who had played for Rickey at Michigan. While still a minor, Sisler, without parental consent, signed a contract with the minor league Akron Champs in 1911. Without his knowledge, the contract was sold to Barney Dreyfuss of the Pittsburgh Pirates. When Sisler later developed into the top college player in the country, a flurry of professional offers came his way, but Dreyfuss had a contract, and he took it to the National Commission—baseball's ruling body at the time—for enforcement. Rickey advised Sisler in his case with the Commission, which eventually ruled that Sisler was a free agent. When Sisler, a future Hall of Famer, signed with Rickey's Browns, a furious Dreyfuss conducted a four-year legal battle with the Browns and the Commission to have Sisler returned to him. Dreyfuss eventually lost the battle, but the bitterly disputed Sisler incident was the spark that led to the eventual dissolution of the National Commission in favor of a single commissioner with dictatorial power.

Following the 1915 season, Hedges sold the Browns to Philip Ball, the owner of the just-disbanded Federal League's St. Louis Terrapins. Ball soon found himself embroiled in legal matters. In 1917, Ball discovered that Rickey had secretly signed a contract with the Cardinals even though he still had five years remaining on his contract with the Browns. Ball had no use for a GM who desired to be elsewhere, but to make a point about the sanctity of contracts, he filed a lawsuit against Rickey to prevent him from leaving the Browns. Twenty-four hours after winning an injunction, Ball dropped the matter and let Rickey go. Later that same year, Ball was sued by two of his players, shortstop Doc Lavan and second baseman Del Pratt, who sought $50,000 in damages for slander after Ball publicly accused them of "laying down" in a game against Chicago. The matter was eventually settled out of court only after the intervention of Ban Johnson and Washington owner Clark Griffith. Ball was also the only owner ever to challenge the authority of Commissioner Kenesaw Mountain Landis in court. When Landis declared outfielder Fred Bennett a free agent on the grounds that the Browns had been hiding him away in the minor leagues, Ball filed a lawsuit, but lost when a federal judge ruled in favor of the broad powers granted to Landis by baseball's owners.

Between 1920 and 1925, the Browns fielded some of their best teams, placing in the first division each year. They set the franchise record for wins in 1922, finishing 93–61, just one game behind the Yankees. Sisler hit .420 and Urban Shocker notched twenty-four wins to lead the team. The Browns' outfield was the best in baseball that season with Ken Williams (.332, 39 homers, 155 RBIs, 37 steals, and the first 30–30 man in baseball history), Jack Tobin (.331), and Baby Doll Jacobson (.317). Rookie left-hander Hub Pruett added some excitement to the season when he struck out Babe Ruth ten times in the first fourteen times he faced the Bambino. Attendance swelled to a franchise record 713,000, providing Ball with a $350,000 profit for the year, $125,000 of which he then doled out to his players and staff as surprise bonuses for a fine season. Ironically, Ball's GM, Bob Quinn, used his bonus to purchase a part interest in the Red Sox in 1923.

After hiring former Cardinal great Rogers Hornsby as manager following the 1933 season, Ball unexpectedly died and the Browns were placed in the hands of executors Louis B. Von Weise, Walter Fritsch, and Carle McEvoy. The three men were easily pushed around by the blunt and abusive Hornsby, which probably explains why "Rajah" lasted nearly four years in the position even though the Browns performed poorly, every player on the team hated him, and the attendance was at an all-time low (just 80,922 *total* in 1935!).

Rookie left-hander Hub Pruett added some excitement when he struck out Babe Ruth ten times in fourteen at bats.

In a desperate bid to get out from under the sad team, the executors offered a $25,000 finder's fee for anyone who found them a buyer. The reward was collected by none other than Branch Rickey, who brought them an investment syndicate headed by Donald Barnes, president of American Investment Company, and his partner, Bill DeWitt. Barnes then fired Hornsby after a Pinkerton investigation revealed the manager engaging in gambling, even using the clubhouse boy as his runner during games.

After managers Jim Bottomley (1937) and Gabby Street (1938) failed to right the Browns' ship, Babe Ruth applied for the job in 1939. Barnes and DeWitt knew that Ruth could help put fannies in the seats, but they passed on the former Sultan of Swat because they were afraid Ruth would be a negative influence on the team's younger players. Instead, they hired Fred Haney, who piloted the team to its worst season ever, finishing sixty-four and a half games out of first with a 43–111 record.

Attendance fell below 100,000 three times in the 1930s and losses were so heavy the Browns had to save money any way they could, like using a goat to keep the outfield grass trimmed. By 1940, the other AL owners were complaining that they were losing money going to St. Louis because their share of the gate was so small. American League president William Harridge was sympathetic to the Browns' plight and convinced the other owners that it would be in everyone's best interests if the Browns had a better team on the field, and to that end, he convinced each of the other seven teams to ". . . go a little socialistic for their own good . . ." and sell the Browns one player for $7,500 each. Only two players turned into anything, aging pitcher Eldon Auker, who won sixteen games, and Walt Judnich, who hit .303 with twenty-four homers. And it wasn't just the team that needed help. Over the off-season, the poorly paid Browns players all received fifteen dollars per week in unemployment compensation.

During the 1940s, the team's fortunes turned around with night baseball. The Browns' first night game took place on May 24, 1940, against the Cleveland Indians. The largest crowd in twelve years — 24,827 — showed up to watch their Brownies lose, 3–2. While the other seven AL teams were allowed to play only seven night games during the season, the Browns, who needed all the help they could get, were allowed fourteen night games, which accounted for half of the entire season's 240,000 attendance.

In 1941, after this was cut back to seven night games, the financial impact was such that the team couldn't even pay its utility bills without help from the league. The Browns, who shared Sportsman's Park with their tenants, the Cardinals, couldn't even pay their half of the maintenance and usher costs. To rescue the bottom line, they dropped five of their farm teams and released their entire scouting staff.

In late 1941, Barnes struck a deal to move the Browns to Los Angeles in 1942. The Cubs' Phil Wrigley agreed to give the Browns his minor league ballpark, Wrigley Field, and cede the territorial rights to the Los Angeles area. Barnes drew up a workable league schedule and arranged for group airline deals, both of which were approved by individual league owners via phone calls; Cardinals owner Sam Breadon offered the Browns a cash gift to help speed up their move so he could have the St. Louis market all to himself. It was a foregone conclusion that the franchise shift was going to be a unanimous thumbs-up; the other AL owners only had to ratify it at the annual winter meeting on December 8, 1941. But on December 7, the plans were blown up along with Pearl Harbor.

In 1942, a guardian angel showed up in the person of Richard Muckerman, president of St. Louis Ice and Fuel Co., who gave the Browns a badly needed cash infusion of $300,000 for a new issue of stock. For his money, Muckerman, who wanted to keep the team in St. Louis, was named the team's vice president. With their bills caught up and a few new players on the field, the rejuvenated Browns responded with their first winning season since 1929, finishing in third place with an 82–69 record.

By 1944, the Browns, who became known as the 4-F Club because of the eighteen 4-F draft status players on their roster, were able to field a competitive team. Never under .500 and no more than three and a half games back at any point in the season, the Browns won their first and only pennant with a record of 89–65. They started strong (10–2 in April), finished strong (18–9 in September and October), and held it together in between (61–54). Over the season's final seventeen games, all at home, the Browns were 14–3, including a season-ending four-game sweep of the Yankees, and they needed every bit of it as they won the pennant by a single game over the Detroit Tigers. In the season finale, a 5–2 win over New York, 35,518 fans showed up, the most ever for a Browns game. For the season, attendance jumped almost 150 percent, from 214,000 in 1943 to 509,000. Even better, the Cardinals won the NL pennant, making it an all–St. Louis Series. It was perfect: The Browns would have fans in attendance every game and there would be no travel expenses.

Unfortunately, after taking two of the first three games, the Browns lost three straight to give the Cardinals the World Championship, four games to two. The Browns' pitching performed admirably with a 1.49 ERA, but the team sabotaged itself with a .183 overall batting average and ten errors responsible for seven of the Cardinals' sixteen runs.

Muckerman, now an enthusiastic owner, bought controlling interest in the team in 1945. In 1946, he spent $750,000 to buy Sportsman's Park from the Ball estate, $500,000 to refurbish the ballpark, and another $750,000 for a new ballpark for the team's top farm club, San Antonio. But when the team fell to third in 1945, seventh in 1946, and last in 1947, with attendance declining to 320,000, Muckerman began to realize that he'd made a bad investment. Over the next two years, Muckerman set about getting some of his money back. He made twenty player deals, sixteen of which brought him cash totaling about $600,000. Then he sold the team to DeWitt and his brother Charley, taking a lesser deal than others were offering so the team would remain in St. Louis.

The DeWitt brothers continued the fire sale, raising another $500,000, most of which went to Muckerman, who had helped the brothers get the team by financing $650,000 of the $1 million purchase price. They also tried to evict the Cardinals as tenants, somehow figuring that they'd have to relocate to another city, thereby leaving St. Louis exclusively to the Browns. The lawsuit ended when a court ruled that the Cardinals had to vacate Sportsman's Park, but not until after the 1961 season.

In 1951, Bill Veeck took control of the team and employed a series of unusual promotions in an attempt to get fans into the park. He used fireworks, clowns, acrobats, free beer and soda, and midget Eddie Gaedel, at 3'7" the shortest man ever to play the game. He also held "Grandstand Managers Day," in which fans participated in the game's management by use of red and

green placards with the words "Yes" and "No." The Browns PR
man held up large signs with proposed moves such as "Steal?" or
"Bunt?" and the "grandstand managers" would hold up the plac-
ard with their choice. The Browns' manager sat in a rocking chair
atop the dugout in street clothes, smoking a pipe as a circuit
court judge tabulated the results and passed them on to the players. That the opposing team would likely know the result of the
vote too was of no consequence since Veeck was just trying to put
butts in the seats any way he could. The league later severely
chastised Veeck for the promotion and forbade its use in the
future.

In spite of Veeck's stunts, attendance over the last three years
averaged an anemic 369,000. Following the 1952 season, Veeck
alienated himself from the other owners when he proposed that
all teams share their television revenue with visiting teams. He
lost the vote, 7–1, and in response refused to sign releases that allowed the televising of games in which the Browns were the visitors, resulting in lost ad revenue for games against the Browns.
The league retaliated by drawing up a schedule that eliminated
St. Louis's lucrative night games.

Figuring his best way out was to relocate the franchise, Veeck
decided to move the club to Baltimore, but to spite him AL owners voted down the move at the winter meeting, 6–2. To stay
afloat, Veeck sold Sportsman's Park to the Cardinals for
$800,000. He then sold his Arizona ranch and several players to
raise more cash. Two days before the end of the 1953 season, fans
hung Veeck in effigy. Then AL owners voted down his move to
Baltimore again, 4–4, and Veeck got word that the owners were
trying to bankrupt him and would dispose of the Browns in a
manner they saw fit.

Two investment groups then stepped in with viable offers to
purchase the Browns. One was from Baltimore, which included
high-powered attorney Clarence Miles. The other came from
Los Angeles, which included Howard Hughes. The AL initially
voted to move to L.A., but after an intense day of lobbying from

Veeck, who convinced the other owners that if Miles didn't get the team he would initiate an expensive lawsuit, the owners reversed themselves and approved the Baltimore offer.

Just when Veeck thought he was finally out of trouble, a St. Louis Browns fan and shareholder of eight shares brought a lawsuit against the Browns in an attempt to keep them in St. Louis. Surprisingly, the fan got an injunction that prevented the move to Baltimore. Veeck knew he would ultimately win the suit, but he also knew that a St. Louis judge would have a hard time ruling against the fan, given the emotional nature of the case, and that a suit could take a year or two. So, in one last indignity, Veeck paid the fan $50,000 for his measly eight shares and moved the team to Baltimore, where they became the Orioles.

J'ACCUSE

THE ST. LOUIS BROWN STOCKINGS
National League
1876–77

There have been three major league baseball teams called the St. Louis Brown Stockings. The second one, a member of the National League from 1876 to 1877, is the only team in sports history to withdraw from its league over a point of honor.

When the National League was created in 1876, the Brown Stockings were charter members, coming over from the disbanded National Association. The owner was wealthy St. Louis businessman John R. Lucas, whose son Henry would later play an important role in baseball history as the sugar daddy of another major league, the Union Association, that operated for one season in 1884.

Right fielder Mike Dorgan hit .308 for St. Louis in 1877.

Their first season was a big success. After opening with a four-game road trip to Cincinnati and Louisville, the Brown Stockings returned to St. Louis to

open their home season with a series against Chicago. The powerful White Stockings were loaded, featuring Cap Anson at third,
Cal McVey at first, Ross Barnes at second, Deacon White behind
the plate, Paul Hines in the outfield, and ace Al Spalding on the
mound—but not loaded enough to keep pitcher George Bradley
from tossing a two-hit, 1–0 shutout in front of 3,000 fans.

St. Louis finished second that season with a record of 45–19,
a feat made far more remarkable by the fact that they managed
it with only ten players on the roster, including Bradley as the
team's only pitcher. Bradley was an amazing specimen, even for
his hardy era. He started all sixty-four games, completing sixty-
three of them, pitching 573 innings of the team's 577 played (outfielder Joe Blong pitched the other four). He led the league in
ERA (1.23) and chalked up sixteen shutouts (still the major
league record for rookies), an incredible number considering
pitchers had to throw underhanded. He also pitched the NL's
first recognized no-hitter, a 2–0 gem over the Hartford Dark
Blues on July 15.

Another significant player that year was forty-year-old Dickey
Pearce, whose career began in 1856 with the Brooklyn Atlantics.
Pearce, one of the first two paid players in baseball history, started
the major leagues' second triple play when the Brown Stockings
defeated the New York Mutuals, 8–0, on June 29. (*See the New York
Mutuals, page 215.*)

The Brown Stockings played their home games at Grand Avenue Grounds, not Sportsman's Park, as most history references
report. (It was the same facility, but it wasn't called Sportsman's
Park until several years later when, after falling into disrepair, it
was spruced up by the Sportsman's Park and Club Association,
which then lent its name to the facility.) The patch of dirt that
was Grand Avenue Grounds saw its first action as a baseball field
in the 1860s, and its last in 1966, when the Cardinals moved into
Busch Stadium.

In 1877, Lucas turned the team over to his nephew John C. B.
Lucas, who named George McManus as manager. Unfortunately,

a series of injuries to key players contributed to the Brown Stockings' fall into the second division that season. While the team was in Louisville for a series with the Grays, however, McManus succeeded in signing several of the Grays to contracts for the 1878 season.

But the trip to Louisville was fateful for another reason: umpire Dan Devinney accused McManus of offering him a $250 bribe to fix a game with the Grays. McManus denied it, but C.B. fired him nonetheless and took over as manager himself. Almost immediately, four Louisville players, including two whom McManus had signed—Jim Devlin and George Hall—were suspended by the Grays for throwing games. The NL upheld the suspensions, and, in the aftermath, St. Louis owner John R. Lucas was accused of knowing about the two allegedly crooked Grays, and looking the other way because he wanted them on his team the following year.

However, the four players who were implicated in the scandal weren't implicated until *after* they signed St. Louis contracts, so there's no way Lucas could have known of their alleged scandalous behavior. He was so outraged at the suggestion that he surrendered the franchise rights back to the National League. The Brown Stockings themselves did not disband, however. The team continued to play as an independent club until 1882 when, after being purchased by Chris Von Der Ahe, it enthusiastically joined the American Association and prepared for war with the National League.

THE REPLACEMENTS

THE ST. LOUIS GUNNERS
National Football League
1934

I n the ninety-year history of the National Football League, only one team has ever been brought into the league in the middle of the season as a replacement for another team.

The Gunners, so named because they operated out of a St. Louis armory, were a major independent team formed in 1931 by sports promoter Bud Yates primarily as competition for the Memphis Tigers, considered to be the top independent team of the era. Yates, who also founded two other independent teams, the St. Louis Blues in 1926 and the St. Louis Veterans in 1932, sought to field teams that could compete with the National Football League teams of the day because exhibitions against them typically attracted the largest paying crowds. And, Yates knew, occasionally the NFL would invite top independent teams to join the league.

But Yates would have to pave his way to the NFL by establishing a powerhouse team capable of beating the Memphis Tigers, whose claim to greatness had been founded in part on their 1929 defeat of the Green Bay Packers, that year's undefeated NFL champions. In 1932, the Gunners were able to hold their own against the Tigers, with a win, loss, and tie in three games, but the Oklahoma City Chiefs, another independent, were now making some noise as the country's best team. To settle the matter, the three teams scheduled two games against each other in 1933.

In the double round-robin series, Oklahoma City knocked off Memphis both times, 14–0 and 20–7. The Gunners tied the Tigers, 13–13, in their first game, then beat them 14–3 in Memphis the second time around. The Gunners also tied the Chiefs in their first game, 0–0. That set up the final meeting between the Gunners and the Chiefs to determine the independents' national champion. In a one-sided affair, the Gunners whipped the Chiefs, 19–0, to claim the title, then proved it was no fluke by compiling a record of 2–2–1 against five NFL teams that year.

By now, the city of St. Louis in general and the Gunners in particular had caught the attention of the NFL, which was considering moving its Cincinnati Reds franchise, which had suffered poor attendance in 1933, to St. Louis. The NFL changed its mind when most of the league's teams balked at traveling to St. Louis, citing the additional travel expenses to a city so far to the southwest from the rest of the league. However, after eight games of the 1934 NFL season, Cincinnati was 0–8 and drawing very few fans—so few, in fact, that the league had no choice but to suspend the team for not paying either its players or its league dues. NFL president Joe Carr arranged a quick sale of the Cincinnati team to Ed Butler and Charles Walsh, who got begrudging permission from the league's owners to move the team to St. Louis. With the rights to a St. Louis franchise secured, Butler and Walsh then contacted Yates and offered to let the Gunners play out the Reds' three remaining league games. Yates agreed.

First, the Gunners hosted the 2–8 Pittsburgh Pirates (now Steelers) in Sportsman's Park, their new home stadium. With the aid of six former Reds players to bolster their roster, the Gunners shut Pittsburgh down, 6–0, in front of a small crowd, then traveled the following week to face the powerful, undefeated Detroit Lions. As expected, the Lions routed the Gunners, 40–7, though St. Louis got high marks for scoring a touchdown, a feat that had eluded seven of the Lions' 1934 opponents. In the season finale for both teams, the Gunners hosted the 6–6 Green Bay Packers, against whom they lost a tough 21–14 game, again in front of a sparse crowd.

The NFL, sensitive to the financial issues that had caused the Cincinnati team to cease operations, was monitoring the Gunners' handling of the payroll, especially in light of the poor attendance at the two games played in St. Louis. Sure enough, Butler and Walsh weren't paying the players either, so the NFL, which had garnished the gate receipts from the two games, took over the responsibility. Unfortunately, there wasn't enough money to pay all the players the money owed them and the NFL "disinvited" the Gunners from the league, replacing them with the Cleveland Rams in 1935. The Gunners were the last NFL team to play in St. Louis until 1960, when the Chicago Cardinals moved south to become the St. Louis Cardinals.

The Gunners continued on as an independent team from 1935 to 1937, then joined the American Football League (a minor league) in 1938, where they remained for two years. When the AFL folded after the 1939 season, a new AFL formed in 1940, this time a major league, and the Gunners applied for membership, but were rejected. After one final season as an independent team in 1941, the Gunners disbanded, as most of the players enlisted in the military at the start of World War II.

KARMIC CASUALTY

THE ST. LOUIS MAROONS
Union Association; National League
1884–86

Millionaire St. Louis realtor Henry V. Lucas was such an avid baseball fan that he built a baseball field on the grounds of his country estate so he and his friends could play whenever they wanted. But this boy in a man's body, who had inherited $2 million worth of real estate, nursed a far grander dream—to own a National League team in St. Louis. Realities intervened: the popularity of the American Association's St. Louis Browns and a National Agreement stipulation that reserved St. Louis solely for the AA.

So Lucas did the next best thing—he formed a third major league, the Union Association, and

DUNLAP.
SECOND BASEMAN.

Second baseman Fred Dunlap led the Union Association with a .412 batting average and an incredible 160 runs and 185 hits in just 101 games.

granted himself the St. Louis franchise. He called his team the Maroons, which was a lighthearted slap at the Browns, whose uniform colors he thought drab. Lucas sold off his real estate holdings to raise the cash needed to launch the league and engage in other equally risky ventures.

After enlisting the support of several wealthy friends, Lucas's new league began play with eight teams and a constitution that mirrored the existing charters of the other two major leagues except for one important distinction: The Union Association would have no reserve clause. This contractual freedom allowed Union Association owners to aggressively go after the services of major league players already in the service of their AA and NL teams. By the time the 1884 season started, about thirty major leaguers had jumped to the UA for bigger paychecks. The rest of the rosters were fleshed out with minor leaguers and amateurs.

Relying on Lucas's deep pockets, the Maroons put together a formidable team. Their final record in 1884 of 94–19 — a winning percentage of .832 — is second best in major league history. The five Maroons starting pitchers finished with won–lost records of 25–4, 24–7, 15–3, 12–1, and 12–2. Second baseman Fred Dunlap led the league in homers (13), batting average (.412), and runs scored (160).

At the gate, teams were enjoying much less stellar performances. While a few of the other teams in the league were financially viable, most were not, a reality that had been glossed over in the rush to form the league. Lucas, ever the league's cheerleader, used his personal fortune to help keep many of the franchises afloat through the season, though several teams folded before the campaign's conclusion.

During the off-season, as the surviving teams were all making plans for the 1885 season, even signing players to new contracts, a rumor surfaced that Lucas was in negotiation with the National League for a St. Louis franchise. Word also leaked that several other Union Association teams were negotiating franchise shifts to the American Association. When this news broke, all Union

Association activity stopped as the other owners waited to see what Lucas would do.

In order to thwart further interference from Lucas and his deep pockets, on April 18, 1885, National League owners admitted the St. Louis Maroons to the league. Having finally realized his dream of securing an NL team in St. Louis, Lucas bade farewell to the Union Association, which promptly folded under the prospect of operating without Lucas's financial support.

Lucas's karma caught up with him. The Maroons finished poorly the next two years and Lucas took a bath. After just two seasons in the NL, he was forced to fold the Maroons. Other equally disastrous investments and a messy public divorce left Lucas bankrupt, and he eventually took a job as a railroad conductor.

ROADKILL

THE ST. PAUL APOSTLES
Union Association
1884

Not even divine intervention from the team's namesakes themselves could have saved the St. Paul franchise, a short-lived beneficiary of major league baseball's chaos.

When the 1884 season began, St. Paul was a successful and popular member of the Northwestern League, the first minor league ever recognized by the National League and American Association, the two established major leagues of the day. The renegade Union Association was launched that same year, and all hell broke loose because the new league didn't recognize the National Agreement or its reserve clause, causing predictable contract jumping by players for higher salaries and financial ruin for many franchises in all three major leagues.

One of the first teams to suffer a financial beating was the Union Association's Chicago Browns. Though Chicago had the population to support two teams, there simply wasn't room in fans' hearts for any other team but their beloved White Stockings, managed by the even more beloved Cap Anson. Not even the incredible pitching of the Browns' Hugh Daily, who tossed a major league–record four one-hitters that year, including back-to-back gems on July 7 and 10, could put people in the park.

So, after compiling a modest 34–39 record, the Browns packed up and moved to Pittsburgh. While a number of teams came and went during the Union Association's one chaotic year in existence, the Browns were the only ones to move their entire operation to another city and take another stab at it. In Pittsburgh, the team renamed itself the Stogies, but the financial problems continued. After just eighteen games and a 7–11 record, the team called it quits following a 3–0 road victory over Baltimore on September 18.

As he'd had to do several times already, league president Henry V. Lucas scrambled to find another team to finish out the season. Cue the St. Paul Apostles. Having just completed the Northwestern League's season, the Apostles were preparing to undertake a postseason barnstorming tour around the country when team owner/manager Andrew Thompson received a telegram from Lucas inviting his team to finish out the season in place of the defunct Stogies. With the prospect of becoming a major league team and Lucas's promise of a franchise spot again in 1885, Thompson accepted.

The Apostles were clearly outclassed in their short time in the majors. Despite the team's .180 batting average, the Apostles managed to win two of their nine games, including a 1–0 victory over the powerful St. Louis Maroons for their first victory. After being thumped 14–1 by the St. Louis Maroons on October 14, the Apostles were scheduled to finish the season with a series in Milwaukee, but they just didn't have the heart. Thompson telegraphed the Milwaukee Grays and asked if they minded much not playing that last series. Milwaukee had no objections and the St. Paul major league franchise was history, having played only nine games—the fewest of any major league team in history—all on the road.

To this day, the St. Paul Apostles, who disbanded after the 1884 season and then reformed and returned to the Northwestern League in 1886, are the only major league team never to have played a home game.

BEATIFIC

THE ST. PAUL SAINTS
Western League
1895–99

Whereas the demise of most teams is typically a story of sadness, frustration, or ruin, the St. Paul Saints had a fairy-tale ending.

After four seasons, the Western Association went bankrupt in 1891, reforming as the Western League in 1894. One of the charter teams of the revamped league was the Sioux City

1895 St. Paul Saints with owner Charles Comiskey.

(Iowa) Cornhuskers, a solid team with both great hitting and pitching. Bert Cunningham (33–18) and Bill Hart (29–16) were a potent one-two punch on the mound, and George Hogriever (.350, 20 HRs, 27 triples, 30 doubles, 93 steals), Frank Genins (.374, 86 steals), and Frank Kraus (.359) paced the hitters.

While the Cornhuskers were busy in Sioux City winning the Western League's pennant with a 74–51 record, Charles Comiskey was in Cincinnati winding down his thirteen-year major league career as a player/manager, the last three of which he spent with the Reds. It was there that Comiskey became friends with Ban Johnson, the sports editor of a Cincinnati newspaper. At the urging of Comiskey and Reds owner John T. Brush, Johnson was elected president of the Western League in 1894.

Following his retirement as a player, Comiskey learned from his friend Johnson that the Sioux City Cornhuskers were for sale, and after due diligence he purchased the team. However, since the Cornhuskers had drawn so poorly in their championship season, Comiskey moved his new team to St. Paul, Minnesota, where his newly named Saints would be natural rivals for the crosstown Minneapolis Millers.

Owning a professional baseball team had long been Comiskey's dream. As a young boy growing up in Chicago, Comiskey's love of baseball was an irritant to his father, a Chicago city alderman. "Honest John" Comiskey wanted his son to be either a businessman or a plumber, but all Charles wanted to do was play baseball, and when he joined a local semi-pro team over the objections of his father, John sent Charles to St. Mary's College in Kansas, where he hoped Charles would be less exposed to the frivolous sport. Instead, and perhaps predictably, Charles met up with Ted Sullivan, the owner of several minor league teams, and soon joined the Dubuque (Iowa) Rabbits, the team that propelled him on his sixteen-year journey as a professional player.

Comiskey's Saints didn't win any pennants during their five-year stay in the Western League, but they did give a good account of themselves. According to the respected Henry Chadwick, editor of the equally respected *1896 Spalding Guide,* the Western League was the strongest of all the minor leagues in the country, and extremely well run by its president, Ban Johnson. The *1899 Spalding Guide* was even more glowing in its praise, and a bit prescient, when it reported that four of the Western League teams, including Comiskey's St. Paul team, were better on the field and at the gate than four of their National League counterparts.

By 1899, Ban Johnson had finalized secret plans to convert the Western League into a second major league. Since the Western League was still bound by its membership in the National Agreement, and was still considered a minor league, Johnson appealed to the National League owners to grant his league, which he was going to rename the American League, status as a second major league. Even though he promised not to place teams in cities that were already home to an NL team, they rebuffed him. An angry Johnson then decided to engage in a stealth war with them in 1900, and he enlisted the help of his old friend Charles Comiskey and his St. Paul Saints.

After officially renaming his league the American League in 1900, Johnson petitioned the NL owners, who were distracted with their own contraction from twelve to eight teams that season, to allow him to put a team in Chicago. The NL agreed to the move with several condescending stipulations designed to put Johnson and his new American League in their place. First, the new Chicago team would have to be a minor league team. Second, as the territorial rights holder to the city of Chicago under the National Agreement, the NL's Chicago Orphans (now the Cubs) would have the right to draft any two of the Chicago AL team's players each season. Third, the team Johnson placed in Chicago could not use "Chicago" as part of its name.

After agreeing to the stipulations, Johnson convinced his friend Charles Comiskey to move his St. Paul team to the Windy City for the 1900 season. Comiskey renamed his team the White Stockings, a stab in the eye of the Orphans, which had gone by the same popular name from 1876 to 1889 before abandoning it. After failing to win a pennant in St. Paul, Comiskey's Chicago team won the first AL pennant, albeit a minor league one.

Then, in 1901, the gloves came off. The American League dropped out of the National Agreement and declared itself a major league. After putting new franchises in Boston (the Somersets) and Philadelphia (the A's) to compete directly with established NL teams, the AL then raided the NL of 114 of its players. And Comiskey's White Stockings won their second straight pennant, their first in the American League, and the former minor league team from little St. Paul was on its way to becoming a mainstay of the only major league ever to successfully challenge the powerful and established National League.

LISTLESS

THE SAN DIEGO SAILS
American Basketball Association
1975

I t was the classic case of a rich boy unhappy with the way the game was going. But when Frank Goldberg, owner of the American Basketball Association's San Diego Sails, took his ball and went home, it had much more dire consequences.

San Diego, founded by Leonard Bloom, joined the ABA in 1972 as the Conquistadors (commonly called the Q's), the first

1975 Topps card of George Adams.

and only expansion team in the history of the league. But the Q's were racked with problems right from the start. The team had hoped to play its home games in the 14,400-seat San Diego Sports Arena, but a feud between Bloom and the Arena's manager, Peter Graham, resulted in Graham's barring the ABA team from the facility for its first two years, forcing the team to play its home games in two inadequate facilities, 3,200-seat Peterson Gym and the smaller still Golden Hall, a ballroom. In addition, the Q's signed former Los Angeles Lakers star Wilt Chamberlain to be their player/coach, but the Lakers sued to prevent it, and Wilt the Stilt was confined to the sidelines. After three losing seasons on the court and at the box office, Bloom sold the team to Frank Goldberg in 1975.

Goldberg had sold his part interest in the Denver Nuggets to become sole owner of San Diego, a team he viewed as a ripe opportunity. By 1975, an NBA-ABA merger looked inevitable, although what form it would take, and when, were uncertain. After purchasing the team, Goldberg made it known that he was expecting nothing less than the same kind of miraculous one-season turnaround that Denver had experienced the year before when it went from an also-ran to a championship contender. He changed the team's name to the Sails and outfitted them in new uniforms with a new color scheme. He secured a lease at the San Diego Sports Arena, brought in some fresh talent, including Dave Robisch, Mark Olberding, Kevin Joyce, Pat McFarland, and Dwight Lamar, and hired legendary University of Minnesota coach Bill Musselman.

But the Sails were just as bad as the Q's. In their season opener, they lost to the Nuggets, 120–108, in front of just 3,060 somewhat curious fans. After losing three of four on the road, the Sails returned home to lose to the lowly Virginia Squires in front of 2,400 somewhat less curious fans, and then upset the San Antonio Spurs before a surprised, but meager, crowd of 1,670.

Already disappointed with the team's poor attendance, Goldberg was further distressed by a rumor that reached him just as the team left on a three-game road trip; a reliable source informed Goldberg that, whenever the NBA-ABA merger took place, Goldberg's Sails would not be part of the new union. By the time the team returned from the road trip, Goldberg had read in *Basketball Weekly* that the reported source of the rumor was Jack Kent Cooke, owner of the Lakers, who, according to the article, wanted no competition in the Southern California market for either fans or his regional cable television network.

On November 12, as the team was preparing to take on the Pacers in its first home game after the road trip, Goldberg simply took his ball and went home. His tantrum reverberated around the league; while some teams were forced into travel limbo for days while the league reworked its entire schedule, most of the Sails players, those not picked up by other ABA teams, were left out in the cold.

Professional basketball did return to San Diego just three years later, when the NBA's Buffalo Braves relocated there for the 1978–79 season, taking the name Clippers. Since Jack Kent Cooke was in the process of selling the Lakers to Jerry Buss that season, he no longer felt the need to have a monopoly in Southern California. And by 1984, the Clippers moved to Los Angeles, where today they share not only the same city, but also, ironically, the same venue, the Staples Center.

SEALS OF APPROVAL

THE SAN FRANCISCO SEALS
Pacific Coast League
1903–57

The San Francisco Seals—and Seals Stadium—should have been protected species; with their disappearance, the last vestiges of all that was the charm and allure of early baseball in America—free alcohol with admission, a separate section for men and gamblers, short fences, quirky ground rules—were gone forever.

> There was an eight-row section under the grandstand affectionately called the "booze cage."

San Francisco was a charter member of the Pacific Coast League when it was formed in 1903. They were first called the Stars, until a newspaper contest in 1907 resulted in naming them after the area's abundant seal and sea lion populations. The team's first home was Recreation Park, but the Great San Francisco Earthquake and subsequent fire destroyed the park in April 1906, forcing the team to move its games across the Bay to Freeman's Park in Oakland for the 1906 season. By 1907, the new Recreation Park had been built eight blocks away from the previous site.

Fondly called "Old Rec," the new ballpark, built without a roof over the grandstand because the weather was always mild and it seldom rained, was a primitive wooden facility with chicken-wire fences. So many of the boards used to construct the stadium were warped that the stadium creaked when a strong wind kicked up. Hitters' eyes would bug out at the sight of the 235-foot sign down the right field line, but the 50-foot-high chicken-wire fence atop the wall turned many would-be homers into singles. The hitters' consolation prize was that, if a ball stuck in the fence, which happened often, it was ruled a home run.

Part of the "charm" of Old Rec was two special seating areas. The first was an eight-row section under the grandstand affectionately called the "booze cage." Before Prohibition, the 75¢ admission included either a shot of whiskey, two bottles of beer, or a ham and cheese sandwich. During Prohibition, soda was substituted for the booze, although many fans brought their own flasks with them. The booze cage was home to all the hard-drinking rowdies and teamsters, and fights in the stands were common. The second was an area about fifteen rows above first base that was the center of gambling activity. Even though gambling was illegal, police looked the other way as gamblers took bets on the game, the inning, the batter, even each pitch. Needless to say, women were not welcome in either area, nor foolish enough to care.

California's mild weather allowed the PCL to play a longer schedule than the major leagues or other minor leagues. In 1905, San Francisco set a record by playing 230 games, in a season that began March 30 and ended December 17. Besides avoiding the heat and humidity of other parts of the country, ballplayers in the PCL were typically paid by the month, which meant they drew two to three months more salary than most players of the day. The long seasons made for some incredible records. Outfielder Jimmy Johnson of the Seals stole 124 bases in 1913. Yankee Hall of Famer Tony Lazzeri, while a shortstop with Salt Lake in 1925, hit 60 homers, scored 202 runs, and knocked in 222. George Van Haltren had 253 hits for Seattle in 1904, but his batting average was only .269 . . . because he had 941 at bats! And in San Francisco's first year, 1903, the team had a record of 107–110, with four pitchers winning and losing at least twenty games each.

In 1909, the Seals had one of the best minor league teams of all time. They finished with a record of 132–80, the third highest win total in minor league history. Only the Los Angeles Angels of 1934 (137–50) and 1903 (133–78) had more. The Seals won their first PCL pennant that year behind 5'5" pitcher Frank Browning, whose 32–16 record included sixteen straight wins, still a PCL record. Another pitcher, Clarence Henley, was 31–10 and pitched the longest shutout in PCL history, a 1–0, 24-inning win over the team's big rival, the Oakland Oaks, a game that somehow took only three hours and thirty-five minutes.

Seals' owner Cal Ewing built a state-of-the-art ballpark in 1914, designed to be the best stadium on the West Coast. But as soon as the team started playing there, they encountered major weather problems that would afflict later Bay Area franchises: strong winds, ocean fog, and general dampness. Fans so hated the conditions at the fancy new ballpark that they stopped showing up. Ewing took such a financial bath that he was forced to sell the team to a new owner, who immediately moved the team back to Recreation Park the following year.

After winning seven PCL pennants in Recreation Park, the Seals won another when they moved into 18,600-seat Seals Stadium in 1931, a new park with lights, but again, no roof. In 1932, Vince DiMaggio arranged a tryout for his eighteen-year-old brother, who did well enough to get a contract, and in 1933 put together a sixty-one-game hitting streak, a harbinger of things to come in 1941 with the Yankees.

The Seals won four straight pennants from 1943 to 1946, which gave owner Paul Hagan big ideas. He was convinced that the Seals and the rest of the PCL should be major league teams and optimistically spent considerable money upgrading Seals Stadium to major league standards while lobbying major league baseball to make the PCL a third major league. Figuring there was no longer any need to groom players to play for other major league teams, Hagan even dropped his team's affiliation with the New York Giants after the 1945 season to play as an independent team.

For six long years, Hagan was rebuffed again and again in his attempts to make the PCL a third major league and got surprisingly little help from his fellow PCL owners in his efforts. Hagan finally gave up and sold the Seals, although his campaign bore some fruit in 1952, when the major leagues recognized the PCL's level of play by granting the PCL "Open" or AAAA ranking. This gave the league preferential status above all other minor leagues and allowed each team to maintain its own system of minor league teams.

And perhaps Hagan's efforts to bring major league baseball to the West Coast played a part in the Giants and Dodgers moving from New York to California after the 1957 season. But when the Giants did relocate to San Francisco, the Seals' long tradition in the Bay Area came to an abrupt end. The Seals moved to Phoenix in 1958 and became the Phoenix Giants, an affiliate of the San Francisco Giants. No doubt the major league Giants were grateful for all the money Hagan spent upgrading Seals Stadium, because that's where they played their home games for the next two years while waiting for Candlestick Park to open.

And although the Seals are now extinct, their proud history is commemorated by the San Francisco Giants' mascot, Lou Seal, and a statue at AT&T Park of the Seals' cartoon mascot from the 1940s.

SOULS ON ICE

THE SEATTLE METROPOLITANS
Pacific Coast Hockey Association
1915–24

I t took a quarter century before an American team finally wrested the Stanley Cup from the grips of the Canadian monopoly it had become since the trophy's inception in 1893. And it wasn't the Boston Bruins, New York Rangers, Detroit Red Wings, or Chicago Blackhawks who did it, but a long-forgotten and short-lived franchise called the Seattle Metropolitans. Even more forgotten is the story of how they graciously gave away a second Stanley Cup victory just two years later.

The Pacific Coast Hockey Association began play in 1912 and the Metropolitans joined three years later. The tiny league had only three teams its first four years, and when Seattle joined in 1915 it mushroomed to four, the most the league would ever have in its thirteen-year existence. The Mets, as they were called, stocked their new team by raiding eastern Canadian teams, primarily those in the National Hockey Association, and more specifically the Toronto Blueshirts. Such player theft was common at the time and sharpened the fierce rivalry between the two leagues. This rivalry eventually led to the Stanley Cup being played between the winners of the two leagues beginning in 1915.

The Seattle Mets opened their inaugural season in 1915, playing to excited fans in Seattle's sold-out Ice Arena. For a dollar, Mets fans saw their team defeat the Victoria Aristocrats, 3–2, and proceed to skate to a 9–9 record that first season, with Bernie Morris finishing second in the league in scoring with twenty-three goals in just eighteen games.

The Mets got off to a slow start in 1916, but poured it on down the stretch to finish at 16–8, good enough to take the PCHA title by one game. With the prolific Morris leading the league in scoring, this time with an amazing thirty-seven goals in twenty-four games, the Mets were headed to the Stanley Cup, set to face the legendary Montreal Canadiens, champions of the NHA.

Under the rules in place at the time, the Stanley Cup was played entirely in one city. Montreal had won the title the previous year while playing all five games at home. The 1916 Mets-Canadiens best-of-five series would be played entirely in Seattle. In addition, because the two leagues played by different rules, the games would alternate between them: Games 1, 3, and 5 would observe PCHA rules, and Games 2 and 4 would use NHA rules. The NHA, for example, played with six-man teams, allowed substitutions for penalized players, and did not allow forward passing in the neutral zone. The PCHA had seven players to a side, did not allow substitutions for penalized players, and did allow forward passing in the neutral zone.

More than 4,000 fans jammed into Seattle's 2,500-seat Ice Arena for Game 1, only to witness a disappointing 8–4 loss to the defending champions from Montreal. But the Mets rebounded and thoroughly embarrassed the Canadiens in the next three games, sweeping them by a combined score of 19–3. The productive Morris led the way with an astounding fourteen goals in the series, including an incredible six goals in the clincher.

The Mets finished first in 1917–18, but faced the Vancouver Millionaires, the second-place team, in a two-game home-and-home playoff to decide the PCHA title, with the championship going to the team that scored the most total goals. The teams skated to a 2–2 tie in Vancouver, but the Millionaires won 1–0 in Seattle, dethroning the defending PCHA and Stanley Cup champs. Vancouver then made the long trek east, where it lost the Stanley Cup three games to two to the Toronto Arenas of the now-renamed National Hockey League.

Seattle finished second to Vancouver in 1918–19, but this time won the playoffs, seven goals to five, setting up the second Canadiens-Mets Stanley Cup in Seattle in three years, a title series that would go down in history as one of the sporting world's most disastrously unique. By the time the Canadiens rolled into Seattle to square off against the Mets, the United States, Canada, and the rest of the world was being ravaged by an epidemic of Spanish flu. Estimates are that between 20 million and 100 million people died worldwide from the epidemic. This was the most terrifying health crisis since the Black Plague of the Middle Ages, and no one was immune, not even seemingly healthy professional athletes.

The 1919 Stanley Cup series stood at two games apiece, with one scoreless tie, when the killer disease struck. Montreal's owner, George Kennedy, and five Canadiens players came down with Spanish flu and had to be hospitalized. One, "Bad" Joe Hall, died. Kennedy never fully recovered and died in 1921 of pneumonia. The Canadiens were devastated. There was talk of allowing Montreal to borrow players from Victoria's PCHA team, but commissioner Frank Patrick vetoed the idea.

Unable to continue, the Canadiens forfeited the Stanley Cup to the Mets, but in a gesture of gracious sportsmanship, Pete Muldoon, the coach and general manager of the Mets, refused to accept the forfeit. The series was declared a draw for the only time in the history of North America's oldest sports trophy.

The following year, in 1920, the Metropolitans won the PCHA title and the playoffs, then traveled to Ottawa to face the NHL's Senators. It was the team's third Stanley Cup appearance in four years. Seattle lost the first two games, then rallied to win Games 3 and 4, forcing a deciding Game 5. Playing under NHL rules, the Senators proved too strong for the Mets, and the 6–1 Seattle loss to Ottawa would prove to be their last shot at the Stanley Cup.

In 1921, a new circuit—the Western Canada Hockey League—was created, and the Stanley Cup playoffs were modified to include its teams. Beginning in 1922, the PCHA and WCHL would play games against each other, counting the interleague contests in the wins and losses in their individual leagues.

This led to some unusual outcomes, as when the Mets finished last in 1922–23 even though they had a 15–15 record. The next year, the Mets finished with a record of 14–16, yet they won the PCHA title!

This of course qualified the team to play in the PCHA play-offs, but without their superstar Bernie Morris, who had jumped to the Calgary Tigers, the Mets lost the two-game series to Vancouver, four goals to three. The Seattle fans didn't seem to care much that year, as attendance had fallen off dramatically. Soon after, the Ice Arena's owner didn't renew the team's lease, and the Mets were put on ice forever. It turned out that the increased popularity of a new twentieth-century invention had presented the owner with a more profitable use for his property: He tore the building down and put in a parking lot.

TURBULENCE

THE SEATTLE PILOTS
American League
1969

The nineteenth century featured many major league teams that lasted just a single season. Since 1902, there's been only one. And it took just the right combination of undertalented players, underfinanced owners, undersize ballpark, and undermining politicians to make sure the whole undertaking was a failure. In short, the Seattle Pilots never had a chance.

The Pilots were born of strife and wrangling. When Charlie O. Finley received permission to move his Kansas City A's to Oakland before the 1968 season, all hell broke loose in Missouri politics, with legislators and other officials in both Missouri and Washington, D.C., threatening lawsuits as well as yet another re-examination of baseball's antitrust exemption. To avert the firestorm, American League officials hastily agreed to prove how "progressive" they were by expanding by 1969 to Kansas City and Seattle.

Having dodged a political bullet, now all the AL officials had to do was find some new owners. For the Seattle franchise, they found what they believed were good ones: William Daley, chairman of the Reading Railroad and former owner of the Cleveland Indians (more of a silent partner, though he owned the majority of the team's stock), and the three Soriano brothers (Dewey, former president of the Pacific Coast League, Max, and Milton, a combined 34 percent). After paying the required $6 million expansion fee, Dewey, who had been designated the team's GM, was faced with fulfilling the AL's three conditions that had been part of the purchase agreement. First, Seattle's minor league park, Sick's Stadium, had to be temporarily enlarged from 15,000 to 30,000 capacity until a new facility could be constructed. Second, Seattle's citizens needed to approve a $40 million bond issue for a new domed stadium. And third, the owners would pay the PCL $300,000 in indemnities for moving into its territory.

Before the season began, the Pilots filled their roster from an expansion draft with a few notable names: Don Mincher, Tommy Harper, Jim Bouton, Tommy Davis, Diego Segui, Mike Marshall,

1969 Seattle Pilots jersey.

and Gary Bell. They also had Lou Piniella, but, in a move indicative of the team's general leadership, traded him away a week before the season started to the Royals for Steve Whitaker and John Gelnar, neither of whom impressed while Piniella went on to win Rookie of the Year honors.

As predicted, the Pilots finished in last place in the West Division with a record of 64–98, but they were one and a half games better than the Cleveland Indians of the East and they did have a few noteworthy individual performances. Among them: Harper's league-leading seventy-three stolen bases; Mincher's twenty-five homers; and Segui's twelve wins and twelve saves. And despite Sick's Stadium's small seating capacity and having the highest ticket price in the AL, the Pilots' attendance of 678,000 exceeded that of the White Sox, Indians, Padres, and Phillies.

But all was not well with the new franchise. Dewey Soriano had refused to pay his team's bill for their spring training facility in Arizona, and the facility's owners eventually filed a lawsuit against the Pilots. In Seattle, the temporary expansion of Sick's Stadium was only partially completed, and Soriano and the city's mayor, Floyd Miller, engaged in a running battle in the press over who was to blame. Miller eventually threatened to have the Pilots evicted. As for the new domed stadium bond issue, the matter was delayed for several years while various interests fought it out in court. Finally, Soriano also failed to pay the PCL its promised indemnity money. By midseason, Charlie O. Finley summed it up for the baseball establishment when he declared, "We made a mistake in awarding the franchise to the Sorianos."

By the end of the season, Daley and Soriano were negotiating with interested buyers in Dallas and Milwaukee. League officials, meanwhile, were undergoing negotiations with Washington theater chain owner Fred Danz in hopes that the Pilots franchise could remain in Washington. So impressed were AL officials with Danz's proposal, they voted him a conditional approval. Unfortunately, Danz didn't have the money he claimed, and the approval was rescinded. Another Seattle group led by Edward Carlson made an offer based on a nonprofit charter, but the AL rejected it. They did, however, keep their options open with Carlson, encouraging him to find a more orthodox way of coming up with his funding.

It was while Carlson was doing as the AL had asked that word leaked out of a tentative $13.5 million deal between Daley-Sorianos and a Milwaukee group. This prompted immediate legal action on all sides. The city filed for an injunction to keep the team from moving; the Sorianos filed for bankruptcy; Seattle citizen Alfred Schweppe, who was trying to buy the team as well, filed suit too, wanting to know how the Pilots could declare bankruptcy when they admitted publicly that they would make $1 million on the team's sale.

With everything in a state of chaos, spring training for the 1970 season was fast approaching. Because the Pilots still had not paid their bill from the year before, the other AL owners all had to chip in $50,000 each to pay for Seattle's spring training costs for both the previous and upcoming seasons.

Matters came to a head in late March. Under cross-examination at the bankruptcy proceedings, it was discovered that Schweppe didn't have the money he claimed to have in order to buy the team, and on April 1 the bankruptcy referee ruled that the sale of the Pilots to the Milwaukee group led by car salesman and future MLB commissioner Bud Selig could proceed. In less than twenty-four hours, the AL approved the sale to Selig's group and the Pilots moved hastily to Milwaukee one week before the season began and were renamed the Brewers.

In the aftermath, the city of Seattle and state of Washington both filed lawsuits against the AL totaling $32.5 million. Washington's U.S. senators, Henry Jackson and Warren Magnuson, predictably announced that they were going to raise the issue of baseball's antitrust exemption. Just as predictably, Major League Baseball announced that the next round of expansion would include a new team for Seattle, as soon as the desired domed facility was built. The residents of Seattle finally settled their squabbling over a new stadium and in 1976, four years later than promised, the Kingdome opened for business and, a year later, welcomed the Mariners.

THE LITTLE CITY
THAT COULD

THE SHEBOYGAN RED SKINS
National Basketball Association
1949–50

When the National Basketball League and the Basketball Association of America merged in 1949 to form the National Basketball Association, resolving a chaotic professional basketball situation, the Sheboygan Red Skins laid claim to being the oldest continuous professional basketball franchise in the country. They not only survived a dozen years in various professional leagues, and under a variety of names, but they thrived, playing in the NBL finals five times, including four consecutive years (1943–46). So when the two rival professional leagues decided it was in their mutual best interest to merge, it was no surprise that Sheboygan was one of the six NBL teams invited to join ten teams from the BAA to form one powerful new league.

Sheboygan built its reputation in the 1930s as a successful industrial league and barnstorming team with a succession of infelicitous nicknames—first as the Ballhorns (after a local funeral parlor and furniture store), then as the Art Imig's (a clothier), and finally as the Enzo Jels (a gelatin manufacturer). Jack Mann, one of the first great black players in professional basketball, starred for the Art Imig's in the 1936–37 season. As the Enzo Jels in 1937–38, the team compiled a 17–3 record, posting wins against some of the leading teams in the country, including the New York Celtics, Harlem Globetrotters, and New York Renaissance.

The NBL had already been playing for a year when the successful Jels were invited to join the league in June 1938, where-upon they changed their name to the Red Skins. Under coach Edwin "Doc" Schutte, a part-time basketball coach but full-time dentist, the team went 11–17 in its first NBL season. Schutte stepped down and was replaced by Frank Zummach, an attorney who used his connections as a former Marquette assistant basketball coach to sign many former Marquette players. Under his tutelage, the Red Skins became consistent winners in the NBL.

In late 1942, the Red Skins moved out of their 1,500-seat auditorium to 3,500-seat Sheboygan Municipal Auditorium and Armory, which boasted the largest court in the NBL—ninety feet by fifty feet—in an era when there was no standard floor size. The move proved to be a good one when the Red Skins won the 1942–43 NBL title under new coach Carl Roth, and thanks in large measure to the addition of guard Buddy Jeannette, an eventual Hall of Famer who joined the Red Skins for the final four games of the 1943 regular season and the playoffs. (Jeannette worked in a defense plant in Rochester, New York, during the week, commuting on the weekends by plane or train to wherever the Red Skins were playing.) In an era of final scores typically in the 30s and 40s, Jeannette averaged an astounding 15.5 points per game. He had a strong supporting cast in Sheboygan in 1943, including the NBL's rookie of the year, Ken Buehler, shooting ace Rube Lautenschlager, and all-NBLers Ed Dancker and Kenny Suesens. After winning the championship, Sheboygan was presented with the inaugural Naismith Memorial Trophy.

The 1943 title would be the only one the Red Skins would take home, though they did appear in the finals the next three years, led by their "twin towers," 6'9" Mike Novak, an All-American from Loyola, and the 6'7" Dancker, who hadn't gone to college but acquired his skills playing in the Wisconsin industrial leagues. By 1944, the Red Skins started reaching outside their local area for players, signing several name players, including Tony Kelly, Al Lucas, Al Moschetti, and Bobby Holm. The eastern players

weren't enough, however, to get the Red Skins another championship, as the Fort Wayne Zollner Pistons (today's Detroit Pistons) defeated the Red Skins in the NBL finals in both 1944 and
1945. Sheboygan was the first NBL team to fly to the West Coast,
where, in 1946, they played and lost two close games to the Los
Angeles Red Devils, who were led by former UCLA star Jackie
Robinson, who would break major league baseball's color barrier
the following year.

By the 1947–48 season, the Red Skins were starting to age.
After they finished with a 23–37 record, their worst ever, and
missed the NBL playoffs for the first time in six years, Sheboygan
cleaned house, replenishing their roster with marquee college
players from around the country, including Kentucky All-
American Bob Brannum. The restocked Red Skins rebounded to
a 35–29 record and a playoff berth in 1948–49, though they were
swept in the Western Division semifinals.

In an era of final scores typically in the 30s and 40s,
Jeannette averaged an astounding 15.5 points per game.

After the season, Sheboygan joined the new NBA, but their
stay was short-lived, just a single season. After starting the season
in impressive fashion (7–2), including wins over the Boston
Celtics, New York Knicks, and Rochester Royals, Sheboygan
faded to a 22–40 final record. There were only two other bright
spots: on January 5, 1950, they beat a Minneapolis Lakers team
that had four eventual Hall of Famers on the floor that night, including George Mikan, who stuffed in forty-two points; and a
week later flashy guard Bobby Cook scored a then-NBA-record
forty-four points against the Denver Nuggets. Despite finishing
fourteenth among the league's seventeen teams in 1950, the Red

Skins qualified for the twelve-team playoffs, thanks to the feeble-ness of their division. They were quickly dispatched by the Indi-anapolis Olympians.

After their first and only season in the NBA, the Red Skins re-alized they were overmatched on the floor and underperforming at the gate. The Armory, the smallest arena in NBA history, just couldn't hold enough fans for the team to turn a profit. In any case, the NBA was shifting from the smaller industrial towns of professional basketball's roots to the big cities with their much larger populations and arenas.

On April 24, 1950, the Red Skins withdrew from the NBA and joined the new eight-team National Professional Basketball League, where they were more among their own kind. The NPBL included Grand Rapids, Louisville, St. Paul, Denver (which moved to Evansville in midseason), Kansas City, and two other former NBA teams, Waterloo and Anderson. The Red Skins were sitting atop the standings at 29–16 when the league folded, an-other victim of inadequate financing. Sheboygan claimed the league title since they had the best winning percentage (.644), a title disputed by Waterloo, who had the most wins (32–24, .571). No playoffs were ever held to settle the matter.

In the summer of 1951, Red Skins owner Magnus Brinkman led a failed effort to form a new league, the Western Basketball Association. Sheboygan played one more season as an indepen-dent barnstorming team, but dwindling attendance spelled their doom, and in 1952 the once-hardy team was quietly moved to the attic of franchise history.

PISSED OFF

THE STATEN ISLAND STAPLETONS
National Football League
1929-32

The Staten Island Stapletons are the only professional team in all of sports history that owed its success to a temper tantrum—the owner's.

Named after the Stapleton section of Staten Island where they played semi-pro football, the Stapletons were formed in 1915 by Dan Blaine, a football-loving man who acquired his wealth from a chain of restaurants. He was also the coach and, in his younger days, the team's halfback. The Stapletons were a respectable semi-pro team that not only played games against other New York area semi-pro teams, but sometimes stepped up and took on established professional teams from both pro leagues, the National Football League and Red Grange's American Football League.

On November 14, 1926, the Stapletons played the Newark Bears of the AFL. Blaine was a proud coach who thought his team was ready for the big time, but when the Bears routed his

1935 National Chicle card of Hall of Famer Ken Strong, who played for the Stapletons all four years they were in the NFL.

team, 33–0, Blaine was livid at how poorly his team had played. Following the game, Blaine went to midfield to congratulate the opposing coach and players.

While engaged in postgame conversation, Blaine discovered from the Bears players that their team's owner hadn't paid them for many weeks due to financial difficulties and they were about to disband. This gave Blaine one of the nuttiest ideas in the annals of team ownership: He fired almost his entire Stapletons team and hired most of the Bears on the spot. He later added some college standouts from New York University, including future Hall of Famer Ken Strong, a speedy halfback who could do it all—run, pass, block, kick, and play defense.

The revamped Stapletons put together a great season in 1928, going 10–1–1, including a 3–1 record against four NFL teams. Convinced his Stapletons were now *really* ready for the big time, he applied for a franchise with the NFL. The only problem was, Staten Island lay in the exclusive territory of Tim Mara, owner of the New York Giants.

As luck would have it, Mara happened to own the rights to a second franchise that weren't currently being used. When the NFL's Brooklyn Lions disbanded in 1926, they still owed Mara a lot of money, so he took the rights to their franchise in exchange for their debt. In 1927, Mara sold the franchise rights to the NFL's New York Yankees, but they, too, disbanded after just two seasons, having not paid the debt in full either. But Blaine was a rich man who was offering cash in full for the franchise rights, and Mara was more than willing to unload the second franchise and recoup the money he'd been owed for several years. Besides, Blaine told Mara, the two teams would become natural rivals because of their proximity and Strong's drawing power.

Blaine's observation proved correct. After hiring Doug Wycoff to be the team's new coach and running back, Blaine's Stapletons started the 1929 season with a pair of wins, then traveled the short distance to the Polo Grounds for their first meeting with Mara's Giants. While nearly every other game that year would be played in front of 5,000–8,000 fans, the October 13 game between the two New York teams attracted more than 30,000 fans. The Giants won, 19–9, but the Stapletons acquitted themselves admirably. In a rematch later that season at tiny Thompson Stadium in Stapleton, an overflow crowd of 12,000 watched as the Giants won again, this time 21–7. The Stapletons finished their inaugural season with an overall record of 6–4–3, and 3–4–3 in the NFL.

The 1930 season proved a bit better for Blaine's crew in several regards. First, they finished with a better record, 8–5–2 overall and 5–5–2 in the NFL. Second, and perhaps more important, the Stapletons defeated Mara's Giants twice in three meetings. After losing 9–7 in front of 20,000 at the Polo Grounds, the Stapletons took the regular season rematch, 7–6, in front of another overflow crowd of 12,000 at home. Because the games were such cash cows for the two teams, they found a way to play a third game that year. They scheduled a postseason benefit game just a few days before Christmas in the Polo Grounds, and the Stapletons won again, this time 16–7.

In 1931, Blaine turned the coaching reins over to two-sport star Hinkie Haines, the only man ever to play on both a World Series winner (the 1923 New York Yankees) and an NFL Championship team (the 1927 New York Giants). The Stapletons also shortened their name to the Stapes. The Stapes took a step backward in 1931, going 6–6–2 overall and 4–6–1 in the NFL, and the Depression cut deeply into attendance, with some games attracting only 1,000–3,000 fans.

By 1932, the situation was getting worse. The Stapes fell to 2–7–3 in the NFL (4–7–3 overall) and they drew only 4,500 in their final game against the Giants. For the first time, Blaine's team lost money, and he asked for, and received, permission from the NFL to sit out a year. As an independent semi-pro team again in 1933, the Stapes went 9–5–1, but the effects of the Great Depression were just too much, and the team suspended operations after the season, officially folded in 1935, and never played again.

OUT OF TIME

THE SYRACUSE NATIONALS
National Basketball League
National Basketball Association
1946–63

As a young man who loved sports, Italian immigrant Danny Biasone made enough money from his bowling alley that in 1939 he was able to fund the operation of a talented semi-pro basketball team, the Syracuse Nationals. In 1946, he paid a $5,000 franchise fee to get his "Nats" into the National Basketball League, one of the forerunners of the National Basketball Association. And by 1954, when the NBA was losing fans in droves and on the verge of collapse, it was Biasone who came up with two ideas that saved the game—and doomed his Syracuse Nationals.

While professional baseball, football, and hockey primarily began on the East Coast and expanded westward, the infant NBL, which formed in 1937, was primarily an upper Midwest–based circuit that expanded east-

Poster of 1950–51 Syracuse Nationals schedule.

ward. When Syracuse joined the NBL in 1946, it became the league's easternmost city. Despite losing records in its first two seasons (21–23 and 24–36), Syracuse made the NBL Playoffs both years—although they were promptly knocked out in the first round each time. In 1948, several NBL teams defected to the rival Basketball Association of America, but the Nats stayed put, fashioning their first winning season, 40–23, behind the solid play of rookie Dolph Schayes. After sweeping the Hammond Calumet Buccaneers in the first round, the Nats were bounced for the second year in a row by the Anderson Packers. Then, following the season, all the remaining NBL teams merged with the BAA to form the NBA.

Led by Schayes, a 6'8" forward/center, Syracuse surprised everyone in 1949–50 with the NBA's best record, 51–13. A future Hall of Famer, Schayes possessed a deadly outside two-handed set shot, and, when overdefended, he was exceptional at driving to the basket. Early in his career, Schayes played almost an entire season with his broken right arm in a cast, which forced him to learn to shoot with his left hand, making him even more dangerous. A twelve-time All-Star, Schayes made the All-NBA first team and second team six times each, and led the Nationals to the playoffs all fourteen years of their existence. By the time he retired in 1964, Schayes was the NBA's all-time leader in scoring (19,249) and games played (1,059).

But the NBA in its early years was hardly the same game as today. It had some serious problems that were not only driving fans away in huge numbers, but threatening the very survival of professional basketball itself. The NBA in the early 1950s more resembled hockey than basketball; players and coaches routinely punched each other out, and fights and fouls were frequent and flagrant, with players sometimes even tackling one another.

But violence was just one of the issues. Basketball was mired in regulations that bogged down the game. Because backcourt fouls brought a lesser penalty than frontcourt fouls, teams routinely disrupted other teams' offenses with relative impunity. Delaying tactics, or "stalling," became the norm, sending frustrated fans home long before the final buzzer. The Lakers, a favorite target of stalling tactics by teams trying to counter their big superstar, George Mikan, lost one game to Fort Wayne, 19–18. Overtime games became ridiculous. In one five-overtime game between Rochester and Indianapolis, the winner of each overtime tip-off held the ball for the rest of the five-minute period, then attempted a last-second shot in hopes of winning the game. Fans littered the court with debris and stormed out. And such games were the rule rather than the exception.

With league attendance falling to frighteningly low levels, something had to be done. Now the answers seem obvious, but only Biasone came up with the solution. First, he suggested that all backcourt fouls result in two free throws, discouraging the endless backcourt fouling in an attempt to steal the ball. Second, Biasone suggested the implementation of a twenty-four-second clock, something he had been pushing for three years. His choice of twenty-four seconds was not arbitrary. After analyzing a number of practice games played without stalling tactics, Biasone discovered that each team averaged sixty shots per game. He divided forty-eight minutes (2,880 seconds) by 120 shots to arrive at an average of one shot every twenty-four seconds.

The fouling and stalling tactics were at their worst during the 1954 playoffs, so the league's owners were quick to implement the new rule changes for the 1954–55 season. The results were immediate. Stalling quickly became obsolete and scoring increased over twenty-seven points per game. Fouls were greatly reduced, making more room for basketball. Fans enthusiastically returned, and the game was saved. And maybe it was karma that Biasone's Nationals won their only NBA title that year, a thrilling series with Fort Wayne that featured a 92–91 last-second win in Game 7.

The irony is that while attendance in the league's big city arenas skyrocketed, smaller-town teams like Syracuse suffered. Danny Biasone, whose two innovations saved the game—and earned him a spot in the Hall of Fame—was soon forced to sell his beloved Nationals to paper magnate Irv Kosloff and his partner Ike Richman. The new owners moved the team to Philadelphia in 1963 and renamed it the 76ers, filling the void left when the Warriors moved to San Francisco after the 1961–62 season.

CHUMP BALL

THE TOLEDO BLUE STOCKINGS
American Association
1884

The Toledo Blue Stockings, one of the country's more successful minor league teams in 1883, took home the Northwestern League pennant. So when owner William J. Colburn was invited in 1884 to join the majors, the American Association, both he and his players thought their ship had come in. And when the Blue Stockings were virtually handed one of the top pitchers in the game, Tony Mullane, they couldn't believe their continued good fortune. Little did they know, however, that it was all part of a master plan that would lead to their ultimate demise.

Pitcher Hank O'Day was 9–28 for the Blue Stockings.

The Blue Stockings came into the AA along with Indianapolis, Brooklyn, and Washington (replaced by Richmond later in the year) as part of an expansion from eight teams to twelve. Toledo had planned on playing the 1884 season with virtually the same team that had won the Northwestern League the year before when pitching ace Tony Mullane was suddenly dumped in its lap at below-market price.

Mullane, it seems, had been a naughty boy. After signing a $1,900 contract for the 1884 season with Chris Von Der Ahe's St. Louis Browns of the AA, Mullane, a thirty-game winner in 1882 and a thirty-five-game winner in 1883, figured he could get more money in the new Union Association that was starting up, and he was right. So, Mullane signed a $2,500 contract with Henry Lucas's St. Louis Maroons of the UA. But in a move that directly targeted the UA, the AA and the National League passed a joint resolution that called for blacklisting any player who jumped his contract. Suddenly, Mullane began to have second thoughts. The UA was, after all, a new league with an uncertain future while the AA and NL were established leagues.

A repentant Mullane approached Von Der Ahe about returning to the Browns, but Von Der Ahe knew he couldn't match Mullane's Maroon contract without setting a terrible precedent for future player negotiations. In a secret meeting between NL and AA officials—who had formed an uneasy alliance to crush the upstart UA—NL president A. G. Mills suggested that Mullane be punished by being banished from St. Louis (and away from Lucas) to one of the league's weaker, more remote teams. Like the poor, innocent Blue Stockings. Besides, Mullane might actually help keep the Blue Stockings respectable until the UA could be quashed.

When Lucas discovered that Mullane was being stashed in Toledo, he took the matter to court and received a restraining order that prevented Mullane from playing any games in St. Louis. This must have brought a smile to Von Der Ahe's face, as his Browns now didn't have to face Mullane in the five games the

Blue Stockings were scheduled to play in St. Louis. Lucas then sent his attorney to Ohio in an attempt to block Mullane from playing there, too, but the judge threw out his suit on the grounds that baseball's internal battles weren't worth the court's time because, said the judge, baseball was just a sport and not a business.

On the field, Mullane lived up to his ace reputation. For the lowly Blue Stockings, who finished in eighth place with a 46–58 record, Mullane was 36–26 while the rest of the staff was a combined 10–32. From August 15 on, Toledo was the best team in the league, finishing the season on a 22–8 run. The team's greatest distinction, however, was that, in defiance of unwritten league policy, it employed the services of two black ballplayers, brothers Fleet and Welday Walker. In Louisville, the Eclipse had refused to take the field against Toledo until Fleet, a catcher, was removed from the lineup. In Richmond, the Virginians threatened mob violence if the Blue Stockings tried to play either of the Walkers in their city. And their reception by their teammates was hardly unambivalent; thirty-five years after his playing days were over, Mullane had this to say: "Fleet Walker was the best catcher I ever worked with, but since he was a Negro, I disregarded his signals and pitched what I wanted."

Toledo's strong finish in 1884 and plans for a competitive 1885 season were all for naught, however. What the Toledo team hadn't known—or figured out from the outset—was that the AA had pressed Toledo and three other teams into the major league as a way of signing players and hiding them from the UA. By tying up as many quality players as possible, the AA would deprive the UA of talent and ensure the league's demise. Then, once the UA folded, the new teams could be contracted out of the league. The AA would once again have eight strong franchises with less competition and lower player salaries.

It worked. The UA called it quits following the 1884 campaign. With his Blue Stockings now contracted out of the league, Colburn decided to disband the team, giving his fellow Ohio team, the AA's Cincinnati Reds, first choice of his players. When

Cincinnati failed to respond, Colburn next made the same offer to Von Der Ahe. The Browns' owner paid Colburn $2,500 for the right to negotiate with four of the Blue Stockings, including Mullane.

After agreeing to a $3,500 deal with Mullane for the 1885 season, Von Der Ahe paid the pitcher $500 down and hid him away in a hotel room for the required ten-day waiting period so no one else would have access to him. But Mullane, up to his old tricks again, pretended to be sick on the ninth day and slipped away, allegedly to visit a doctor. Instead, the rogue pitcher met with a representative of the Cincinnati Reds and signed a $5,000 deal, accepting a $2,000 down payment.

When Von Der Ahe uncovered Mullane's chicanery, he brought fraud charges against the pitcher. When the dust settled, Mullane didn't go to jail, but had to return both down payments, and was kicked out of baseball for a year for unethical conduct. Apparently, Mullane learned his lesson. After playing for four different teams in his first four seasons, following his suspension Mullane played the next nine seasons with one club, the Cincinnati Reds.

ONE-ROUT WONDERS

THE TONAWANDA KARDEX
American Professional Football League
1921

The Tonawanda (New York) Kardex are fondly remembered, if at all, as the shortest-lived professional football franchise. Their year in the sun was 1921. After five years of impressive semi-pro league play, the team decided to make the bold jump to professional league play and joined the American Professional Football League. From 1916 to 1920 the team was known variously as the All-Tonawanda Lumberjacks, the Tonawanda Lumbermen, or simply the Jacks. They chose Lumbermen as their official name upon joining the APFL, but when an office supply company offered to sponsor them, they unofficially took the company's name — Kardex — as their own.

The Lumbermen were emboldened to move up the ladder after a strong showing in 1920, when they finished 7–1 on the season, including two wins over the Rochester Jeffersons of the APFL, 6–0 and 14–3, the second of which was among the first Thanksgiving Day Classics. They had a strong defense, only once allowing

c. 1921 football helmet.

more than six points in a game (a 35–0 loss to Buffalo). What's more, even though the Lumbermen played their home games at Tonawanda's high school field, Lumbermen Stadium, they often drew crowds of 3,500 or more, impressive for the time.

And so, in 1921, the Lumbermen joined the APFL along with the Minneapolis Marines, Evansville Crimson Giants, and the then-fledgling Green Bay Packers. (Bids from teams in Davenport, Iowa, and Gary, Indiana, were rejected.) The league, however, admitted Tonawanda on the condition that they play all of their games on the road. As the *Tonawanda News* reported, "There will be eight or ten such teams to do the touring to the big cities, where the large 'dough' lies, thereby covering the [costs of the] season."

The season began uneventfully with a 0–0 tie against the Syracuse Pros and a cancellation with another non-league team. That set the table for a November 6 match in Rochester against the Rochester Jeffersons, the team they had twice defeated the year before. It would be Tonawanda's first professional game. The Jeffersons were having a tough year. By the time they met the Kardex, they were 0–3 on the season, having lost a nail-biter to Chicago, 16–13, in the season opener before getting whitewashed by Buffalo, 28–0, and by Akron, 19–0.

More than 2,700 fans showed up in Rochester, no doubt fearful of a repeat of the previous year's losses to Tonawanda. Instead it was the Jeffersons who manhandled the Kardex, 45–0. Apparently, Tonawanda was not familiar with the adage, "Win some, lose some." The team never recovered from the rout. In fact, they disbanded, never to play again, in the APFL or anywhere else.

Amazingly, while its football team lasted but one game in the pros, the Kardex Company is still in business to this day.

BUNCH OF BULL

THE TORONTO TOROS
World Hockey Association
1973–76

Probably no other professional sports team in history suffered as many underhanded tactics at the hands of a competitor as the Toronto Toros of the World Hockey Association.

The Toros were not one of the WHA charter franchises in 1972, but rather came into being a year later after a very strange set of circumstances led the Ottawa Nationals franchise to relocate to Toronto after the WHA's first season. The Nationals made the playoffs, but they had performed much better on ice than at the gate, drawing only 3,000 fans per game. With the first round playoffs about to begin, the City of Ottawa, owner of the Ottawa Civic Centre in which the Nationals played their home games, demanded a $100,000 payment to guarantee the team's two scheduled playoff games with the New England Whalers. Nationals owner Nick Trbovich either couldn't or wouldn't come up with the money, and moved his team's playoff games to Toronto's Maple Leaf Gardens, home of the National Hockey League's Toronto Maple Leafs.

Maple Leaf Gardens was owned by Harold Ballard, who

TOROS

GOALIE

GILLES
GRATTON

1974 O-Pee-Chee
card of Gilles
Gratton.

also owned the Maple Leafs and had been one of the most vocal opponents of the new WHA. Under normal circumstances, the Nationals wouldn't have been able to rent their competitor's home arena, but Ballard was experiencing an unusual problem of his own: He was sitting in prison after being convicted of fraud, theft, and income tax evasion. Though he hated the idea of renting his arena to a lowly WHA team, he saw it as a chance both to pick up some badly needed cash and improve his public image. (That image had been further damaged when Ballard, estranged from his family, had made the ill-advised decision to cancel a youth hockey game scheduled for the Gardens when he found out his grandson was going to play.)

The Nationals lost their two games against the Whalers, but drew better than they had in Ottawa, and after the season Trbovich sold the team to John Bassett, Jr., son of former Maple Leafs minority owner John Bassett, Sr., a millionaire media mogul who several years before had had a serious falling out with Ballard when both were part owners in the Maple Leafs. Before the 1973–74 season began, the younger Bassett moved the Nationals to Toronto, renamed them the Toros, and took up residence at Varsity Arena.

The WHA had opened for business announcing that they would not use, or recognize, the reserve clause, and Bassett, like Trbovich before him, was very aggressive in signing NHL players away from their teams. This player war led to several bitter lawsuits between the NHL and WHA, and many lawsuits between the individual teams and the players. Bassett ratcheted up the animosity between his Toros and the Maple Leafs when he signed former Maple Leaf star Carl Brewer and nearly signed another Leaf star, Darryl Sittler, for a $1 million deal, forcing Ballard, who had already lost many of his players to other WHA teams, to pay Sittler much more than he wanted in order to keep him.

The Toros had done very well at the gate in their first season in Toronto, averaging over 8,000 per game at Varsity Arena, and Bassett was flush with cash, but hardly content. He had his eye on something bigger, namely playing in Maple Leaf Gardens. Bassett believed this was a distinct possibility because, despite all the legal fighting and harsh words, the NHL and WHA were actively engaged in settlement talks that led many to speculate on just what kind of merged league would result. Bassett felt Canada's largest city had room for two teams—Ballard's Leafs and his Toros.

Bassett approached Ballard, now out of prison after serving one year of his nine-year sentence, and they struck a deal—a pricey one for the Toros—in which the Toros could share the Gardens for $15,000 per game. Bassett agreed to the high price because he felt that his Toros would soon be an NHL team and draw even more fans than ever.

When the Toros showed up for their first practice, however, Ballard refused to let them use the Maple Leafs' locker room. Bassett was forced to build his own at a cost of $55,000. Then, just before the puck was dropped for the Toros' first game, the lights in the Garden inexplicably dimmed, whereupon Ballard informed Bassett that lights would be extra—$3,500 per game extra. Bassett was furious, but stuck. Then Bassett was told that many of the fans were complaining that the Gardens' customary seat cushions were missing. When confronted, Ballard barked, "Let 'em buy their own cushions!"

To make up the revenue lost to Ballard's confiscatory practices, Bassett brought in many unusual promotional events, none stranger than the time he challenged superstar daredevil Evel Knievel to a goal-scoring contest. Knievel was given four chances to score penalty shots, at $5,000 per goal, against Toros goalie Les Binkley. The daredevil made two of four, walking away with a cool ten grand.

To add insult to injury, the Toros posted a terrible 24–52–5 record in 1975–76. Bassett, tired of Ballard and with no NHL-WHA merger yet in sight, moved the Toros to, of all places, Birmingham, Alabama, where the team changed its name to the Bulls and the public address announcer had to explain what icing was to the area's confused fans.

HELL IN TROY

THE TROY TROJANS
National League
1879–82

I n Greek mythology, the city of Troy fell to the ruse of the Trojan Horse. In the 1880s, the Trojans of Troy, New York, fell to the forces of early organized baseball, which included stiff competition, overly flexible scheduling, and some of the smallest crowds to ever watch a professional game.

Troy's population in 1879 was just 57,000, well below the National League's required minimum of 75,000. But in 1878 Troy had a pretty good ball club—although the Haymakers of Lansingburgh weren't exactly from Troy, but the town just north of it. They were members of two leagues at the same time, the New York State Association and the International Association. The NYSA was a peculiar league that played games, but not for any pennant or title; its sole purpose seemed to be proving to the NL, the only major league at the time, that it couldn't single-handedly control professional baseball.

Hall of Famer Mickey Welch collected 69 of his 308 career victories with Troy from 1880 to 1882.

As part of its plan to destroy the impudent NYSA, the NL offered franchises to Troy, Buffalo, and Syracuse (all of whom belonged to the same two minor leagues), provided that all three of them agreed to drop out of the other two leagues. All three jumped at the chance in time for the NL's 1879 season, and the Haymakers of Lansingburgh were rechristened the Troy Trojans.

Troy, essentially a minor league team promoted by expedience to the majors, was clearly outclassed in 1879. The Trojans, who finished dead last with a 19–56 record, were a weak-hitting group, led by rookie and eventual Hall of Famer Dan Brouthers, who hit .274. Staff ace George Bradley was a lousy 13–40, but his scintillating 2.85 ERA was evidence of just how poor the team's run production was. Troy's fortunes improved dramatically in 1880 with the addition of four more rookies, all of whom would eventually enter the Hall of Fame. Utility man Buck Ewing, first baseman Roger Connor, and pitchers Tim Keefe and Mickey Welch constituted perhaps the greatest addition of rookie talent to a single team in the history of major league baseball. The team improved to a respectable 41–42, good for fourth place, new ace Mickey Welch chalked up a 34–30 record with a 2.54 ERA, but Tim Keefe, foreshadowing his future greatness, was 6–6 with an ERA of 0.86, the lowest in major league history.

The Trojans had a few other notable characters on their team as well. Fred "Dandelion" Pfeffer, a second baseman, was the first infielder to cut off the catcher's throw to second on a double steal attempt and cut down the runner at the plate. Terry Larkin, a thirty-one-game winner with Chicago in 1879 before coming to Troy in 1880 and collapsing with an 0–5 record and 8.76 ERA that knocked him out of baseball, would later shoot his wife and a policeman before needing three attempts to get his own suicide right with a razor in a mental institution. And Bob Ferguson, the player/manager of the team and one of the nineteenth century's biggest stars, wore a belt that read, "I AM CAPTAIN," in case anyone was wondering.

But Troy's 1880 season was not all roses. One of the conditions the National League imposed on Troy was that the team stop playing its archrival, Albany, one of the remaining NYSA teams on which the NL wanted to clamp down. But the natural rivalry between the two cities, just five miles apart, drew large crowds and from the beginning the Trojans thought they could have it both ways. They ignored the NL's injunction and scheduled exhibition games with their rival on some of their off days.

On May 15, 1880, when an away game against the Providence Grays was rained out and the Grays scheduled a makeup game for May 17, an off day for both teams, Troy faced a conflict with an exhibition game they had scheduled on that day with Albany. Unwilling to sacrifice the big payday, Troy readily accepted the forfeit to Providence and headed back to New York. Providence owner Henry Root was incensed and demanded a vote to expel the Trojans from the league for not playing a scheduled league game, which had been one of the hot-button issues that prompted the NL's very creation. So sure were some of the NL owners that Troy would be expelled that Boston and Providence began negotiations with some of the Trojan players. But, in a surprise vote, Troy survived when the majority of the NL owners argued that Troy didn't violate the league's requirement to play a scheduled game since no game had originally been scheduled on May 17.

The 1881 season, the Trojans' third in the league, featured both highlights and humiliation. On July 4, Mickey Welch pitched and won both games of a doubleheader. On September 10, Roger Connor hit the first grand slam in major league history. On the other hand, the Trojans lost their lucrative exhibition games with Albany when the team disbanded before the 1881 season. Then, on September 27, when the Trojans lost 10–8 to the eventual league champs, the Chicago White Stockings, it was in front of twelve paying fans, the lowest attendance total in major league history (tied by Buffalo in 1885). Needless to say, NL officials started to worry about the Troy franchise's viability.

As tenuous as Troy's hold was, by 1882 they had survived six of the NL's eight charter teams. New York and Philadelphia had been kicked out for failing to complete their schedules in 1876. A year later, St. Louis, Louisville, and Hartford all left the league due to financial problems. Cincinnati had been given the boot in 1880 for leasing out its park to amateur teams for Sunday games and selling booze in the ballpark. The time was ripe for the formation of a second major league.

The new league that started play in 1882, the American Association, was racy. It played Sunday games, charged only twenty-five cents admission (half of NL ticket prices), had no reserve clause in its player contracts, and not only sold beer and whiskey in their ballparks, but *encouraged* its sale, since many of the AA owners also owned breweries. The advent of the AA also drove player salaries skyward as its six new major league teams demanded quality players. Many of the remaining NL teams felt the financial strain. Troy was now in such dire financial straits that the NL had to step in and subsidize the Trojans (as well as the Worcester franchise) for most of the 1882 season. Troy's final home game of the year drew a paid attendance of just twenty-five.

> The new league not only sold beer and whiskey in
> their ballparks, but *encouraged* its sale, since
> many of the owners also owned breweries.

At the NL's winter meeting on December 6, 1882, NL owners voted to contract, leaving Troy and Worcester out in the cold. The Trojans, who in 1879 were invited *into* the NL in order to stave off the competition, were now being booted *out* of the league in order to stave off the competition. Troy and Worcester, however, were granted honorary memberships in the NL, a status they still hold to this day. (In fact, should either city field a professional team even today, the National League would be required to play four games a year in each city.)

Most baseball history sources claim that the Trojans moved to New York and became the Giants, but it isn't true. The NL wanted a team in New York starting in 1883 and granted a new franchise, the New York Gothams, to tobacco merchant John Day, who eventually changed its name to the Giants. Day, who also owned the New York Metropolitans of the AA, merely purchased the contracts of seven of the released Trojans. Day assigned four of them to the Gothams and three to the Metropolitans. The rest of the besieged Trojans scattered to other teams.

NO JOKE

THE VERNON TIGERS
Pacific Coast League
1909–1925

I f ever a baseball team reflected and embraced the great American social changes of the early twentieth century—the advent of automobiles, movies, Prohibition, and burgeoning sports obsession—it was the Vernon Tigers.

The Tigers were founded in 1909 in the tiny Los Angeles County community of Vernon (still the smallest incorporated city in California with a 2000 census population of 91) to compete in the Pacific Coast League, the top minor league in the country. Owner Peter Maier, a wealthy meat-packer, placed the team in Vernon for one reason: It was one of only two "wet" towns (tiny Venice was the other) in all of L.A. County.

When Maier built the new 7,000-seat Maier Park for the team, he built it adjacent to Doyle's Bar, which billed itself as "the longest bar in the world." With thirty-seven bartenders and thirty-seven cash registers, it could easily hold more than 1,000 patrons, all of whom were warned by a sign over the bar, "If your children need shoes, don't buy booze." Two years before, the city fathers decided to make Vernon a sporting town, and Jack Doyle, the bar's owner, did his part by opening Vernon Avenue Arena next door to his bar. The Arena, the site of many twenty-round world championship boxing matches over the years, drew thousands of Angelinos into the tiny town.

When Maier built his new ballpark in 1909, he not only recognized the natural relationship of baseball to beer, but also anticipated the era of the automobile by including eighty parking spaces just outside the outfield fences, making it the first drive-in ballpark. In the left field corner, the park boasted a separate entrance directly from Doyle's bar, a convenience that Vernon left fielder Jess Stoval often made use of between innings.

After four seasons in Vernon, Maier and Vernon city officials had a falling out over some city charges for his ballpark. Maier was so incensed that he dismantled the ballpark in its entirety—stands, clubhouses, and fences—and moved it to the tiny coastal town of Venice, fourteen miles away, where Maier already owned a brewery. After reassembling Maier Park, he christened his new team the Venice Tigers and organized a parade for Opening Day in 1913 that snaked twenty miles from downtown Los Angeles to Venice, attracting thousands of fans along the route. Local schools declared it a half-holiday and let children out so they could attend the exhibition game with the Chicago White Sox.

1919 Zee-Nuts candy card of Vernon owner and movie star Fatty Arbuckle.

Maier had miscalculated. Wet or not, Venice was still fourteen more miles from Los Angeles than Vernon and fans didn't appreciate it. Attendance plummeted, sometimes to just a few hundred per game. Despite the PCL's lengthy seasons, sometimes more than 200 games a year (Vernon was 113–98 in 1914), Maier's team was awash in red ink.

After two years of heavy losses, Maier conceded that his Venice experiment had failed. So, after mending his political fences with Vernon's city officials, he dismantled his outfield fences once again in 1915 and moved the ballpark back to Vernon, in the process expanding its capacity to 12,000. But, after the

1918 season ended early because of World War I's fight-or-work order, Maier had had enough. He sold the team to movie star and bon vivant Roscoe "Fatty" Arbuckle.

Arbuckle didn't care that much for baseball, but bought the team to please his business manager and close friend, Lou Anger, whose wife was the sister-in-law of Vernon's ace pitcher, Byron Houck. After purchasing the team, Fatty developed a taste for being a celebrity owner. His Hollywood status attracted other celebrities, such as Buster Keaton, Tom Mix, and Al St. John. Fatty and his friends were soon dressing up in Vernon uniforms to perform various burlesque routines at the ballpark, often even accompanying the team on road trips.

Fatty's comedy act (and serious bank account) helped bring Vernon its first PCL pennant in 1919. Because Prohibition ended the legal sale of alcohol at his ballpark on June 30, hurting attendance, Arbuckle made arrangements to play the team's Sunday and holiday games in Los Angeles's Washington Park whenever the Angels were out of town. With his riotous routine and the Tigers' sterling play, sober crowds of 25,000 were not uncommon.

But near the end of the 1919 season, antics of another sort took center stage. Rumors persisted that some PCL players were involved in throwing games for gamblers. PCL president William H. McCarthy banished a number of players from the league, including Vernon's first baseman, Babe Borton. Criminal charges were brought before a grand jury, which accepted Borton's extraordinary defense that he hadn't thrown any games, but had merely bribed opposing players to lose games for their teams, and Borton was cleared of any wrongdoing.

Weary from the effects of the drawn-out scandal, Fatty sold the team. At a press conference announcing the sale, he told the press that he was tired of spending all his time promoting the team and not his movies, and that all he got to do was "be president and sign checks." He also complained that he wasn't sleeping well, wasn't having any fun, and his stomach hurt all the time.

He only bought the team to please other people and now it was time for him to be done with baseball and all its scandals.

But he was done only with baseball. Less than a year later, Arbuckle was arrested for the murder of Hollywood playgirl Virginia Rappe during a wild party in a San Francisco hotel. After three trials, Arbuckle was ultimately found innocent, but the damage to his reputation was done. Unable to work in Hollywood for ten years under his own name, Arbuckle took the alias "Will B. Good" to gain work. On June 28, 1933, he signed a film deal with Warner Brothers. The next day he died of a heart attack.

As for the Vernon Tigers, Los Angelinos just wouldn't travel to tiny Vernon to watch a baseball game that featured neither celebrity clowning nor access to booze, and in 1925 the team moved to San Francisco, where it became the Mission Reds.

UNGENTLEMANLY

THE VIRGINIA SQUIRES
American Basketball Association
1970–76

T he Virginia Squires just never seemed to get anything right. From where to call home, to what players to put on the floor, to public relations, to simple business operations, the Squires were geniuses of disorganization and controversy. Ironically, had they survived just one more month, they might be members of the NBA today.

1974 Topps card of Jim Eakins.

Before settling in Virginia in 1970, the Squires had played in Oakland for two seasons as the Oaks and one year in Washington, D.C., as the Caps. While in Oakland, the embattled Rick Barry led the Oaks to the 1969 ABA title, a championship fraught with controversy when Barry jumped his contract with the cross-bay San Francisco Warriors to join the Oaks. But even with a championship in hand, the Oaks' primary owner, pop singer Pat Boone, was facing a bank foreclosure because of the financial strains imposed by poor attendance.

With no other option, Boone sold the team to Washington, D.C., lawyer Earl Foreman, who moved the team to the nation's capital for the 1969–70 season. Before the season began, Barry was again the center of controversy, stating, "If I wanted to go to Washington, I'd run for president!" Barry refused to report to the team until the ABA forced him to, thirty-three games into the season. Perhaps Barry knew something owner Foreman didn't, because the attendance in Washington was just as meager and inattentive as it had been in Oakland.

Dismayed at his team's first-year performance, Foreman was unexpectedly shown a way out of his predicament. Merger talks with the NBA were already under way, but the presence of Foreman's team in Washington was one of the stumbling blocks. Abe Pollin, owner of the NBA's Baltimore Bullets, wanted to move his team to Washington, but not if he had to compete with the Caps. Since the ABA owners knew that a merger would be good for everyone, they convinced Foreman to move his team to Virginia for the good of the league, assuring him that they would not forget his sacrifice once the merger was worked out.

Foreman moved his team to Virginia and renamed it the Squires in time for the 1970–71 season, deciding to make them a migrant regional team, splitting their home games among the cities of Norfolk, Hampton, Richmond, and Roanoke. But if Foreman thought the move would be the beginning of some semblance of peace and prosperity, he hadn't reckoned on Rick Barry—again. In August of 1970, *Sports Illustrated* featured an article about Barry and the Squires in which he said he didn't want his children growing up in the South and speaking with a Southern accent, saying things like, "Hi, y'all, Dad." The article set off a storm of controversy that was a public relations disaster the Squires were unable to contain. Less than a month later, the Squires traded Barry to the New York Nets for a draft pick and $200,000.

Although the Squires had given up one of the best players in history for a song, behind players like Charlie Scott, George Carter, Ray Scott, and Doug Moe they were good enough to win the ABA's Eastern Division with a 55–29 record. On the flip side, the decision to make the Squires a regional team proved disastrous. While the team averaged around 5,000 per game in Norfolk, they were lucky to attract 1,000 in Hampton, and this put Foreman into deep financial doo-doo that only a miracle could pull him out of.

That miracle arrived the next season in the person of college standout Julius "Dr. J" Erving, who left the University of Massachusetts after his junior year to join the Squires. Erving's signature high-flying slam dunks created a sensation around the league and helped the Squires make the playoffs again, though for the second year in a row they were knocked out in the second round. The following year Erving, who was joined late in the season by superstar George Gervin, led the ABA in scoring and the Squires to the playoffs before the Kentucky Colonels knocked them out in the first round.

The addition of Erving and Gervin helped the Squires' attendance, but only modestly so, as their multiple hometowns diluted fan interest. Moreover, another public relations disaster struck the team before the 1973–74 season when Erving attempted to jump to the Atlanta Hawks of the NBA. A legal battle erupted, with Atlanta, the Milwaukee Bucks, and the Squires all claiming the rights to Erving. In addition, the Squires sued Erving for damaging the team's reputation by trying to break his contract. When the legal hassle was finally settled out of court, Erving was sent to the ABA's New York Nets along with Willie Sojourner for George Carter, the draft rights to Kermit Washington, and an undisclosed amount of cash.

The damage to the team's image was severe. Furious over both Erving's attempted defection and his ultimate loss, Virginia fans stayed away in droves. Midway through the 1973–74 season, Foreman sold Gervin to the San Antonio Spurs, further igniting his own fans' furor against the team, and attendance plummeted along with the Squires' fortunes. They fell to 28–56.

Foreman couldn't make his payroll in 1974 and one player, Barry Parkhill, even took him to court over a bounced paycheck. The situation got so bad that Squires players refused to take Foreman's checks, once threatening to boycott a road game in Indiana until they were paid. A strike was averted only when minority investor Wylie French appeared with a satchel full of cashier's checks.

To keep the team's doors open, Foreman continued selling off his team's better players—Warren Armstrong, Billy Paultz, and Swen Nater—leading to disastrous records in 1974–75 (15–69) and 1975–76 (15–68), easily the worst two season records in ABA history. The Squires almost folded in February 1976, but a $250,000 bank loan and cash from the sale of advertising banners inside the arena kept them alive until the end of the season. On May 10, 1976, Foreman was unable to pay a $75,000 league assessment (as a guarantee against team expenses and salaries) and the following day the league disbanded the Squires.

Just a month later, the NBA-ABA merger went through, giving each surviving ABA team either a spot in the NBA or a large cash settlement for being contracted out.

BUM RAP

THE WASHINGTON SENATORS
American League
1901–60

I f ever a team had an undeservedly bad reputation, it was the Washington Senators, which was taunted its entire existence for being a patsy. Early vaudevillians teased them: "Washington . . . first in war, first in peace, and last in the American League." In 1955, the Broadway musical *Damn Yankees* began a 1,019-performance run that poked fun at the lowly Senators, who needed the help of the Devil himself to overcome the Bronx Bombers and win the pennant. In 1958, a hit movie of the same name added insult to injury and widened the audience for the bashing of the Senators.

As for being "last in the American League," the Senators finished in last place ten times in their sixty-year existence, but so

Trolley car ad featuring Walter Johnson.

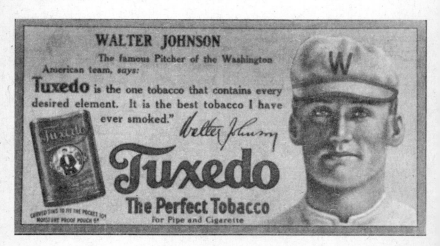

did the Boston Red Sox in the same sixty-year period. And the Athletics were even more pathetic, finishing last twenty times in the same sixty years. Over in the National League, the Phillies finished last twenty-one times between 1901 and 1960, yet they were called the Whiz Kids. Wags easily could have written, "The only thing they ever did for sixty years was whiz on their fans," but they didn't.

Moreover, the Senators won three pennants in those sixty years, the same number the Cleveland Indians won in their first ninety-four years. Those three pennants were also two more than the St. Louis Browns ever won and only one fewer than the White Sox, who needed 104 years to win four pennants.

Off the field, longtime Senators owner Clark "The Old Fox" Griffith, through his extensive Washington political connections, was very instrumental in helping baseball survive some very tough times. During World War I, when Congress was considering shutting down baseball as a nonessential business, it was Griffith who convinced Washington politicians to let baseball continue, albeit with a shortened schedule. He arranged for each team's ballplayers to conduct patriotic on-field marches and drills—some of them led by then Assistant Secretary of the Navy Franklin Roosevelt—using baseball bats instead of rifles. The World War I strategy paid off in World War II when Roosevelt, by then the U.S. president, insisted that baseball *must* keep playing to support the morale of both civilians and the troops, even though baseball's executives had volunteered to cease operations.

Along with Ban Johnson and Charles Comiskey, Clark Griffith played an important role in the transformation of the American League from minor to major league in 1901. When the upstart AL raided the established National League for 114 of its players in its first year of existence, it was Griffith, at the time a star pitcher, who was responsible for convincing many of the NL players to jump leagues. And Griffith was a "company man" who performed whatever role Johnson and Comiskey needed in the AL's early years. At their request, he managed the Chicago White

Stockings in 1901–02. When Johnson moved the Baltimore Orioles to New York in 1903, he sent Griffith along to be the Highlanders' new player/manager, the AL's inside man in baseball's preeminent city.

While Griffith was doing Johnson's bidding in New York through the 1908 season, the Senators were muddling their way through eleven consecutive second-division finishes, half a dozen managers, a tragic player death, and poor attendance. The attendance problem was partially rectified with the shift of the nearby Baltimore franchise to New York in 1903. The player who died under mysterious circumstances was future Hall of Famer Ed Delahanty, who, after being kicked off the team's train near the International Bridge between Ontario and New York for being drunk and disorderly, fell, jumped, or was pushed into the Niagara River. His body washed up several days later, missing his money, watch, and jewelry.

The Senators were also experiencing difficulty on the ownership side. Waiting to find the right ownership group for the fledgling team, Johnson held controlling interest into the 1904 season, when he finally sold out to a group of Washington businessmen led by sports promoter William Dwyer. But after a 38–113 record in 1904, Dwyer unloaded the team to Thomas Noyes, the ownership group's biggest financial backer, whose family owned Washington's *Evening Star.*

Noyes changed the team's name to the Nationals in 1905, an unpopular move with fans who continued to call them the Senators. In 1906, the team suffered another tragic player death when twenty-one-year-old Joe Cassidy, the best defensive shortstop in the league, died of typhoid fever.

On the positive side, outfielder Clyde Milan and pitcher Walter Johnson were both signed on the same 1907 scouting trip by injured backup catcher Cliff Blankenship who had been sent specifically to check out the pair. Milan, a lifetime .285 hitter, played his entire sixteen-year career with the Senators. Johnson, considered by many to be the best pitcher in history, spent twenty-one seasons with the Senators, racking up 417 wins, the most in AL history and second most ever, trailing only Cy Young's 511. The fireballing Johnson, who led the AL in strikeouts twelve times, pitched 110 shutouts despite refusing to pitch inside on batters because he feared injuring or killing them. Johnson, whose best year was 1913 when he was 36–7 with a 1.14 ERA, could pitch on short rest if need be, as he proved in 1908 when he shut out the Yankees three times in four days.

The Senators' rotation of four knuckleball pitchers
kept the team in the race all year.

Griffith, brought in by Noyes as manager in 1912, was given a 10 percent stake in the team, which actually made him the club's largest shareholder. Griffith asked his old friends Ban Johnson and Charles Comiskey for a personal loan so he could buy a larger share of the team, but both men refused, citing their belief that Washington's chances of staying viable were slim, and the trio's relationship was damaged.

Griffith cleaned house when he took over, dropping ten of the club's aging veterans within a few weeks. He rebuilt the team with younger players and the team responded, finishing a surprising second for the first time in team history. When Noyes died unexpectedly that summer at the age of forty-four, the ownership consortium named a longtime friend of Griffith's, Ben Minor, as the new president. In 1913, Griffith gave Frank Navin, owner of the Detroit Tigers, a $100,000 check for the purchase of Ty Cobb. When Navin expressed surprise that Griffith actually had that much money, Griffith admitted that he didn't, but if Navin would give him two weeks, he would have the money. Navin considered the offer while Griffith made plans for a promotion to sell 100,000 tickets for one dollar apiece to raise the money in case Navin said yes. But, two weeks later, Navin gave Griffith his check back, deciding to keep his franchise player.

Griffith's team finished second again in 1913, then placed in the middle of the pack for the next decade, a marked improvement over the team's first decade. Then, in 1924, the Senators shocked the baseball world by winning their first pennant, two games ahead of those damn Yankees. Griffith had improved the team significantly by bringing in future Hall of Famers Bucky Harris at second and Goose Goslin in the outfield, along with third baseman Ossie Bluege, who anchored the Senators' infield for eighteen years. The aging Walter Johnson, near the end of his career, led the way with thirteen straight wins down the stretch, finishing with a 23–7 record and 2.72 ERA. President Calvin Coolidge joined the raucous capacity crowds at Griffith Stadium as the Senators won an exciting seven-game Series against the New York Giants, benefiting from two freakish bad-hop hits over Giant third baseman Freddie Lindstrom's head in Game 7.

In 1925, Griffith brought in thirty-six-year-old Stan Coveleski (20–5), thirty-one-year-old Dutch Ruether (18–7), and forty-year-old Vern Gregg to help Johnson (20–7) on the mound and the Senators repeated as AL champs, finishing eight and a half games ahead of the Athletics. The World Series was another exciting affair, but this time the Senators lost to the Pittsburgh Pirates in seven.

Right after the 1932 season, following seven years of mostly first-division finishes, the last four under manager Walter Johnson, Griffith named twenty-six-year-old Joe Cronin as his new player/manager. When Griffith asked Cronin what he needed to get the Senators over the hump and back into the winner's circle, Cronin gave him the names of three pitchers—Earl Whitehill, Jack Russell, and Lefty Stewart. Within two days of that December's winter meetings, Griffith had purchased all three pitchers from their respective teams. Cronin was as good as his word, using the three new additions along with Alvin Crowder (24–15) to guide the Senators to a 99–53 record, seven games ahead of the

Yankees, giving Washington its third AL pennant. Future Hall of Famer Heinie Manush (.336) paced six Senators who hit at least .295. But in the World Series, it was the Giants' pitching staff that dominated. Carl Hubbell won twice and the New Yorkers sent Washington home in five games.

Over the next twenty-seven years, the Senators finished in the first division only three times, but two of those years were during World War II. Griffith used his friendship with Washington politicians and draft officials to gain many extended deferrals that other teams couldn't get. Between being able to keep his better players and his use of Cuban and other Latin players who weren't subject to the draft, Griffith helped his team to two second-place finishes in 1943 and 1945. In the 1943 race, a tight one with the Yankees, Griffith and Senators fans were drooling over the prospect of another pennant. On July 3, the Senators and Yankees were tied atop the AL standings when the fickle finger of fate intervened. Griffith had been successful only in obtaining temporary deferrals for his players, and by the second half of the 1943 season, the deferrals were expiring en masse. The Senators faded in the second half, finishing in second place, a distant thirteen and a half games behind New York.

After the Senators fell into the cellar in 1944, Griffith didn't think his team stood much of a chance in 1945, so he scheduled a lot of doubleheaders during the season to free up his stadium on weekends in August and September so that he could earn some extra money by renting it out for football games. But the Senators' rotation of four knuckleball pitchers kept the team in the race all year. The crash diet of doubleheaders—forty-five in all, including fourteen in the heat of August and ten in September and often four and five in a row—backfired. It physically wore down a team that finished second to the Tigers by only a game and a half!

The war years also saw Griffith's nephew, Calvin, taking a more active role in the team. Calvin and his sister, Thelma, had come to live with their uncle Clark at early ages when their parents were unable to afford a house full of children. Calvin, whose full name was Calvin Griffith Robertson, legally changed his name to Calvin Robertson Griffith, though he was never legally adopted by Clark. Calvin had another sister, Mildred, who married Joe Cronin.

After finishing fourth in 1946, the Senators were a second-division team for the last fourteen years they were in Washington. With a decaying stadium, a dwindling fan base, and the added competition from the nearby Baltimore Orioles who had relocated from St. Louis in 1954, Griffith was seeking a new home for his team when he passed away at the age of eighty-five on October 27, 1955. Calvin and Thelma each inherited 26 percent of the team (insurance broker H. Gabriel Murphy owned the other 48 percent) under the strict condition that neither could sell their share without the other's permission. Calvin took control of the team and Thelma rubber-stamped his decisions. Murphy, who didn't like the way Calvin ran the team, tried for years to wrest control of the team through a number of lawsuits, none of which succeeded.

Because the franchise's poor financial condition was well known, a number of cities wooed Calvin in an effort to get him to relocate to their city. Former baseball commissioner Happy Chandler led a Louisville group that offered to build the team a new stadium and underwrite guarantees of one million fans per year for the first three years. Representatives from Minneapolis and San Francisco offered similar proposals. A group from Los Angeles made a serious offer, but wanted the team in place for the 1957 season. Calvin couldn't take the L.A. folks up on their offer, claiming he had unbreakable radio contracts. Earl Warren, Chief Justice of the Supreme Court and former governor of California, worked behind the scenes in an effort to get the Senators to move to San Jose, but that effort ended when the Giants announced they were moving to San Francisco.

All the speculation about a possible move damaged Calvin's credibility with Washington fans and the team's attendance figures tumbled badly, to 5,000–6,000 per game from 1955 to 1958. On January 15, 1957, Calvin published a statement in the *Washington Post:* "This is my home. I intend that it shall remain my home for the rest of my life. As long as I have any say in the matter, and I expect that I shall for a long, long time, the Washington Senators will stay here, too. Next year. The year after. Forever."

At the city of Washington's urging, Congress considered building a new stadium for the Senators. But when Calvin found out that the new stadium would be built in the predominantly black section of northeast Washington instead of the more affluent western or southern suburbs, he balked, and the discussions ended. The final solution came quickly in 1960. American League owners knew it was in their best interests to relocate the Senators, so they agreed to a Minnesota move. To keep Congress off their backs, which was threatening to investigate baseball's antitrust exemption, the league's owners agreed to expand by two cities, Los Angeles and Washington. The NL had long since voted to expand in 1962 to Houston and New York, but the AL put its plan into hyperdrive, and in a matter of months expanded first, a year before the NL. The L.A. team became the Angels, the Minnesota team the Twins, and the Washington team, with promises of a new stadium, became the second Senators.

While the nation's capital was left with an expansion team that finished over .500 only once in the eleven years it remained in Washington (before moving to Arlington, Texas), the Minnesota Twins—with a Griffith-engineered nucleus that included Earl Battey, Don Mincher, Harmon Killebrew, Zoilo Versalles, Bob Allison, Camilo Pascual, and Jim Kaat—had an AL pennant flying over Metropolitan Stadium by 1965.

ATHLETICALLY INCORRECT

THE WASHINGTON SENATORS
American League
1961-71

Appropriately, the only major league team whose demise can be blamed on political expediency was the team that played in the city most known for its political expediency. When the city of Washington lost the Senators in 1971, it marked the ninth time a major league team had failed in the nation's capital. This so-called "second" Senators team was hastily created by the American League under pressure from Washington politicians to replace the previous Senators team that left for Minnesota and became the Twins following the 1960 season. But

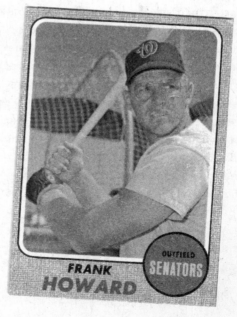

*Senators slugger
Frank Howard on
his 1968 Topps
card.*

the replacement team was pretty much doomed to fail before it ever took the field in 1961.

The eighth Washington team, the Senators of 1901–1960 (yes, Virginia, there were seven major league teams in the nation's capital at different points in the nineteenth century) was a charter member of the American League, and had a lot going for it. It was owned and operated by a professional baseball family, the Griffiths. Many Hall of Famers had graced its roster over the years, including, among others, Walter Johnson, Ed Delahanty, Sam Rice, Goose Goslin, George Sisler, Al Simmons, Early Wynn, Lefty Gomez, and Harmon Killebrew. And this "first" Senators team had made three World Series appearances.

Yet in spite of the stability, tradition, stars, and three AL pennants, the team still failed and moved to Minnesota. What made anyone—hopeful fans, placating baseball officials, or extortionist Washington politicians—think that this replacement team was going to succeed when the previous one hadn't? Sadly, it didn't matter, because putting a successful team on the field wasn't the primary motive for creating the replacement Senators. AL officials just wanted to pacify Washington politicians who were threatening to revoke baseball's antitrust exemption, and keep them off their backs.

In a classic case of haste makes waste, the Washington politicians got exactly what they deserved: a team of scrubs, hastily thrown together in two months, owned by an underfunded group led by Washington bureaucrat Elwood Quesada, head of the Federal Aviation Agency. Quesada hired longtime Senators first baseman Mickey Vernon, a local favorite, as the team's manager, hoping the former two-time AL batting champ would help put fans in the seats. But the 1960 team had drawn 743,000 in a 154-game season before departing for Minnesota. The 1961 team, in an expanded 162-game schedule, drew only 597,000, a drop of 2,300 per game. In their last homestand of the season, the Senators drew fewer than 20,000 fans for eight games, including two games against the Twins that drew an astoundingly meager combined attendance of 3,478. There were cocktail parties in town that drew bigger crowds.

Things seemed to be looking up for the Senators in 1962 when they moved into their new home, D.C. Stadium (later renamed R.F.K. Stadium), and attracted 42,143 for Opening Day. They even witnessed pitcher Tom Cheney strike out twenty-one Orioles in a sixteen-inning complete game win, still the record for most strikeouts in one game by one pitcher. Behind the scenes, however, trouble was brewing. Quesada was engaged in a running battle with his GM, Ed Doherty, whom he accused of being prejudiced against black players, of which there were only two in the entire Washington organization.

After the team finished in last place with a 60–101 record, Quesada fired Doherty. Two months later, he sold the team to an investment group headed by two bankers, James Johnston and James Lemon. Early in the 1963 season, the new owners fired Vernon and replaced him with another legendary hitter, Gil Hodges, but the Senators sank even lower, finishing with a record of 56–106. Hodges was able to increase the team's win total every season for the next four years (62, 70, 71, 76) before being replaced by Jim Lemon (not the co-owner, but another popular former Senator) in 1968.

Under Lemon, the Senators fell to 65–96 and drew just 546,000 fans. The only excitement in 1968 was provided by Frank Howard, the 6'7" slugger famous for his mammoth home runs. In one stretch of twenty at bats, "Hondo" clubbed ten home runs. Aside from Howard's league-leading forty-four home runs, there was little to cheer about, especially for the owners, who put the team up for sale. Initially it appeared the team was going to be purchased by comedian Bob Hope, who went so far as to announce Bill DeWitt as his choice for GM. But when Hope was faced with a serious eye operation, he withdrew his bid. This left only Bob Short, a hotel magnate from Minnesota (and treasurer of the Democratic National Committee), as the sole bidder.

Short purchased the team for $9 million and soon thereafter

installed Ted Williams as his new manager for five years at $100,000 per season. Williams had an immediate impact on the Senators, helping raise the team batting average twenty-five points. He led the team to what would be their only winning season in 1969, finishing 86–76. The fans responded, too, setting a record attendance of 918,000 for the "second" Senators.

Over the next two years, the Senators' win totals dropped to seventy and sixty-three, as did attendance, to 824,000 and 655,000. Much of the Senators' energy in 1970 and 1971 was spent dealing with issues surrounding two new additions, Denny McLain and Curt Flood. McLain, a thirty-one-game winner for Detroit in 1968, had fallen into disfavor after being suspended for his connection with gamblers. Ted Williams was a vocal opponent of the trade for McLain that sent pitcher Joe Coleman to the Tigers, and his unhappiness proved prophetic. Coleman won eighty-eight games for Detroit, including two twenty-win seasons, while McLain won a grand total of ten games for Washington.

Flood was in the process of challenging baseball's reserve clause, a battle of historic consequences for major league baseball. Most teams would have nothing to do with Flood, but the maverick Short decided to give him a chance. After a protracted battle over contract language (neither Flood, the Players' Association, nor MLB wanted Flood's appearance on the field for the Senators to affect or alter in any way their position in the bitter lawsuit), Flood finally took the field. But after only thirty-five at bats, Flood fled to Europe and became a recluse, never to play major league baseball again.

By 1971, Short was in severe financial trouble. He stopped paying the rent on R.F.K. Stadium and issued an ultimatum to the league: either find a local buyer willing to pay $12 million for the team, or he would move the Senators to Dallas–Fort Worth.

Commissioner Bowie Kuhn struggled mightily to save the franchise and came up with Joseph Danzansky, owner of a supermarket chain and the president of the Washington Board of

Trade, but Short rejected his $8.4 million offer. Kuhn next pleaded with World Airways chairman Ed Daly to buy the team and save it for Washington, but he refused. With no other option, Kuhn and the league's owners had to approve the team's move to Dallas–Fort Worth, where it became the Texas Rangers in 1972.

After the second Senators team left Washington, Kuhn tried his best to secure another team for the city. He nearly had a deal to relocate the San Diego Padres, but it fell through just days before the 1974 season began. Then, in 1975, he concocted a plan in which every team would play two games in Washington, but the owners eventually quashed that scheme. When the AL expanded again in 1977, Kuhn tried to steer one of the teams to Washington instead of Toronto, but he failed in that effort too.

After exhausting every imaginable idea, Kuhn finally gave up trying to secure a "third" Senators franchise for Washington. And those other senators, the ones given to pontificating and bloviating under the Capitol dome against reexamining baseball's decades-old antitrust exemption, apparently no longer felt the need for a new team to embarrass the nation's capital.

SLOW TO CATCH ON

THE WILMINGTON QUICKSTEPS
Union Association
1884

In their humiliating second professional season, the Wilmington Quicksteps learned that, in an era of rampant free agency, money talked and players often walked.

After the move to professional baseball began to sweep the country in 1871, it took several years before the Wilmington,

1861 sheet music of the song "Home Run Quick Step," which inspired the team's nickname.

Delaware, area, a stronghold of amateur baseball activity, felt cosmopolitan enough to have its own pro team. The natural choice for the first pro team from the city was the Wilmington Quicksteps, who took their name from a popular baseball song of the day, "The Home Run Quick Step." By the mid-1870s, they already had several paid professionals on the roster who toiled side by side with talented amateurs. And the Quicksteps were already good enough to tour the East Coast and Midwest, holding their own against all the top teams in the country, including the Chicago White Stockings and Cincinnati Red Stockings, among others.

Problem was, the Quicksteps' professional opponents recognized the great talent on the Wilmington team and lured the better Quicksteps away with lucrative contract offers. To keep the team intact, the Quicksteps were going to have to put all of their own players under contract.

In 1883, the Quicksteps finally took the plunge and turned pro, joining the Inter-State Association with other regional teams such as Allentown and Harrisburg. After Wilmington finished sixth with a 27–48 record, the minor league reorganized under the new name "Eastern League" (no connection to today's Eastern League) and the 1884 edition of the Quicksteps, now with some major league caliber players on the roster, came into their own. When the season ended on August 15, the Quicksteps had run away with the title, compiling a 51–12 record. They were so dominant, in fact, that several of the teams dropped out of the league before the season ended. Worse, their own fans stopped attending their boringly one-sided games. The Quicksteps were a foregone conclusion to win the pennant.

On the bright side, several major league teams had noticed just how good the Quicksteps were and scheduled exhibition games in Wilmington. The Quicksteps defeated two major league clubs, the Union Association's Baltimore Monumentals and the Washington Nationals, at the Wilmington Baseball Grounds, two home games that *did* draw large crowds.

The St. Louis Maroons were running away with the pennant by mid-August in the Union Association (in what turned out to be its only year of existence), and when the Philadelphia Keystones dropped out of the UA in August, Maroons owner and league founder Henry Lucas scrambled to find a replacement. On the recommendation of several teams who had played the Quicksteps, Lucas offered Wilmington's manager, Joe Simmons, the chance to take the place of the disbanded Keystones. Lucas guaranteed the Quicksteps a better-than-normal fee of seventy-five dollars a game for all road games, to be paid directly from the league office. For home games, they could keep all their gate receipts, less the visiting team's sixty-dollar fee. Simmons quickly agreed and the Quicksteps' long desire to become a major league club was realized.

Wilmington began its venture into major league play with a ten-game road trip, five games in Washington followed by five more in Boston, but the team almost immediately ran into trouble. Because the team had finished its Eastern League season, the Quickstep players felt they had completed their contractual obligations. After only two Union Association games, shortstop and star slugger Oyster Burns jumped to the Baltimore Orioles of the American Association for $900 a month, six times his Wilmington salary. Outfielder Dennis Casey joined Burns in Baltimore for a hefty increase as well. Then, when the Quicksteps played an exhibition game against the Philadelphia Phillies, catcher Tony Cusick relocated himself to the Phillies when they offered him $375 a month, $225 more than he had been making. At least Cusick's batterymate, Ed Nolan, rejected a similarly lucrative offer from the Phillies.

In spite of losing three of their four big stars, the Quicksteps won their first game against the Washington Nationals, 4–3, behind the fine pitching of Dan Casey. After losing their second game in tough fashion, 4–2, the Quicksteps were embarrassed in the final three games of the series, losing them by a combined score of 36–5. After losing five more games in Boston to the Reds, the Quicksteps' record stood at 1–9, and stepping up to the major leagues no longer seemed like such a great idea.

Their fans concurred. When Wilmington returned home for a three-game series against the Cincinnati Outlaw Reds, surprisingly few of them turned out to watch their new major league team win its home opener, 3–2, behind Ed Nolan. It was the last game the depleted Quicksteps would ever win. They lost their next seven home games, falling to 2–16, which was bad enough, but when league honcho Lucas realized that Wilmington was not going to be a long-term answer to his league's needs, he refused to pay the Quicksteps their promised money.

There was nowhere to go but down. On September 15, the Kansas City Cowboys came to town for a series. During pregame warm-ups, Manager Simmons looked into the stands and saw that not a single fan had showed up for the game. Knowing he was on the hook for a guaranteed appearance fee of sixty dollars to the Cowboys, Simmons called his players in from the field and told the Kansas City manager he was forfeiting the game. His next move was to disband the team, completing the great amateur team's humiliating decline. Wilmington's foray into major league baseball had been an embarrassment for players and fans alike.

After receiving word that the Quicksteps had dissolved, Lucas quickly replaced them with the Milwaukee Brewers of the Northwestern League for the final twelve games of the season. In 1885, a new Wilmington team formed, this one called the Blue Hens, and joined the Eastern League. But Wilmington fans, burned once, stayed away in droves. After compiling a 5–28 record, the Blue Hens were sold and moved to Atlantic City in June.

ABOUT THE AUTHOR

At the age of sixteen Dennis Purdy began filling spiral notebooks with Major League Baseball statistics, records, and standings—all for his own enjoyment. He played both semi-pro baseball and fast-pitch softball. In 1976 he had a two-day tryout with the Minnesota Twins in Metropolitan Stadium, and though it did not lead to a pro career, it did deepen his love of the game.

In 1978, at the age of twenty-five, Dennis developed what he believed was a winning system for wagering on baseball games and moved to Las Vegas to test it. It worked, and Dennis also became an expert in both blackjack and poker. Dennis then spent the next twelve years as a police officer, juvenile delinquent services worker, car salesman, and undercover informant for various police agencies.

In 1990, after authoring a successful book on automobile advertising, Dennis started his own trade show promotion company, specializing in baseball card and coin shows, which he operated until 2006. In 1995, Dennis created *The Vintage & Classic Baseball Collector* magazine, a journal of baseball's rare collectibles and its history, which he sold in 2000 to devote more time to writing books. His first novel was published in 2002, followed by six more books—on baseball, football, poker, and blackjack—and a screenplay, *Shoeless Joe*, for which the movie rights have been optioned. Dennis lives in University Place, Washington, with his wife, Kathy, and their four children.